ISRAEL - ISLAND OF SUCCESS

—

This book takes up the challenge of looking into the mechanism of Israel's success: Why is Israel a success? Is this success sustainable? What is Israel's probable future?

Noga Kainan and Adam Reuter

ISBN: 1979817170
ISBN-13: 9781979817172
Library of Congress Control Number: 2017919696
CreateSpace Independent Publishing Platform
North Charleston, South Carolina

Quotes from the Book

Israel is the largest American aircraft carrier in the world that cannot be sunk.
—Alexander Haig, former US secretary of state

The kind of innovation going on in Israel is critical to the future of the technology business.
—Bill Gates, Microsoft's former CEO

The United States is the best place for entrepreneurs in the world, followed by Israel.
—Eric Schmidt, Google's former CEO

Microsoft is almost as much an Israeli company as it is an American company.
—Steve Ballmer, Microsoft's former CEO

CONTENTS

INTRODUCTION

Israel is developing capabilities to win its many challenges - as a result of the struggles that Israel has to face that are described in this book. Even the name "Israel" comes from the biblical story of Jacob, father of the nation, after winning against all odds in the fight against the angel of God (Genesis 32:22–32).

The State of Israel, throughout the years of its existence and even before it was founded, has overcome enormous challenges: severe natural ones, such as water scarcity and the global desertification process; human challenges, such as the absorption of immigrants, including Holocaust survivors and many others, who brought languages and cultures from seventy nations, including parts of Africa, Islamic countries, and the former Soviet Union; military and political threats and actions aimed to destroy Israel; and many other challenges. Despite it all, and perhaps because of it all, Israel is a success. Why? In many of the interviews we conducted during the collection of material for this book, we heard the same sentences: "Because of the challenges, we succeeded"; "Because there was no choice—we had to find a solution"; "We had to win; otherwise we would die." It seems that overcoming threats shapes Israelis' ability to create a better future.

As for the future of Israel, Matt Ridley[1] defines a "rational optimist" as one whose positions are derived not from gut feelings but from observation of the evidence. We, too, writers of this book, whose feet have been rooted for many years in the economic and business world, have not reached our optimistic positions based on feelings but rather by observing the global and local statistics, academic studies, and interviews we held with more than 120 senior executives, entrepreneurs, and experts. The data indicates that we can be rationally optimistic about the future. Israel stands on stable ground and has the strength to cope with all the existing and future challenges.

However, even if we agree that the current situation is good, the question remains whether Israel is deteriorating and withdrawing or constantly improving. Our research indicates that in the vast majority of subjects, Israel has improved compared to its past results (though in the minority of subjects, there is some stagnation). We found no evidence of withdrawal or deterioration.

The success presented in this book cannot be attributed to any political party or personality. Most of this success can be accredited to the character of the Jewish people and their heritage and values, mostly to the ways in which such character, heritage, and values have been assimilated into modern Israel.

Moreover, we learned that Israel is constantly reinventing itself. People have the courage to invent the future and build it with their own hands and especially with their brains. Israel is united by its mission to build the first Jewish independent state after two thousand years of exile, to build a strong shelter for all Jews suffering from anti-Semitism, and to create values for the world.

The history of Israel teaches us that the ability to predict any specific future based on the past does not work. Israelis' rebellious and revolutionary way of thinking creates the State of Israel in their image—a vivid country, that is always in the process of building something better. Its future is constantly redefined by a people with little or no mental or behavioral fixation.

In many ways, Israel is an island, and its residents live in this sense. Although geographically it is not, in practice, for years, it has been isolated from its hostile environment and lives as a "state surrounded by enemies."

It is an island of stability, an island of sanity, the only Western democracy in the Middle East, whose economic, social, and cultural power separates it from its neighbors and places it among the world's most successful countries.

In the film *The Third Man*, Orson Welles, as the famous crook Harry Lime, says, "In Italy, for thirty years under the Borgias, they had warfare, terror, murder, and bloodshed, but they produced Michelangelo, Leonardo da Vinci, and the Renaissance. In Switzerland, they had brotherly love, they had five hundred years of democracy and peace, and what did that produce? The cuckoo clock." Lime was not accurate—the cuckoo clock was invented in Germany, and Switzerland was neutral for only two hundred years, but this statement might explain the Israelis, who live in a hostile environment and yet invent, innovate, and succeed.

In April 2018, Israel will celebrate seventy years of its existence. No nation can compete with its achievements in such a short period, but Israelis are not satisfied. Driven by a history of pogroms, hatred of Jews, death, and poverty, Israelis want to make sure that history will not repeat itself. It is impossible to speed up the process of building a state, a people, and a society, just as it is impossible to speed up the growth of a tree. There is a biological-psychological-social time that these processes require, and in this regard, even the hyperactive nature of Jews and Israelis will not help.

An entire chapter is dedicated to highlighting the challenges, doubts, and risks facing the State of Israel, in addition to those listed throughout the book. We also offer some solutions that we think should be considered.

The book is intended to encourage all those who are interested in Israel to be rational optimists—to know the facts and to draw the appropriate conclusions. We invite our readers to relax in their chairs and join us in a revolutionary journey through the success of Israel, its mechanisms, and its future. It is a worthwhile journey.

EXECUTIVE SUMMARY

The State of Israel is facing many challenges—problems related to social disparities, poverty, and anti-Semitism that have turned into extreme anti-Israelism, ethical issues, the high cost of living, inordinately high property prices, an excess of regulation, structural challenges—and all these in addition to a complex and demanding security situation. We refer to these challenges throughout the book and devote chapter 14 in its entirety to them.

Nevertheless, despite all the challenges, the overall picture indicates that Israel is an economic and social success story. That is certainly the case when compared to those OECD countries that are quickly losing their growth engines. The book relies on approximately two hundred interviews and quotes from key people in the economy, and its conclusions are optimistic.

The Israeli economy has four advantages:

- The global advantage: Israel's global advantage stems from its being a nation of immigrants: the global nature of generations of wandering Jews, the existence of Jewish and Israeli anchors across the globe, its people's proficiency in numerous languages, and education that is geared toward global openness.

- The entrepreneurial advantage: Due to the Israeli culture that en-courages entrepreneurs, Israel became the "startup nation," with all the economic advantages driven by it.
- The technological-scientific advantage: This combines academic research with high-tech applications, which has made Israel a global R & D center and a prizewinner in cutting-edge research in a variety of fields.
- The demographic advantage: This derives from its being a country with a relatively young population and high birth rates compared to the Western world coupled with the process of integrating two large sectors—ultra-Orthodox Jews and Arabs—in education and job markets.

At the same time, there are three revolutions taking place in Israel, which are at different stages of evolution:

- The triumph over the desert, which led the parched country to integrative capacities of legislation, management, and operations, and water economy technology serve as an example and model studied by other countries. Today, Israel can trade in water and knowledge in this field, in a world that is getting warmer and succumbing to the process of desertification.
- Inexpensive energy that emanates from the huge gas reserves was discovered in Israel's territorial waters, and it has an impact on the developing trade in energy in addition to a relative advantage for the energy industry.
- Transportation infrastructure in general, and public transportation in particular, which, for many years, was a stumbling block to Israel's growth, has gained momentum in the form of investments and development in recent years.

It is very reasonable to assume that when the four advantages and the three revolutions attain their full effect, Israel will achieve even greater economic success than it has now, primarily compared to the prevailing sluggishness in the economies of developed countries.

Israel's economic success is not an outcome of a temporary process, but it derives from the nature of its populace and its ability to adjust to the global reality.

By their very nature, Israelis are a global people who are housed on a small island and are part of a crowded network of ties to the big world outside. They are people who sanctify learning and education in an environment that rewards knowledge. Above all, they rebel against conventions, are not prepared to accept the existing situation, and develop creative solutions in order to survive under difficult conditions. They are a people who know how to convert tough challenges into groundbreaking successes.

The challenges faced by the State of Israel are still very real and existential. For some of them, only time will solve, whereas the remaining ones will require mobilization at the national level to achieve change. Some are internal challenges, and others are geopolitical threats. The book highlights the challenges associated with each of the topics it discusses and presents additional challenges in a special chapter devoted to the subject.

When asked about it, Israelis answer that they are happy with their lives. In fact, Israel is ranked number eleven on the World Happiness Report 2017. That is surprising because in view of the existential challenges, they have no reason to be pleased. The book explains why they are happy—and they have a very good reason to be.

ON PESSIMISTIC AND OPTIMISTIC FORECASTS

Simon Dubnow, the most prominent Jewish historian and demographer of the nineteenth and early twentieth centuries, thought that the establishment of the Jewish state was a pointless exercise. He wrote in his book, *Letters on Old and New Judaism, 1898*:

> In one hundred years from now [in 1998], there will be half a million Jews in Palestine…As such, political Zionism is a three-fold utopia: a dream about the opportunity to establish a Jewish state in accordance with international law; the idea that a significant proportion of world Jewry emigrating there; and the illusion that this will provide a solution to the fate of the whole Jewish people.

At that time, Dubnow may well have had good reasons behind his prediction, but in fact, in 1998, Israel, the state of the Jewish people, founded fifty years earlier, was home to around 4.7 million Jews, around 39 percent of the world's Jews. In 2018, the number of Jewish residents in Israel stands at around 6.7 million, making it the largest population of Jews in the world. Just one hundred years ago, 99 percent of Jews lived outside the borders of the historical homeland; then they began to return, and one hundred years later, in 2018, around 46 percent live in the land of their forefathers, and this proportion is steadily growing.

Dubnow's prediction proved false, but he was not alone. According to some experts, Israel is always on the brink of extinction or disappearing. There were predictions that Israel would not survive the War of Independence, not the Six-Day War, and certainly not the Yom Kippur War. There also were dark forecasts about wars that Israel did not participate in but just stood aside—for example, the first Gulf War in 1991. There were bitter predictions about its gloomy future during the terror period of suicide bombings, the intifadas, and every time the Iranian nuclear program was mentioned.

There were predictions that it would be left without enough energy sources, such as during the Arab oil embargo after 1973, that it will be left without water sources because it is located in a semidesert area with a rapidly growing population, and that it would collapse economically. Various predictions were published in the 1950s, at the end of the twentieth century, and at the beginning of this century. Throughout its history, there have also been predictions that the Jews will become a minority due to the high natural increase of the Arab population.

All predictions were false. Reality proves that Israel, despite everything, is thriving.

Part I
A Global Nation on a Small Island—A Very Dense Network

I

THE MANIFESTATION OF JEWISH VALUES

NEW COUNTRY, NEW PEOPLE, NEW MAN

Dov Kehati did not put a mezuzah on his door. Nothing convinced him. There were no persuasions or requests or pleas. He had an angry conversation with God, who had enabled the murder of his family and his people in the Holocaust. He did not set a mezuzah and refused to speak Yiddish. He concentrated on planting trees on Mount Carmel, having ideological arguments with his friends, and building his family. He was not alone. Many of the first pioneers from the Second Aliyah (the second wave of immigration to Israel) and those who followed made a barrier between themselves and Judaism. They built a new country, a new people, and a new man—a new Jew who would be a laborer or farmer, muscular and strong, a warrior and man of honor. Only in the evenings, when he was tired of building all this newness and when he thought no one was paying attention, ancient tunes, Chasidic songs from the Beit Midrash where he studied and was considered a genius, would sneak into his heart.

Like those songs, so too did Jewish values sneak into the new state. Jewish social phenomena hundreds of years old merged into the new Israeli phenomena, which were only decades old, and created something new.

The Jews are dispersed geographically but have connections from their distant places of residence. Benjamin of Tudela described the Jewish diaspora as part of his travels in the twelfth century. He coined the term "wandering Jew" in the context of geographical dispersion without a single base country. The frequent deportations from their places of residence taught them flexibility, forcing them to search constantly for new sources of livelihood based on their higher education and trade skills. This began from earlier periods of commercial caravans that passed through the Middle East in ancient times and became stronger as the global transport and trade system improved.

In the nineteenth century, Yaakov Reuter was released from the Russian czar's military, where he was frequently subjected to anti-Semitic attacks. He wandered south, crossed the border, and settled in Manchuria in the northern part of China. Over time, he set up a large trading house for paints. The first store was established in the Chinese city of Harbin and then another in Tenzin. Jacob was not satisfied with his Chinese customers, and together with his brother Mithia, he also sold colors and sugar cubes to Mongolian customers. The goods were transported in long convoys on camels on weeklong journeys, in the extreme Mongolian climate, to the Mongolian capital of Ulan Bator. In return, the Mongols provided them with the skins, furs, and intestines of sheep, goats, and cows. The skins and fur were sold to the Chinese and the intestines to the sausage industry of California.

Jewish globalism is the powerful engine behind worldwide travels that many Israelis carry out these days. From speedboats on the Mekong to leisurely cruises on the European rivers, from trekking Nepal to bicycle trips in Tierra del Fuego—anywhere and everywhere, you can hear Hebrew and meet Israeli travelers.

The path of Israeli maturation includes a Holocaust memorial trip to the extermination camps in Poland during high school and a trip to India or South America for a few months after military service. The young Israelis are exposed to very different cultures and adopt this adaptability when they travel years later to meet with investors in New York, run farms in remote countries, or provide technical support services to Israeli software companies worldwide. The global perception of the Jewish heritage characterizes the Israelis and is inherent in them.

A NATION OF IMMIGRANTS

In Russian restaurants, music is filled with inner joy and emotional turmoil. On the tables, there are plenty of salads on plates, one on top of the other in a kind of strange pyramid that threatens to fall. The music moves the legs and the hearts; the vodka flows. "Oi, Odessa!" all the dancers sing together with the band's singers, as well as "Get drunk from the magical nights of Moscow," and a love song for "Utka" (the duck). The babushkas (grandmothers) dance with their grandchildren; the sexy women and the handsome young men all dance and sing passionately. Drunk and tired, they all leave the restaurant to go out into the street. It's not Odessa; it's not Moscow; it's the beautiful promenade of Bat Yam, Israel. On the left is the kiosk of Rachamim, and on the right are three young Ethiopian Jews. There are plenty of Russian restaurants in Israel: in Ashdod, Netanya, Tel Aviv, and in Beer-Sheva, and in all of them there is a Russian joy of life, which has slowly been assimilated into Israeli music.

The rate of immigration to Israel is an average of more than twenty-five thousand per year in the last five years. Immigrants are about a quarter of Israel's population and about a third of its workforce. Forty percent came from the former USSR; 25 percent from Arab and Islamic countries; 20 percent from Europe; 3 percent from the United States;[2] and 3 percent from Ethiopia, South America, India, and other places.[3]

From biblical times until today, immigration to Israel has been called *Aliyah* (climbing up), and emigration from Israel is called *yeridah* (going down). These are highly emotional expressions, glorifying those who are coming and judging those who are leaving.

Today, 80 percent of all Jews live in two large concentrated areas: Israel and the United States, followed by Russia and France, which are in a rapid process of losing the Jews with the rise of anti-Semitism and anti-Jewish violence. In 2010, Israel became the largest place of residence for Jews.

In this count, we include hundreds of thousands of sons and daughters who, according to Jewish law, are not Jewish, and therefore are degraded as "others" by official records in Israel, even though they were entitled to come to Israel under the Law of Return. They are the flesh of the Jewish people and must be treated as such.

Seven out of Israel's twelve prime ministers were not born there. The new immigrants have been the backbone of the fabric of life in Israel.

Many studies show that countries that have positive migration of an educated and working population who want to integrate have a better economic position. Notable examples are the United States, Canada, and Australia. The immigrants bring with them demands for housing, education, and health care and thus help the economy to grow.

Eric Weiner, author of *The Geography of Genius*,[4] said research shows that in dealing with a problem in a familiar field, it is easier to find a solution among a homogeneous group of people, but in solving a problem in a new or unknown field, solutions are better found with a variety of perspectives. Weiner shows that today, the countries where genius and creativity grow are usually nations with open immigration systems and willingness to borrow or steal ideas from other places. In ancient times it happened in Athens, where Greeks borrowed ideas from the Phoenicians, in Egypt, and in Babylon. It is also happening today in the Silicon Valley, which magnetizes peoples from all over the world. Ideas are not necessarily born there, but they learn to walk there. They come there, develop, and grow. Ultimately, Weiner explains, talented immigrants who bring ideas and initiatives with them are a powerful economic and cultural driving force.

A community that wants to encourage creativity and cultivate geniuses should encourage cultural heterogeneity, said Dean Keith Simonton, a professor at the Department of Psychology at the University of California, Davis, and one of the world's leading researchers on creativity.

Israel did not absorb immigrants because of the good and abundance they brought with them. Sometimes the immigrant absorption was too heavy and demanding for the young country. But Israel took them in because of its mission as a home for the Jewish people. However, in doing so, Israel enjoys the significant assets that the immigrants brought with them: understanding of world cultures, connections with the populations in their countries of origin, and extensive knowledge of languages. A professor of languages from the United States who spent several weeks in Israel expressed his amazement at the Israelis' ability to communicate in so many languages. "I have been to dozens of countries in the world, but I have never encountered a country in which it doesn't matter on what language you speak, there will be always someone whom you can communicate with." This is a significant contribution to the Israeli economy, which we call in this book *the global advantage.*

A study by the OECD[5] regarding the integration of immigrants in the receiving countries states that Israel has one of the largest immigrant populations, with the first generation of immigrants constituting 23 percent of the total population. In only two countries, the rate of first-generation immigrants is higher: Switzerland and Australia. When we add to this figure the second generation of immigrants, Israel jumps to second place in the list after Switzerland.

The comprehensive study found that Israel is among the few countries in which the participation rate of immigrants in the labor force is higher than that of veteran citizens. Israel is a nation where immigrants feel less discriminated against. The poverty rate among immigrants in Israel is among the lowest in the developed world. Even with respect to the rate of self-owned homes, it turns out that the new immigrants in Israel are in excellent shape relative to other OECD countries.

Another indicator examined was the percentage of those receiving citizenship from the new country after at least ten years. Not surprisingly, in Israel, obtaining citizenship for Jewish immigrants is almost automatic, and therefore it is in first place, with almost every immigrant receiving a citizen's certificate very quickly.

The participation rate in the parliamentary elections is also very high compared with immigrants in other countries and is almost identical to that of veteran residents.

The same is true in the education system. The study found that literacy ability of immigrant children is very close to that of native Israelis—third highest among OECD countries on literacy and fourth in the rate of children staying in school.

One of the main difficulties of the immigrants in the various countries is learning the language and the culture of the absorbing state. In Israel, the immigrants are absorbed in ulpan.[6] New immigrants learn Hebrew at a level that enables conversation, reading, and basic understanding of text. In addition, they learn subjects of Israeli culture, history, and geography—all with no tuition fees.

Each immigration brought special challenges to its absorption. Migration is always a traumatic process for the immigrant and involves dramatic changes in all areas of life. It should be noted that even though Israel is an immigrant country, there is also, on one level or another, xenophobia, which was directed at all immigration when it occurred. Today it is mainly directed at Ethiopian immigrants. Their uniqueness in the color of their skin, culture, and social structure has pushed them to the margins of Israeli society. A major important and moral challenge that has not yet been completed is their unconditional absorption, adoption, and assimilation into the social fabric.

HOLOCAUST AND REBIRTH

"The Holocaust is not the reason for the establishment of the State of Israel. The Jews have immigrated to the Land of Israel throughout their years of exile," writes futurist Prof. David Passig in his book *Israel 2048*.[7]

The Holocaust advanced the declaration of the State of Israel. The victorious countries of World War II found it difficult to look in the eyes of the survivors. They had to do the only moral action possible, and that was to agree to the establishment of the State of Israel.

But the Holocaust also wiped out millions of Jews—men and women, children and infants—who had the potential to become citizens of the new state.

The world's Jewish population is currently estimated at 14.2 million. Together with those who identify themselves as "partial Jews" and those who are not Jewish according to the Halacha[8] but are eligible for aliyah to Israel, the total number is approaching eighteen million.

———

Lt. Col. Aryeh Oz (then Harry Klausner) was hidden as a child in the Holocaust in the attic of a Dutch family:

> One day I heard strange sounds that I did not know. I ran to the window and there was a flock of planes passing just above the house. I quickly counted 12 planes…only 10 returned. Since then, I have heard many more planes and in my imagination, I sat with the crews on airplanes and I was part of them. One night a British pilot whose plane had been shot down was brought to the farm. Although he remained only a short time until he was collected by members of the underground, its appearance and uniform remained engraved in my memory to this very day. I knew, without a doubt, that I would be a pilot like him. "I'm going to be a pilot," I said, walking upright and proud for the first time.[9]

———

"Until a few years ago we did not have a past, we did not want the past, we were not ready to deal with this trauma," said four Holocaust survivors, pilots in the Israeli Air Force, who embarked on a journey in the wake of their lost childhood, their silent youth, and their lives as pilots in Israel. They came to Israel, each in his own way. They wanted to be like all Israelis, the Sabras[10], not like those Jews in the Holocaust who "went like sheep to the slaughter." In the 1950s, there were 350 pilots in the Israeli Air Force, 138 of whom were Holocaust survivors. They were a symbol of Israelites and a little more.

Stusho Porcellina, later called Col. (Res.) Yesha'ayahu (Shaya) Harsit, navigator in the Israeli Air Force, was born in Warsaw.[11] At the age of five, he was cut off from his happy childhood and became the victim of a saga of escapes, starvation, poverty, and an endless struggle for survival on the vast plains of the Soviet Union. After the Second World War ended, his family boarded the *Exodus* immigration ship on its way to Israel—it held 4,554 refugees from the horror. The young people on board sang songs to the future homeland. Only Israelis are able to understand the built-in oxymoron in this expression "future homeland." They lifted the blue-and-white flag and sang the *Hatikvah*, the future anthem of Israel and their current "secret weapon."

Two days before they arrived at the Port of Haifa at 2:30 p.m., two British battleships gored the *Exodus* with all their mighty force. After a bitter struggle, the wrecked ship surrendered and was dragged to the Port of Haifa. The refugees were transferred to the deportation ships that returned them, not without a struggle, to the port of origin in France, and from there, when they refused to evacuate, to the land of the inferno—Germany. Only after the establishment of the State of Israel, the Porcellina family boarded the ship *Mala* to their "new homeland."

Shaya Harsit arrived as a new immigrant. But he wanted to take root and to become Israeli quickly like the native-born Israelis: a Sabra. "I wanted to look like them," he writes in his book. "And in order to do so, I had to shed my skin, to give up my experiences and my separate identity. If my friends wore their berets behind their head, I stuck it to my neck, if they were bold and daring, I stuck my neck out on the line for them." In a pilot course and throughout his years as a fighter in the air crew afterward, Harsit did not talk about his past as a survivor child from the war. "But I was not the only one who remained silent," he writes. "All this wonderful group was silent, everyone felt alien to the Israeli way of life, and everyone tried to forget the past, to resemble their friends and to merge with Israelites." He married Tzipi, who also came from the horrors of Europe, and they have three daughters and nine grandchildren. Harsit is one of those who won the Holocaust, even if he still bears it as eternal scars on his soul.

———

Three Israeli F-15s, along with a fueling plane, flew on a four-hour flight from Israel to Poland. The Israeli Air Force agreed to participate in an air show that it was invited to in Radom, Poland, under one condition—to conduct a special flight over Auschwitz-Birkenau. One flight for all those Jews who were murdered in the Holocaust, for all those whom only one airstrike over Auschwitz could have saved.

It was already nearing the end of the Second World War, and despite their victory, Britain and the United States chose not to bomb the extermination camps and railroads, leading to the slaughter of millions of Jews. Every day that was postponed, another twelve thousand Jews were murdered. To this day, there is no satisfactory explanation for this terrible decision.

The flyover, which took place on September 4, 2003, was led by Amir Eshel, who later became commander of the Israeli Air Force. The three pilots and three navigators shook history and reminded everyone that "at the right time, there was not a single flight for us."[12] From May until the end of November 1945, there were twenty-eight hundred flights by the Allies over Auschwitz. During this period, all Hungarian Jewry was murdered. The planes were there, above the gas chambers, above the crematoriums. They were in the air, and they did not stop the murder.

"We pilots of the Israeli Air Force, flying over the skies above the camp of horrors, arose from the ashes of the millions of victims and shoulder their silent cries, salute their courage, and promise to be the shield of the Jewish people and its nation—Israel," said the grandchildren who flew over the ashes of their grandparents.

"And the world was silent," Elie Wiesel said in his book about Auschwitz in astonishment and incomprehension. Why was the world silent? In the documents of that period, it was explicitly stated that one of the considerations not to intervene in the genocide of the Jewish people—which was well known at this time to Western leaders, including Churchill and Roosevelt—stemmed from the dilemma of who would take care of all these Jews. What country would absorb them? No one wanted them. The State of Israel did not exist yet. "A noble deed," Elie Wiesel called the flyover of the Israeli pilot.

When the Germans invaded Poland, seventeen-year-old David Azrielovich (later Azrieli) fled his home in the town of Maków Mazowiecki, Poland. At the end of the war, Azrieli discovered that his parents, younger brother, and sister were murdered in the Holocaust. In the Soviet Union, he joined the Anders Army[13] in order to reach the land of Israel. The journey through Uzbekistan, Iran, and Iraq was long.

"During the months of my service in the Anders Army, my commitment to Zionism was due to the anti-Semitism that prevailed in it," Azrieli recalls in his memoirs[14] about his service in the Anders Army.

A Jewish family in Iraq helped Azrieli escape from Anders's army.

I was dressed in the clothes of a poor Arab peasant—an old shirt, slacks and sandals—and I decided that I would pretend that I was deaf and mute, to prevent mishaps because of my lack of knowledge of the language and customs. While saying goodbye all the family gathered around me and the father gave me three silver coins, to pay if necessary to any troublemakers. At that time, the Jews of Iraq lived in fear of the Arab anti-Semitic violence, and I had no doubt that if I was caught, I would be killed, but they will be severely punished. I knew that the Jews who helped me were endangering their lives. Up until today I'm deeply grateful to them for their courage and generous assistance.

Azrieli brought about a change in consumption habits in Israel when he established the first enclosed mall, Ayalon Mall. In 2007, the third tower was completed in the skyscraper complex named after him, the Azrieli Center. The round, square, and triangular buildings sealed their mark on the skyline of Tel Aviv. In 2010, Azrieli completed the group's IPO on stock exchanges in Tel Aviv and London, the largest offering by a private company in Israel, in which 25 percent of the shares were sold for NIS 2.5 billion.

His daughter, Dana, a second-generation Holocaust survivor, left her home in Montreal at the age of seventeen and immigrated to Israel, first as a volunteer at Kibbutz Zikim and later in Kibbutz Ortal. After graduation, she began working as a lawyer.

> It was important for me to tell his story, about a 17-year-old boy who remained optimistic and uses his luck and connections to the right people to escape from the Nazis and to survive. It was a story that influenced his worldview and my life, too. I'm not a generation that has a sense of "I deserve it," I feel I have a lot of luck. This story gave me the frame and proportion that everything can turn over in one day.[15]

Dana Azrieli currently serves as the chairperson of the board of directors of one of the leading and strongest groups in the Israeli economy, and she is owner and manager of fifteen shopping and commercial centers in Israel. David Azrieli died in July 2014, surrounded by his family; he was loved and successful, not as had been planned for him by the Nazis.

Sano-Bruno's Enterprises, Ltd. was founded in 1965 by Bruno Landesberg. The company was first issued on the Tel Aviv Stock Exchange in 1982 and is a leading Israeli company in the manufacture of nonfood consumer goods, including toiletries and hygiene and cleaning products for the industrial, institutional, and domestic markets. In 2017, Sano had about sixteen hundred employees, and its revenue was about NIS 1.5 billion.

Landesberg was born in Czernowitz. After the death of his father, the family moved to Bucharest, and with the Nazi occupation, he fled with his younger brother to the east, back to Czernowitz. There he met Raya, his future wife, with whom he fled from Nazi terror to the Soviet Union. Bruno attended university in the Soviet Union and from there immigrated with his family to Bukhara, where their eldest son, Alex, was born. Toward the end of World War II, Bruno returned to Bucharest and completed his studies. He enlisted in the Communist underground and was given a certificate of recognition for his participation in the antifascist struggle. In March 1952, he immigrated to Israel with his wife and son.

At first, he worked in the Defense Ministry, and finally, in 1958, he mortgaged his home and all his property to establish the Southern Marketing Company. In the early stages, the business became illiquid, and Landesberg considered closing the company. For his living, he lectured about marketing and sales, but after winning a scholarship to specialize in international marketing at Harvard University, he founded a small company called Sano, which specializes in aerosols and cleaning products. Today, his son Alex is leading the company, and his grandson Yuval is the CEO. They are second and third generation to the Holocaust. Despite this all, "I am an optimist," Landesberg said. "If not for that I would have never got to where I am now. I was always a fighter, I always dared to do things and I always thought I would succeed."

———

Somewhere in a small pit in total darkness, a boy named Felix Zandman lived for seventeen months. He hid with his uncle, Sander Fridowitz, and three other Jews under the home of a brave Polish woman named Anna Puchalski. There in the pit, his uncle taught him mathematics and physics—in a whisper, orally, in the dark. "Sander was an excellent mathematician and had an extraordinary mathematical memory," says Zandman.[16] Algebra and geometry, formulas, and mathematical theories became the center of their lives and an incessant dialogue that kept their sanity in a narrow hole shared by three other survivors. Three lay on the ground, one stood between the legs of the laying down, and the fifth sat on the bucket that they used for their body wastes. Every two hours, they moved in place to prevent muscle cramps and spasms—day and night for seventeen months.

Later, Dr. Felix Zandman founded Vishay, one of the largest electronic components manufacturers in the world, employing, as of 2017, twenty-six thousand employees in seventy plants worldwide, six of them in Israel, and with a turnover of $2.8 billion.

The Smithsonian science museum in Washington, DC, presents Zandman's invention as one of the eighteen greatest scientific achievements of the twentieth century. This is a patent that paved the way for minimizing all electrical and electronic appliances. Another invention of his own, Photo Stress, allows the testing of metal reinforcement and is the basis for the construction of any aircraft. For this invention, Zandman was awarded the Legion of Honor of the French Republic. Zandman translated his inventions into a worldwide industrial empire. The special name, Vishay, is the name of a small village in Lithuania where his grandmother grew up and lived before the outbreak of World War II.

However, Dr. Zandman's final victory was the acquisition of the German corporation Telefunken. During World War II, the company collaborated with the Nazis, employed forced labor, and supplied infrastructure to Auschwitz. When Zandman, the Jewish boy from the pit, bought the German factory, the Israeli flag flew over it. At the moment of signing, he took a yarmulke[17] from his pocket, covered his head like a religious Jew, and signed with the leaders of German industry.

THE HIDDEN REFUGEES

They are not refugees. They never viewed themselves as refugees, even though they had been forcibly expelled from countries where they had lived for centuries and all their property had been taken away. The Jews of Arab and Islamic countries immigrated to the land of their forefathers and built their homes, their families, and their futures. The comparison between them and the Palestinian refugees is astonishing.

People can become chronic refugees if they and their environment insist on preserving their refugee status. The Palestinians are a good example for the outcome of preserving a refugee status. Every Palestinian citizen is given an average of a thousand dollars a year. More than 60 percent of the gross domestic product of the Palestinian Authority (PA) comes from donations. In 2009 and 2010, the PA received donations totaling $4 billion a year. Since 2005, donations to Palestinians have more than doubled. Accumulated funds that the Palestinians received from all sources—only from 2005 to 2015—amount to $25 billion. The great tragedy of the Palestinians is their success in deviating from the international rule in which a refugee is only a member of the first generation. In doing so, the Palestinians have sentenced their children and grandchildren, for all generations, to remain detached from their ability to build their lives and happiness.

Today, seventy years after the expulsion of most Arab and Muslim Jews from their countries, the former Jewish refugees live with honor, free from the past, while Palestinian refugees still suffer in refugee camps throughout the Mediterranean and need support from international institutions.

Throughout history, Muslim countries discriminated against individuals and non-Muslim communities, including the Jews. In most places, the Jews were defined as protected persons and were therefore entitled to certain protections under the law or wishes of the rulers, but they were always perceived as "doomed." With the increasing involvement of the European powers in Islamic countries, the Jews gained a built-in advantage, stemming mainly from their education and family and community ties. The growing demand for bankers, commercial and financial managers, customs brokers, merchants, and so on gave the Jews opportunities. Communities grew and prospered, Jewish institutions were built, and individuals and families became rich.

Expulsions, riots, nationalization of the property, and layoffs caused desperate Jews to lose almost everything they owned. A great deal of Jewish property was left in the Muslim countries when the Jews were deported from there. Both the US Congress[18] and the Israeli government[19] recognize Jews who have been expelled or fled from Arab countries as refugees. In recent years, the Israeli government has been evaluating the Jewish property that has been nationalized by the Arab states.

The US Congress estimates that the number of Jewish refugees from Islamic countries is 850,000.

———

In Egypt there was an ancient and glorious Jewish community from the time of the prophet Jeremiah after the destruction of the First Temple in Jerusalem. In the beginning of the nineteenth century, under the leadership of Muhammad Ali Pasha and his descendants and under European influence, Egypt underwent modernization and industrialization that brought about a blossoming of the Jewish community there. The Jews knew both cultures—Arab and European—had trade ties, family ties, and a cross-border community. The Egyptian Jewish community numbered forty to eighty thousand people at the time.

Beginning in the 1930s, following fascist propaganda on one hand and the Egyptian Muslim national awakening on the other, an atmosphere arose against minorities, including Copts, Greeks, and Jews. Particularly cruel and specific propaganda was directed against the Jews and included translations of Nazi and anti-Semitic documents into Arabic. The incitement led to the outbreak of riots against the Jews in 1938 and later in 1945. The UN Partition Plan and the establishment of the State of Israel in 1948 were grounds for new riots.

The Egyptian government took part in the persecution of the Jews. On the eve of the declaration of the State of Israel and the invasion of the Arab armies into the territory of the young state, the Egyptian police arrested Jews throughout Egypt, imprisoned them in detention camps, and released them only after a year and a half. The Jews were accused of supporting Zionism. Hundreds of Jewish shops and businesses were expropriated. After the defeat of the Egyptian military during the War of Independence, the harassment increased and lasted for many months. The insecurity led many of the Jews to leave. During Gamal Abdel Nasser's regime, Jewish community institutions were closed, including schools and hospitals. In November 1956, mass layoffs of Jews were carried out, and expropriation of Jewish property by the government was deepened.

Following the persecution, about thirty thousand Egyptian Jews were forced to leave. The government confiscated all their property, and they were forced to sign a declaration that they had no claims from Egypt and would never return. Many Jews were forced to sign a declaration that they "donated" their property to the Egyptian government. Thousands of Jews were ordered by the authorities to leave, with permission to take a brief-case and a small amount of cash.

The Sinai Campaign in 1956 led to the almost total expulsion of Egyptian Jews. Expulsion orders were issued against thousands, and much property was expropriated by the government. The government conduct-ed arrests and employment dismissals among Jews. The Jews sought a way to escape, and a few thousand of them did so on ships that had been hired by the Red Cross for this purpose.

———

With the withdrawal of France from Algeria and the enactment of a new citizenship law that prevented non-Muslims from obtaining citizenship, almost all the Jews left. Many Jewish institutions were expropriated by the Algerian authorities, and even the Great Synagogue was confiscated and turned into a mosque.

———

In 1967, the Libyan government announced that the Jews had to leave Libya temporarily. Each of them was allowed to take property worth only fifty dollars. The rest was left behind. In 1970, the Libyan government enacted additional laws that expropriated all Jewish property left in the country.

———

Morocco had the largest Jewish community in Islamic countries. There has always been a rise of rabbis and leaders from Morocco to the land of Israel. Among the immigrants of the nineteenth century, in addition to many others, there was Haim Amzalag, who was one of the founders of Neve Tzedek and participated in the purchase of land in Rishon LeZion and Petah Tikva, the Moyal family, and the Shlush family, who were among the founders of the first neighborhoods in Tel Aviv.

In 1948, with the establishment of the State of Israel, there were approximately 205,000 Jews in Morocco. Following a series of riots and murders, Moroccan Jews were pressured to leave..

After independence of Morocco in 1956, prohibitions were imposed on Jewish emigration and the removal of Jewish property. From 1961 onward, the Moroccan authorities agreed to allow Jews to leave, for a fee, to Israel for every immigrant. Jews were allowed to take with them only sixty dollars per person. Much property was left behind.

———

Of all Jewish communities, it seems that the Babylonian community (Iraq) was the first, according to Psalm 137:1: "By the rivers of Babylon, there we sat down, yea, we wept, when we remembered Zion". [20] Under the British Mandate, the legal status of Jews was identical to that of Muslims. According to their proportion of the population, they were given five seats in Parliament, the right to run educational and religious institutions independently, and the right to be accepted for government service. This status was maintained even when Iraq gained independence in 1921 under the reign of King Faisal I.

During this period, there even was a Jewish minister of finance, Yehezkel Sasson, also known as Sir Sassoon Eskell. The wealth of the Sasson family and its philanthropic activities inspired the nickname "the Rothschilds of the East" and an abundance of books and articles written about them.

In 1933, Ghazi came to power as king of Iraq and brought back discrimination and harassment against the Jews. Anti-Semitic and anti-Zionist propaganda of the Nazis and the influence of Haj Amin al-Husseini, the mufti of Jerusalem, penetrated the regime as well as the hearts of the incited masses. In 1941, the Farhud massacre occurred, during which 180 Jews were murdered and 240 injured, 586 Jewish shops and businesses were looted, and 99 Jewish homes were destroyed. This marked the beginning of the end of the Jewish community in Iraq. The movement to escape to Israel increased.

The Iraqi government decided that every Jew could leave the country on the condition that he renounce his citizenship and property. The Iraqi government, too, wanted to construct Iraq on the economic base of Jewish property - and they did so. As part of Campaign Ezra and Nehemiah, which began in April 1950, more than 120,000 Jews fled to Israel. In the years that followed, the Ba'ath regime continued to harass the Jews, denied them freedom of movement, and confiscated their property. About fifty Jews were killed by hanging. The escape from Iraq continued for all those years until there were no Jews left.

———

The impressive capabilities of the Jewish refugees of the Islamic countries, with their personal and communal strengths and powers, and the commitment of the absorbing State of Israel, allowed them to succeed in rising up and reaching the successes described later on, presenting a mirror image to the Arab states. If the Arab nations have wanted to, they could absorb the Palestinian refugees and prevent their grief and pain from afflicting their children and grandchildren. They could have been rehabilitated, as were the Jewish refugees of the Arab countries upon their arrival in Israel. The same is true for Israeli Arabs who are given a springboard by the state that does not exist in the Arab countries (apart from the Gulf states). There are Israeli Arabs who did this; there are Israeli Arabs in the process. "Enough complaining and feeling sorry for ourselves," says Dr.

Dalia Fadila, dean of Al-Qasemi College for Science and Engineering in Baka al-Gharbiyye.

AND THEY ALL TOUCH EACH OTHER

Mutual responsibility is an ancient Jewish term determined by Chazal[21] as a moral and a Halacha rule—all people of Israel are guarantors of one another. Its original meaning is that every Jew bears responsibility for the observance of his or her friend's mitzvoth[22], but in modern times, the expression is different in meaning: every Jew is responsible for his or her friend's life and welfare. The Israelis brought this value to extreme, as the value of one Israeli soldier in captivity or the aid of one Israeli tourist in a disaster zone knows no bounds.

The mutual guarantee is the basic principle of the State of Israel. In fact, for that principle Israel was founded: to serve as a national home for the Jewish people. Every Jew in the world who feels threatened is invited to immigrate to Israel and receive citizenship. In fact, all Israelis are building and defending with their lives this shelter for every Jew, if and when needed. This is the essence of the State of Israel, and this is the purpose of its existence. It is the "insurance certificate" of all Jews in the world.

Beyond all the variance, Israeli society is very small, and all the rules of "small world" apply to it. Israelis will discover within a few minutes that they are acquaintances of old age.

The poet Yehuda Amichai wrote:[23]

What a mess in this little land,
what a confusion! The second son of the first husband
goes to his third war, the Second Temple
of the first God was destroyed every year.
My doctor takes care of the intestines
of the shoemaker who was repairing the man's shoes
who defended me in my fourth trial.
On my comb—hair that does not belong to me,

and on my handkerchief cold sweat.
In addition, the memories of others stick to me...
And they're all infected one another and everyone
touches each other and leave
fingerprints...

Israeli society is, as noted, a very dense network characterized by strong connections between individuals as a result of a sense of common destiny, as the state is constantly under existential threat. The dense network is further reinforced by significant encounters in the people's military, which will be discussed later.

The great physical density, the small nation, and the close network of connections have led to high caring, human warmth, and great induction in mutual assistance between Israelis. One of the most prominent of these cases was the presence of thousands of Israelis at the funeral of a lone soldier who immigrated to Israel to serve in the military, leaving his entire family there. Another notable case was the public war to return captive soldier Gilad Shalit under the slogan "He is the child of us all."

Vast numbers of Israelis volunteer to open their homes and host strangers during bombing attacks on civilian towns in the Galilee and around the Gaza Strip. The same happened during the burning of forest on Carmel Mountain. Many of the victims interviewed in the media emphasized the great help they had received from all sides.

The crowded Israeli network also has disadvantages. Sometimes it leads to a feeling of suffocation that causes people to need temporary or permanent physical distance. Some find that this close network intervenes too much in their personal lives. Sometimes it is expressed by constant comparison and competition.

We find in Israel that there is an unusual phenomenon of intergenerational relations. The help of parents for their children is something deeply embedded in the DNA of the Jewish people. The character of the Jewish mother, who cares endlessly for her children, is well known. A study of intergenerational assistance, cited by the Kohelet Research Institute, found that the elderly population is a major source of household transfers, such as "time transfers." More than 60 percent of adults in Israel provide baby-sitting services to their grandchildren at least once a week, compared with only 45 percent in the OECD. Money transfers are the highest among the twelve developed countries examined in the study. The money is used to finance basic needs such as: the purchase and renovation of apartments, large procurements, family events, and educational studies.

But mutual responsibility is also the cause of the spectacular phenomenon of contribution among strangers. This was best described by a street study published in early 2016 by Moran Kleper, a correspondent on Keshet's television show *The Morning of Keshet*, who went out to examine whether Israelis were reaching out to one another. He pretended to be a blind person, went out into the street, and asked passersby to help him cash a NIS 20 bill, but he gave them a NIS 200 bill. How many helped him? The results surprised even the Israelis—everyone helped him. "We stopped dozens of people," says Kleper. "We interfered with them in their daily routine, and they not only helped me, while they turn my attention to 'my mistake,' but also offered help in crossing the street. All of them, without exception, reached out for help."

We shall present here three examples from various fields that illustrate the deep mutual responsibility that comes from the Jewish communities in the diaspora, as expressed in Israeli society: "Gift of Life" for kidney donation, "First Hug" for abandoned babies, and "Ofanim," which teaches children in the far periphery.

Gift of Life: One morning, Lior Frishman called his sister Sarit and told her quietly that he had donated a kidney. She remembers that she laughed and told him, "Don't fool me," and hung up. After a few minutes, knowing her brother, she realized that he was not laughing. She called him back and checked out the details. His parents did not know. Except for his wife and a close friend, no one knew. Lior, who was twenty-three years old, religious, and the father of a child, had become the youngest altruist donor of kidneys in Israel.

Many recoil when it comes to organ donation, even after death. Quite a few retreat even when it comes to organ donation to a relative who needs it. To donate an organ in life and to a complete stranger is a rare act, very rare. Still, the Gift of Life Association, which began operating in 2009, succeeded in harnessing Fishman, as well as more than 320 Israelis who committed the ultimate altruistic act and donated a kidney to other Israelis, who were complete strangers to them.

The association was founded by Rabbi Yeshayahu Haber, an ultra-Orthodox Jew and head of a yeshiva[24] in Jerusalem. He was shocked by the death of a nineteen-year-old boy from a bereaved family who had been waiting for a kidney donation. As a result, he decided to dedicate his life to encouraging people to donate kidneys, and he set up the association for this purpose. According to Fishman, Israel has become a "light unto the nations": it is first worldwide in live organ donation. It ties closely to faith, since almost all donors are religious.

At the state level, there is also an important economic aspect. Every kidney donor saves the state between NIS 3.5 million and NIS 5 million from dialysis to hospitalization. In other words, with more than 320 donors, the Gift of Life organization has already saved the Israeli health system NIS 1.25 billion in its seven years of activity.

First Hug: "It's hard work; mentally - it's not simple. It's not easy at all; not everyone can handle it," Rina says with moisture in her eyes. Rina is a tough operations manager at a financial company that deals with debt collection from hundreds of companies. Most of the employees in the company where she works do not know her volunteering story. She does it discreetly. "Embracing a baby is the most amazing thing in the world, but to think that he was abandoned—is very difficult."

Every year, about three hundred babies are abandoned in hospitals. These babies usually have long stays without dedicated parental care. The medical staff, in charge of rooms laden with babies, takes care of the physical care and health of the infants, but due to the daily burden, they are often unable to provide for the babies' emotional needs.

First Hug was founded in 2004 by Michelle Koriat, CEO and owner of TransCom Global Ltd. First Hug volunteers spend a few hours each day with the baby, giving warmth, love, and touch. They play, sing songs, and read stories. This ensures that the baby will not be exposed to too many individuals and will be able to identify the volunteers, like in a real family. First Hug volunteers make sure babies have a home environment as much as possible, which includes mobiles, picture books, and toys. "There is no shortage of volunteers," Rina notes. "There are more than enough good women."

Ofanim: "My father was a construction worker, and my mother worked in a community center as a cook," says Dr. Haim Dahan, a high-tech entrepreneur who has a master's degree and a PhD in computer science. As a teenager, he met by chance with Prof. Bergman of Ben-Gurion University, who decided to expose the young boy to the computer world. "After those meetings, I realized that I had to learn computers; that's all I wanted.

"The brothers who were born before me, not less smarter than me, turned to basic subjects. The brothers who were born after me—all of them have a master's degree. When I grew old, I understood that I want to give children with a similar background, a push."

Ofanim takes old buses, removes all the seats, and installs computer stands instead. The buses reach the children's homes, which are located far from the cities. Participants in the activities usually come from low socioeconomic backgrounds as well as from the Arab and Bedouin sectors.

COMMITTED TO SOCIETY

Various researchers who reviewed the development of social responsibility in Israel argue[25] that, unlike the way it developed in North America and Europe, it was not a result of coercion, either social or legal. When social justice protests started in Israel in the summer of 2011[26], the social responsibility of companies was already well established in the collective consciousness and in their implementation.

Until the social protest of 2011, the world was simple for companies and their managers. Social contribution was perceived as a good and important thing for the business community. The protest completely changed the rules of the game. The demand from the companies' leaders was no longer a contribution and volunteering-only demand but rather something much more complex. The new demands included different and, at times, contradictory characteristics: lowering the prices of products in parallel with the payment of fair wages to employees, contributing to the community without reducing profits for institutions' investors, welfare conditions for employees without raising prices due to these additional costs, streamlining without layoffs, and other opposing expectations. The paradigm has changed.

"I got up one morning, and suddenly I was the bad guy," says Zion Balas,[27] CEO of Strauss Israel. "I come from a middle-class family with a socialist sentiment. I never thought I was the bad guy. From a company loved by all, we became a hated company. It was a sharp and frustrating transition. It took me a few days to digest, and then the seeds of today's wage plan were sown. In retrospect, one of the advantages of the social protest is that it redefined, at least for me, the role of the CEO in terms of social responsibility," said Balas while raising the employees' wages. "But alongside the desire to benefit the workers, I also have a responsibility toward the shareholders, and this is a step that will cost tens of millions of shekels a year. My job is to ensure that it does not harm the financial stability and profitability of the company."

Strauss social's sustainability report shows that the paradigm has indeed changed. The company is contributing to the community with significant amounts that are growing each year, but this is only the margin of a very complex report. It represents a new world view that includes a strategic partnership with the various circles in which the company operates. Regarding the employees, the report refers to the diversity of workers and managers (Arabs, ultra-religious, women, and so on), the development of workers abilities, and their safety and welfare.

As far as consumers are concerned, Strauss is trying to understand and respond to their different preferences as well as promote adequate nutrition and a healthy lifestyle. As for Strauss's commitment to the environment and the community, the report talks about the company's desire to "deepen our relationships with suppliers to ensure they understand and uphold responsible standards in terms of human rights, labor rights and environmental responsibility."

Many companies in Israel today issue a social report describing their social commitment far beyond donations. For example, Israel Discount Bank, which was the first bank to publish a social report in 2005, writes that their social report is based on the perception that a corporation owes a report to society and the environment in which it operates, not just to its shareholders. The adoption of this approach leads to an expansion of the scope of the report, referencing a wide range of issues, with the aim of addressing the range of social, environmental, and economic issues that concern all the stakeholders of the reporting corporation. (Stakeholders means anyone to whom Discount Bank affects or is affected by: its clients, employees, suppliers, shareholders, the community, and the environment). The social report complements the corporation's financial statements. While the first presents the corporation's economic performance, the other presents the way things are done, the degree of importance that the corporation attributes to the aspirations of its stakeholders, and its efforts to promote issues that require improvement.[28]

The Health System Committed to the Sanctity of Life

The sanctity of life has meaning in Judaism. In the Mishnah[29], we find that sustaining one's soul is equal to sustaining the whole world. Humanism is a basic value in Judaism, and Jews have gone out of their ways to save lives.

The sanctity of life inherent in Israel's culture is perhaps the main reason for the achievements of the health system in Israel. From the international data and assessments, an unequivocal picture emerges regarding its achievements: "Israel is the No. 4 in the world in the quality of the health system," says Bloomberg L.P.[30] "Israel has one of the most enviable health systems among the OECD countries," says the organization's comparison report.[31]

Dr. Mark Britnell, who reviewed health systems around the world, published a book titled *In Search of the Perfect Health System* at the end of 2015 in which he concluded his research:

> If I had to build the best health care system in the world, I would choose the British universal medical coverage, the French freedom of choice from whom to receive treatment, the Nordic preventive medicine, the American R-and-D, the Japanese elderly, the Singapore information systems, the Australian mental health system and the Israeli health maintenance organization (HMOs).

Indeed, the progress of medicine, the improvement in the quality of life, the assimilation of preventive medicine, the education about proper nutrition and physical activity, the early diagnosis of many diseases, and the improvement in the availability of medical services and medication all led to high life expectancy in Israel.

The reality has also made Israel's emergency medical services—whose personnel are frequently trained in emergency security situations—especially good. In many cases, Israeli doctors succeed in saving people when most of the world has already given up.

According to the World Health Organization, Israel is in eighth place in life expectancy, with that of men standing at 80.6 years and ranked fifth in the world, and women's stands at 84.3 years and is currently ranked ninth.

The Israeli Central Bureau of Statistics compares[32] the mortality rates for the common causes of death—cancer, ischemic heart disease, and cerebrovascular disease—indicating that mortality rates in Israel are lower than in most OECD countries. An analysis based on data from the International Agency for Research on Cancer[33] shows that Israel ranks first in the world in the survival of cancer patients.

Such good results also appear in other medical fields. For example, as caesarean section is a dangerous surgery and should be avoided as much as possible, its rate in Israel is the second lowest among the OECD countries and stands at only 15 percent of all live births.[34]

There is no shortage of physicians in Israel. The average ratio of physicians in Israel is 3.3 per thousand residents, higher than the OECD average of 3.1. However, the distribution of doctors between the center and the periphery does not meet the needs of the periphery. There is a significant shortage overall of nurses and hospital beds. The number of nurses is 4.8 per thousand residents compared with 9.1 in the OECD. The number of general hospital beds is 1.8 per thousand residents; it is 3.3 in the OECD.

Despite these problematic data, the health system functions at a high level. How? Part of the explanation is that community health services manage to significantly reduce hospital loads by early screening of patients who need hospitalization and those who can spend their sick days in bed at home.

Dr. Chanan Meydan[35] and his colleagues were among the leaders of a study that examined the fluctuations in the number of hospitalization days in the internal wards of Israeli hospitals (2000–2012). The data examined relate only to hospitalizations that are especially relevant to the elderly, and they show that despite the rapid growth of the elderly population as a result of the increase in life expectancy, the system has succeeded in preventing a significant increase in the number of hospitalizations. "This is due to the strong emphasis placed in Israel on community medicine—that is, health maintenance organizations—that they provide patients the medical treatment without the need to hospitalize them," says Dr. Meydan.

The length of hospitalization in Israel is one of the shortest in the world. Patients there spend an average of 4.3 days in hospitals compared to an average of 6.5 days in the OECD countries. Despite the short duration of hospitalization, the rate of readmissions is among the lowest.

Community medicine is provided in large clinics and with better funding compared to other countries. As a result, the health services enable the management of chronic diseases such as diabetes, which are prevalent in Israel but whose hospitalization rate is among the lowest. The efficiency of the hospitals is also relatively high, perhaps because there is no other choice; hospital bed occupancy is 98 percent compared with 75 percent in the OECD.

One of the assets of the Israeli health system is the long-term database of health organizations. No other country in the world can present decades of historical data on the scope of health care, morbidity, and behavior patterns like the health maintenance organizations in Israel, which have insured all residents of Israel for years. On this basis, it is possible to develop management information systems as well as medical research.

Eli Defes, who was the director general of Clalit Health Services, refers to the information system that was developed there. The system, called Ofek, was developed by the Israeli company DBMotion and adopted by the Ministry of Health as a national system. It connects all hospitals and community clinics to prevent wrongful or unnecessary treatments. It is considered one of the most advanced systems of its kind in the world.

Prof. Ran Balicer, director of the Clalit Institute for Research, explains. "Innovation and digital medicine are an existential and necessary need for health organizations today, and with the constant rise in chronic morbidity, to the point that it is becoming a norm, new approaches are needed to deal with the new challenges. Wise use of medical data is necessary to enable new approaches of this kind."

"There is a common phenomenon worldwide of repeated hospitalizations of older adults returning within thirty days of discharge from hospital," says Prof. Balicer. "We were surprised to discover, after running this study, that despite the short time of hospitalization, we were in less repeated hospitalizations. This is due to the unique integration between the hospitals and the community. We used algorithms on our data to predict who will return to rehospitalization. For those peoples we create special programs to prevent their need for rehospitalization. We succeeded in reducing readmission amount of five percent."

Nissim Alon, CEO of Leumit Health Services, refers to three main indicators for examining the health system: justice, equality, and efficiency. "Justice means, among other things, the level of insurance coverage; does it cover the entire population or only its share? In Israel, the coverage is universal, and all citizens of the State of Israel and all permanent residents are covered by national health insurance." The medical coverage in Israel is also one of the most extensive. "There are countries in the OECD whose coverage does not include drugs," he explains. Regarding the freedom of choice, he says, "The Israelis also have the ability to choose the medical institute and the physician they prefer and to change it at any time. It does not exist in many places."

The second main indicator is social equality. "Pay as much as you can and receive medical services as your needs, a mechanism in which rich and healthy subsidize the poor and the sick." The third factor is efficiency. "The national expenditure on health in Israel is 7.6 percent of the GDP, one of the lowest in the OECD, where the average is 9.4 percent. It means savings budget of NIS 20 billion every year, and we are still considered to be one of the best health systems in the world," Alon emphasizes.

Other successes are related both to the medical system and to cultural characteristics. The desire to have children is especially important to Israelis. It is not surprising then that about 4.1 percent of Israel's children are born from fertility treatments—the first place with a huge gap in comparison to the world[36].

Health tourism to Israel has also developed as a result of its excellent medical services. From around the world, wealthy tourists, mainly from third-world countries, arrive for surgery and complex treatments. This phenomenon requires, of course, maintaining a balance between the income it brings and the scope of allocation of health resources, doctors, beds, and so on to public health.

Finally, it should be noted that there are additional explanations for the high life expectancy of Israelis that are not related to the capabilities of the medical system. There is a theory that the people of the Mediterranean are healthier because of the Mediterranean diet. In addition to Israel, Spain and Italy are also among the top ten countries with the highest life expectancies of both men and women.

According to a Taub Center study published in December 2016, an analysis based on a sample of more than 130 countries found, somewhat paradoxically, that military service adds more than three years to the life expectancy of Israeli men. Given the characteristics that affect life expectancy in each country—levels of wealth and education, health system characteristics, and overall demographic profile—the Israeli advantage is greater and even expands over time. In OECD countries, women live an average of five and a half years longer than men, whereas in Israel, where women's military service is shorter and often requires little physical effort, the gap is only three years. In three out of the four countries enjoying the highest life expectancy in the world, men are required to serve in the military. Of the five leading countries in the OECD index, only one (Japan) has had no type of compulsory military service in the last thirty years.

Arab men in Israel can enjoy a life expectancy of seventy-seven years, which is higher than almost any Arab country. The life expectancy of Arab men in Arab countries ranges between seventy-nine years in rich Qatar, seventy-six years in the equally wealthy UAE, seventy-four years in Saudi Arabia, seventy-two years in Jordan, sixty-nine in Morocco and Egypt, and sixty-six in Iraq.

FEWER DIE ON THE ROAD

In Israel, the number of fatalities from road accidents is lower than in all other European countries except the Scandinavian nations, the Netherlands, and Britain. The number of road traffic fatalities per capita in Israel is sixth lowest in the world. In Canada, the number of fatalities per hundred thousand residents is nearly double, and in the United States, it is almost four times higher.

One main hypothesis is that rapid rescue and advanced medical knowledge in emergency situations is the reason for this phenomenon.

ADDICTED TO THE DEVELOPMENT OF LIFESAVING TECHNOLOGY

The British website, Information Is Beautiful, published[37] a fascinating new world map that illustrates how each country is characterized. The statistical information was gathered in an in-depth study that included online information on various subjects, data from the World Bank, and even the number of Guinness World Records. The map is full of data, some surprising and some even strange. Puerto Rico is first in the consumption of rum, Greece in the number of cheese eaters, Namibia in the number of road accidents, and Argentina in the amount of horse-meat for food.

Sometimes it turns out that stereotypes are true to reality: North Korea is first in the military population relative to population size, Peru is indeed the kingdom of cocaine, and Honduras is the queen of murders. Not surprisingly, South Africa tops the table with exports of platinum and Chile in exports of lead. Of the two hundred countries, only a few were ranked first in something that was no more than a curiosity, something that really matters to humanity. Here they stand alone: Taiwan in the number of patents, Croatia in kidney transplants, Switzerland in innovation, Cuba in the number of doctors per capita, and Israel, which ranks first in the world in terms of medical research.

There is not enough time or space to cover all Israeli developments regarding saving lives, so we present only a few. We do not relate to the economic value of these initiatives but to the value motivation of developing medical technology, which has made Israel one of the leading centers in the world specializing in these fields.

Ran Poliakine, an inventor in every fiber of his being, is involved in at least three specific projects dedicated to saving lives. One of them is QinFlow, a startup that provides a unique solution to a critical medical problem: the need for rapid heating of fluids for blood transfusions in the field. The device is thus far used by paramedics, intensive care teams, and trauma centers, and it has helped to rescue earthquake, avalanche, and accident victims.

Another project by Poliakine is Wellsense, which involves a system called M.A.P that uses the first intelligent textile technology to prevent pressure ulcers in hospitalized patients and patients in nursing homes. The system is already in use in medical institutions in several countries and may eliminate this terrible problem in the future.

The third project in which Poliakine is involved is called Years of Water and is designed to save the third world from a lack of clean water. It consists a portable device known as the "water elephant," manufactured by the company, which is a container of about five liters. A sixteen-watt ultraviolet-light-emitting lamp eliminates bacteria, viruses, and protozoa within eight seconds of contact with contaminated water. The power is produced by a hand winch, which eliminates the need for chemicals, electricity, running water, filters, or other expensive items. The water elephant solves the problem of freshwater at the household level, thus making it unnecessary for government agencies or private donors to maintain community wells and other solutions in the villages.

The company EarlySense has developed pioneering technology aimed at promoting preventive care in hospitals and improving patients' medical conditions. The product, which is installed under the patient's bed, measures the pulse, breathing rate, and movement. According to the company, the system is currently installed in approximately fifty hospitals in the United States, Europe, and Asia. In 2015, the system saved twenty-seven thousand hospital days and prevented 583 patient deaths and 415 resuscitations due to early identification of symptoms in patients.

Given Imaging is the first company in the world to develop pellet endoscopy technology. It engages in the production and marketing of visual inspection methods for the human digestive system. The technology is based on tiny cameras located in capsules that can be swallowed to create pelvic endoscopy. Given Imaging has pills for imaging of the esophagus, the small intestine, and the colon. In addition, the company has developed an RF pill that checks for intestinal obstructions that can cause the imaging pill to get stuck.

"InSightec develops an operating room—without surgery," says Dr. Kobi Vortman, CEO of the company. "The treatment is based on magnetic imaging that transforms the body into a transparent, focused beam of sound waves that destroys growth by heating without damaging the environment." InSightec is the only company in the world with US Food and Drug Administration (FDA) approval for the use of this technology and has won numerous awards and accolades, including the selection of the company's work as "a technological breakthrough" by the World Economic Forum in Davos.

BioSense Webster was the first company to be established and sold by a cardiologist. Prof. Shlomo Ben-Haim developed a method to navigate within the coronary arteries to reach a precise point within the heart and weld it in a way that will balance heart-rate disturbances. The procedure for welding the heart was, at that time, at the beginning of its development, and it suffered from a barrier—the doctor did not know exactly where he or she was welding. In 2000, the company was bought by Johnson & Johnson for $427 million, and it became the highest high-tech company sold in Israel at that time. BioSense Webster, which currently employs more than two hundred people, was later merged with the parent company's catheters department. It records sales of more than $1 billion a year and is an independent unit that is a partner in the development of Johnson's overall cardiology strategy.

In the fight against cancer and degenerative and chronic diseases, the drug Copaxone, which is known for billions of dollars in revenues it has delivered to Teva over the years, is just one of the developments. Many Israeli companies and scientists are world leaders. Among the most prominent are "nano-skeletons" for the destruction of cancer cells by Prof.

Machluf and the drug Azilect for Parkinson's disease by Profs. Youdim and Finberg, all from the Technion. Exelon is used for the treatment of dementia and was created by Profs. Weinstock-Rosin, Chorev, and Dr. Ta-Shma. Doxil for cancer treatment is from Profs. Bernholz and Gabizon, both from the Hebrew University of Jerusalem.

There are unusual patents, such as Prof. Haick's of the Technion development "NaNose" for rapid detection of cancer through the oral breath sample. There are ongoing research projects such as the understanding of the cells responsible for degenerative diseases and the technological uses, conducted by Prof. Gazit, Drs. Adler-Abramovich, Levin and Arnon of Tel Aviv University, and a new method for activating immune cells to treat cancer by Prof. Eshhar of the Hebrew University of Jerusalem.

II

THE LAND OF OPPORTUNITIES

The Israeli dream of personal, economic, and social success is perhaps based on the American dream but goes far beyond it. Israeli society demands equality: between Ashkenazim and Sephardim, between residents of the center and the periphery, between women and men, and between secular and religious. This is a value-based society that allows mobility, which contributes to its cohesion.

"The number of new rich in Israel, as a result of the realization of high-tech companies and technological entrepreneurship, is exceptional in relation to everything we know," says a senior investment banker at J. P. Morgan Chase & Co. "When I first came here, twelve years ago, and I looked for clients, I have been told to meet about twenty rich families that ruled the Israeli economy at that time. Since then, almost all the tycoons have disappeared or their power has fallen, and there has been a large-scale enrichment of people who have accumulated their fortunes in the high-tech sector, so now there are hundreds of wealthy families and individuals, some of them very young people. The majority of them came from the Israeli middle class."

But accumulating capital from the high-tech industry is only a small part of the picture. The Israeli dream is of an increase in the individual's quality of life and an increase in one's social status. This dream of social mobility and the many examples of its realization are what motivate

Israelis to realize their talents and personal abilities independently of the circumstances of their birth.

CLIMBING THE SOCIOECONOMIC LADDER

There are six main factors for socioeconomic mobility in Israel: high-tech and technological entrepreneurship, business entrepreneurship and management, the military, academia and medicine, politics, and the media. These promote those who use them far beyond the socioeconomic conditions of their parents and family.

Maj. Gen. (Ret.) Orna Barbivay, a former general in the Israel Defense Forces (IDF), was born in Ramla. Her parents raised eight children in difficult economic conditions. "From a very young age I worked in a variety of jobs, from washing floors for an elderly blind woman to a babysitter for the children of the hospital doctors," she says. "I did everything to bring some money to my mother, to make it easier for her. I did homework while lying on the floor, because there simply was not a table." From preparing homework on the floor to becoming general staff in the military, Barbivay climbed the ladder while realizing the Israeli dream. There are few countries in which such social mobility is as possible as it is in the State of Israel.

Shlomo Eliahu was born in Baghdad, Iraq. When he was a child, he immigrated to Israel with his parents and eight brothers and sisters. At the age of fifteen, he began to work, initially as an apprentice in a metalwork shop, and later as a delivery boy for Migdal Insurance Company. His military service was postponed because of the polio he suffered as a child. Rising up in Migdal, He bought it, the largest insurance company in Israel. In 2011, Forbes estimated Eliyahu's fortune at $1.1 billion.

During the Second World War, Avram Hershko's father, a schoolteacher, was taken to forced labor camps in the Hungarian military and was taken prisoner by the Soviets. His mother, brother, and he were imprisoned in the ghetto and then to a concentration camp in Austria. In 2004, Prof. Avram Hershko, together with Prof. Aaron Ciechanover and Prof. Irwin Rose, received the Nobel Prize in Chemistry. They discovered and described the ubiquitin system responsible for the breakdown of proteins in the cell, leading to a breakthrough in cancer research and neuro-degenerative diseases in the brain.

The last three chiefs of staff in the Israeli military came from immigrant families who fled to Israel without any property. Lt. Gen. Gadi Eisenkot, the current chief of staff, was born in Tiberias to Meir, a native of Marrakech, and Ester, who was born in Casablanca. Eisenkot grew up in Eilat and studied at an evening school while working during the day. He holds a BA in general history from Tel Aviv University and an MA in political science from the University of Haifa. He completed his military and security studies at the US Army War College in Carlisle, Pennsylvania.

The former chief of staff, Lt. Gen. Benny Gantz, was born and raised in Moshav. His mother was a Holocaust survivor from Hungary, and his father came from Transylvania. His parents immigrated to Israel aboard the illegal immigrant ship *Chaim Arlosoroff* and were expelled by the British to a refugee camp in Cyprus. Later, they came to Israel and were among the founders of the cooperative Israeli settlement Kfar Ahim.

Before him, Lt. Gen. Gabi Ashkenazi served as chief of staff. His mother fled from Syria at the age of ten in a secret operation of the Palmach, and his father was a Holocaust survivor from Bulgaria. They all started from nothing.

Ada Yonath's parents emigrated from Poland and ran a grocery store in Jerusalem. During her studies, Yonath worked to help support her family. After her military service, she studied chemistry and biochemistry at the Hebrew University of Jerusalem. She received her PhD with honors from the Weizmann Institute of Science and was a postdoctoral fellow at Carnegie Mellon and MIT. Upon her return to the Weizmann Institute of Science, she established a research lab for ribosomes, where she is working today. Learning the ribosome structure has enabled a better understanding of how existing antibiotics work and to develop new drugs. In 2009, Prof. Ada Yonath received the Nobel Prize in Chemistry.

"This was the phone call that changed my life," said Dr. Masad Barhoum, general director of the Galilee Medical Center in Nahariya about the call he received from an IDF officer in the middle of the night; the officer told him that there were wounded from Syria. "'We are ready,' I replied without thinking," Barhoum recalls, adding that Nahariya Hospital (Galilee Medical Center) is supposed to provide medical services to Jews, Christians, Muslims, and Druze, who constitute the human mosaic in the Galilee. But Syrians? Those who see us as enemies? Since then, the hospital has treated more than two hundred Syrians, and more than three thousand Syrians have been treated in Israel—war victims seeking medicine with their sworn enemies—the melodrama in full. "When you cross the hospital gates," he said, "the Jews cease to be Jews, the Muslims stop being Muslim, and I stop being an Arab." Dr. Barhoum delivered this moving speech to the AIPAC conference in Washington.

Zadik Bino was born in Basra, Iraq. When he was six, his family fled to Israel. As a young boy, he assisted his parents at a neighborhood grocery store they ran. After his discharge from the military, where he served as a mechanic in the air force, he was promoted to a junior position at Hapoalim Bank, and he progressed rapidly in the banking system until he was appointed CEO of First International Bank and later chairperson of the board. For two years, Zadik Bino served as CEO of Bank Leumi, and during the following years, he purchased shares of Paz Company until he owned control of the company and issued it on the stock exchange. Later, he bought the oil refineries in Ashdod. He became the owner of FIBI, with all its daughter companies, including First International Bank, where he once worked.

After his military service, Shlomo Shmeltzer, born in Haifa, married Atalia and worked for her father, Victor, in his garage. Since he did not see a future as a mechanic, with the help of his father-in-law, he bought two small cars. In 2015, the turnover of Shlomo Group car rental, which he founded, is about NIS 6.7 billion.

Yitzhak Tshuva was born in Tripoli. When he was six months old, his parents and their eight children immigrated to Israel and lived in a transit camp in Netanya. At the age of twelve, Tshuva began to work to help support the family and learned in the evenings. After his discharge from the IDF, he began his independent career as a construction contractor in Netanya. Today, Tshuva has direct and indirect holdings in many areas in Israel and abroad, and his fortune is estimated at more than $4 billion.

When Hilla, a twenty-eight-year-old flight attendant cured of cancer, brought a firstborn son to the world after having ovarian tissue transplanted that she had removed a decade earlier, it was thanks to Prof. Joseph (Yossi) Lessing, who was ahead of his time with innovative technology. Prof. Lessing was born in a refugee camp in Austria to Holocaust survivors from Poland. His mother, Chava, lost her first husband and two daughters in the Warsaw Ghetto. After the war, she met her second husband, Yossi's father. The family was absorbed in Israel in the Beer Yaakov transit camp. Later, Prof. Lessing served as director of the obstetrics and gynecology department of Ichilov Hospital in Tel Aviv. Lessing cannot forget the caesarean operation he carried out together with Prof. Fouad Azem, an Israeli Arab born in Taibeh. His hands shook slightly as he held the baby that was brought out of Hilla's womb. In an excited voice, he broke the tense silence in the operating room when he announced, "Welcome home, boy" just before the baby's crying filled the space.

There are countless other examples in all areas of life. Israel is full of them: the politics, culture, and art of the descendants of immigrants whose parents fled to Israel from the death countries in Europe and from the terror in Muslim countries in the Middle East. The way from the transit camp, from the kibbutz, or from the urban slums to the peak of success was not easy. It is not easy still, but it exists. The Israeli dream is within the reach of every talented, diligent, courageous, and visionary person in this country of immigrants.

EDUCATION AND EDUCATION AGAIN

All Israelis have a "Jewish mother," and some of them have a Polish Jewish mother. The famous American writer Dan Greenberg has already written that "in order to be a Jewish mother, you do not have to be neither a mother nor a Jew." A Jewish mother could be all the Arab fathers and mothers, Jews, veterans, new immigrants, ultra-Orthodox, religious and secular, urban and rural, Mizrahi and Ashkenazi, Ethiopian immigrants and Ukrainian, those who came from France and South America, and all the parents who believe in education and push their children.

Yossi Vardi, one of the leaders of the Israeli Internet industry, told the ultimate story about the Jewish mother when he presented the founder of Google to the participants in the President's Conference in Jerusalem. Sergey Mikhaylovich Brin is a Soviet-born American Jew who, together with Larry Page, developed Google during their PhD studies at Stanford. When Google was established, the two stopped their studies and devoted their time to develop the company. Only Sergey's mother continued to lament for years, saying, "Google shmugel, what about the PhD?"

The "Jewish mother" can sometimes be a Druze father. Col. (Res.) Dr. Salman Zarka, director of the Ziv Medical Center in Safed, was born to a Druze family of eight children from Peqi'in. His father worked in plastering, flooring, and other hard physical labor, and he understood that in order to live a good life, his sons must have a good education. "Look at my hands," the father used to say, and he stretched out his hands to show his young son. "It's farmer's hands, used for hard work. Look at the cracks I have in my hands—you do not need those hands." Every summer vacation, the father would take his son to work with him, and he always told him, "This is for you to learn and understand that you do not want a life like mine. You want to learn and succeed."

The Zarka sisters were brought up differently. A custom in the Druze sector was that for girls, when they reached the seventh grade and when the first signs of femininity began, their studies were stopped, and until they found a husband, they worked in the sewing shops. When Salman was already a student at the Technion Medical School, he came home one day and heard the argument between his younger sister and their father, during which his sister demanded to learn nursing. The father resisted with all his power and gave up only when Salman threatened that if his sister was not allowed to go to school, he would leave the medical school.

———

Israelis finds it difficult to accept the relatively low grades of Israeli pupils in international comparison tests. The national pride and self-perception of a people and a culture of learning are damaged. There is also great concern at a possible connection between the low achievements of the students and the future prosperity of the country.

The existence of such a relationship has been refuted in all studies, and the Israeli reality proves this time and again. Israel is one of the world's leading countries in the number of patents registered per capita, far ahead of the countries that achieved high scores in the international tests. Israel has scientific, technological, artistic, and other achievements at the highest levels in international comparisons.

Can the gap between the results of Israeli children in tests and the high-tech reality be explained by the deterioration of the education system? Will the learning system that produced the Israeli geniuses of the past continue to create the geniuses of the future?

The data indicate that the education system in Israel is better itself and not deteriorating. A significant improvement in student achievements has shown in recent years: Israel is ranked eighth in the world at the rate of improvement in results. The percentage of those eligible for matriculation in the Jewish sector has risen, and the most significant advancement is taking place in the Arab sector, where the Druze segment is particularly prominent.

The outstanding Israeli Arab students aspire to reach higher levels than in the past, and some of them integrate in prestigious professions in medicine, pharmacy, and premedicine in numbers that grow steadily. This trend also exists in the fields of computers and engineering. "A quarter of the computer science students at the Technion are Arabs (far more than their share in the population)," says Yoram Yaacobi, Microsoft's CEO in Israel.

This gap between the students' achievements in international comparison tests and the high-tech, research, and patents developed in Israel, has another explanation, in our opinion, that is rooted in one of the characteristic of Israelis: the rebellious nature that prevents them from accepting rules. There are quite a few stories about senior research and technology students who were failing or average students. It is exactly the same rebelliousness that will make the failing or average student into a successful entrepreneur or science researcher. Of course, students in countries where the value of obedience to a teacher is sacred from an early age, such as the East Asian countries, lead the international comparison tables.

However, it seems that one of the most important reasons is the per-pupil investment in the education system. A high proportion of children in the education system make it difficult to allocate financial resources to enable optimal scholastic achievement. Israel spends a higher GNP on education than the OECD average, but because of the large number of students, the investment per student is lower than the average. Here, Israel's demographic advantage as the youngest country among the developed countries becomes a disadvantage. The size of the classrooms and the number of students per teacher weigh heavily on the education system.

The results of the tests are really disturbing for a different reason: they reflect the social gaps that exist in Israel. The best results were obtained from students from Hebrew-speaking schools, the secular education system, and higher socioeconomic statuses. Instead of being an instrument of social mobility, education expresses gaps. This issue requires immediate attention by the relevant authorities.

———

As she sat on a golden throne in one of her golden palaces, the Thai princess Maha Chakri Sirindhorn gave the medals to each of the winners of the 2009 Asian Physics Olympiad. "Before the ceremony, we had to train for two hours on how to walk properly how to bow to the Princess properly," recalls silver medal winner Itamar Hasson, who won a gold medal at the International Olympic Games in Mexico later on.

The Israeli youth delegations to the International Science Olympiads in mathematics, physics, chemistry, robotics, and computers return with medals almost every year. In the summer of 2013, Israel's representatives reached an unprecedented achievement, with nineteen members of the delegation receiving Olympic medals. In the summer of 2016, a delegation of Israeli high school students won six medals at the International Mathematics Olympiad. At the International Physics Olympiad that summer, Israeli high school students obtained five Olympic medals.

———

Private expenditure on education in Israel is much higher than the OECD average. Most of the private investment in education is devoted to academic studies. Almost half of the adult population in Israel has an academic education. Thus, Israel ranked third in the world, behind Russia and Canada, and far above the OECD average. Due to the highly educated immigrants from the former USSR, this is especially evident in the older population, whose percentage of academics in Israel is twice as high as the OECD average. But even at the younger ages, the percentage of students studying in higher education in Israel is higher than the international average, thus causing the need to compete with the countries that have a higher percentage of students in higher education than Israel, such as Luxembourg, Lithuania, Ireland, Canada, Russia, and South Korea.

Even in the ultra-Orthodox sector, which had not been integrated into higher secular education in the past, the trend is changing. Yehuda Morgenstern, a fourth-year student at the Technion's Faculty of Industrial Engineering and Management, says that high yeshiva graduates have very little knowledge, if any, of mathematics and English. The graduates of the higher yeshivas are intellectually sharp but without sufficient knowledge in any field relevant to work.

These things are starting to change. Rabbi Yaakov Litzman, the health minister, a member of Yahadut HaTorah, and former chairman of the Finance Committee in the Knesset, says openly: "Anyone who cannot study [at the yeshiva] will go to work, and this includes preparing himself for the studies relevant to the work life." The Israeli government surrenders again and again to the ultra-religious demands for exemption from the state's curriculum. "Ironically, it is the state that perpetuates the gaps in knowledge and skills, thereby increasing the future budgetary cost of programs designed to reduce these gaps."

But there are also other opinions on the subject. "Anyone who understands the ultra-Orthodox world realizes that forcing a core curriculum is the wrong way; except creating antagonism, it will not do anything, and when you hurt people, people all gather together, tighten the lines, remove the thorns. I do not believe in coercion, but in massive support for ultra-Orthodox integration in academia, in colleges, to open options for them, to put in a stimulating window and let the processes do their part," says Dr. Shmulik Hess, a yeshiva student from Safed. Hess joined the military, later became a brilliant student in pharmacology, did postdoctoral fellowships at Harvard and MIT, and then founded a biotech company called Valin Technologies, which sells tens of millions of dollars of insulin knowledge to China. But the number of ultra-Orthodox workers is rising dramatically. "There will always be Torah scholars, but the massive masses do want to make a decent living."

———

Beit Jann is a Druze village in the Upper Galilee. The Druze maintain a unique religion that split from Shi'ite Islam in the eleventh century; it comprises about 1.5 million people. Almost all the Druze live in the geographical area that includes Syria, Lebanon, and northern Israel. The Druze community in Israel, some 150,000, is loyal to the country and its institutions and serves in the military (most Arabs in Israel don't).

Beit Jann is very low in the socioeconomic ranking. For years, as expected due to the village's low socioeconomic status, the students were at the bottom of the national comparison tests.

Surprisingly, in 2013, Beit Jann was ranked third in terms of the number of students who received a matriculation certificate. One year later, 100 percent of the students in the village were eligible for matriculation; in 2014, the village was rated in the top three, with 94.3 percent.

Not only Beit Jann, but also Maghar, which has Druze, Arab, Christian, and Muslim residents, reached 81 percent in 2014, while the Arab Muslim village, Deir al-Asad, reached 76.2 percent, and the Bedouin village, Lakiya, in the south had 75 percent entitled to matriculation.

The reason? A special project in which fifteen schools implemented in, which was developed by Nissim Cohen, director of the Rashi Foundation's Yeholot, and funded by the Ministry of Education, philanthropists, and donations from companies like Check Point.

The uniqueness of the project is that it fosters the worst students in schools, who are at risk of dropping out of the education system. They are in the tenth grade and begin an acceleration program designed to complete educational gaps and provide them with confidence in their abilities and pride in their achievements. They study for long hours, including nights and vacations, and are examined frequently, receiving close personal support from their teachers. Educational indicators are also integrated and measured, including students' self-efficacy, focus and internal control, sense of belonging, aspirations for academic education, and overcoming behavioral problems. In all these indicators, there was a significant improvement among the students in the program. The enlistment in the IDF among male Druze graduates of the program rose, and graduates of the first class even began to study at higher education facilities.

———

Alongside the value of education, it is important to note other educational values, including the "acceptance of the other," which is different. "Ten years ago, if a child in a wheelchair could not come to school because of accessibility problems, they would say, sorry, but we do not have money for accessibility; there are other priorities," says Dr. Eran Uziely, head of special education in Achva Academic College, which has been following this issue for nearly three decades. "Today, the awareness of the students' needs has risen, and no one can think of saying such a thing. Much has changed, in the field of integration and treatment of children with special needs. Israel today is very advanced on integration." It's not enough, but it is moving in the right direction. This is part of the mutual guarantee that exists in the DNA of the state. The subject has become very central and focused, with much more budgets and understanding of the system.

———

Another educational value to which the education system devotes great efforts is "zero tolerance for violence." Violence in general and violence in schools in particular have a high public profile. The education system devotes ongoing and focused efforts to dealing with this issue. Some are more successful and some are less, but the results show improvement. According to the Israeli police, there has been a sharp drop in violence committed by minors in schools.

Over the years, there has been a downward trend in the rate of reporting on various forms of violence, mainly at the elementary and junior high levels. There is no doubt that the ongoing war declared by the Ministry of Education against violence must continue with full vigor and perseverance.

ACADEMIA AND RESEARCH

Elon Lindenstrauss is the first Israeli to win the Fields Medal, described as the mathematical equivalent of the Nobel Prize, which is not awarded in this field. Lindenstrauss was born in Jerusalem and studied at the university's high school, where he won a bronze medal at the International Mathematical Olympiad at the age of eighteen. He joined the elite IDF program, Talpiot, and received his first degree in mathematics and physics from the Hebrew University. He has done postdoctoral studies at the Clay Mathematics Institute and Princeton University, and since 2009, he has divided his time between the Hebrew University of Jerusalem and Princeton University.

Eight Israelis have won the Nobel Prize since the beginning of the twenty-first century, so Israel is ranked as a world leader in the Nobel Prize winners per capita, more than 50 times its share of world population. Since Israel's founding, more than 22 percent of the Nobel Prize recipients have been Jewish or semi-Jewish, and the number has increased to 31 percent in the twenty-first century, with 41 percent of the Nobel Prize winners being Jewish scientists. Jews account for only 0.2 percent of the world's population, and according to Nobel, their scientific contribution is two hundred times their weight in the world's population.

"They ask me why there is such a high percentage of genius among Jews," laughs Erik Weiner, author of *The Geography of Bliss*.[38] "The reasons for this are complex. I do not think it's a genetic matter. I believe that there is a cultural issue here—Judaism is a culture of literacy. The Jews in Europe studied Talmud[39] at a time when many [Europeans were] still illiterate. Moreover, the fact that the Jews were outsiders played a decisive role. It is known that the sense of alienation and being an outsider is an internal combustion engine that pushes people into something, and the Jews are not only the chosen people, they are also the challenged people."

In their book *The Chosen Few*,[40] Prof. Eckstein and Prof. Botticini described the development of literacy in Judaism and its results. In 70 AD, most Jews were illiterate farmers. In 1492, the year of the expulsion from Spain by Isabella the First of Castile and King Ferdinand the Second of Aragon, the Jews were mostly urban educated and specialized in medicine, commerce, and money management. This radical change from illiteracy to education was not the result of anti-Semitism, the persecution of the Jews, and their restrictions, but of changes in the Jewish people itself.

During this period, the implementation of a new norm requiring every Jewish man to read and study Torah and to send his sons to school began. As a result of the establishment and expansion of Muslim substitutions, there has been a process of urbanization and growth of trade, and the demand for professions that have given a significant advantage to literacy has increased. The prestige of the educated Jews rose in an age when only a few knew how to read and write.

The achievements of Jews in research and academia also contributed to the culture of the debate with the existing text in the Talmud, the education to revolt the given and conventional reality, to question it in conventions that are essential to a religious minority that wishes to preserve its heritage, the desire to create a better world, and an aspiration for personal progress. Those attributes were intensified in modern Israel, when people were called to maximize their abilities in order to succeed against all odds.

Whatever the reasons, we find Jews and Israelis among the contenders and winners of all the important international prizes.

The Nobel Prize is not awarded in computer science. The most important prize in this area is the Turing Award. As of 2017, Israel is in third place among the world's countries in the number of award winners. The Gödel Prize is the second most important in the field of computer science. More than a third of the prize winners are Israelis.

Scientists at the Israeli Academy are working on the next big idea. In mentioning only some of the fields, they are active in innovative treatments for cancer, the atlas of the human brain, the development of giant planets, sleep disorders, identification of explosive molecules, regulation of oil and gas drilling, development of cardiac patches, renewable energies, and more.

Israel is a world leader in the number of per capita publications in mathematics, and about a quarter of Israeli publications are in clinical medicine, followed by physics, chemistry, and engineering. Israel ranks fourteenth in the world in the number of scientific publications per capita, followed by France, Germany, and the United States.[41]

A relatively new immigrant to Israel is physicist Prof. Jeff Steinhauer, a native of Los Angeles who completed his doctorate at the University of California (UCLA) and then two postdoctoral studies. In his study published in August 2016 in the journal *Nature Physics*, Steinhauer shows how sound particles are emitted from black holes in space. The study presents new findings that support the Hawking radiation theory, which was proposed more than forty years ago and focuses on the claim that black holes are not "absorbers" but emit electromagnetic radiation. "This is an experimental confirmation of Hawking's prediction of the thermodynamics of the black hole," Steinhauer says, participating in a CNN article in his laboratory at the Technion. Experts estimate that the study could pave the way for a Nobel Prize for Stephen Hawking.

CERN is the largest and perhaps the most important scientific project in the world today; it deals with the discovery of new subatomic particles, especially the famous "God particle." "There are thousands of scientists there, but the involvement of Israelis in CERN is far beyond Israel's relative weight," says Avi Blizovsky, a science reporter for thirty years who founded the Hayadan website, which covers scientific topics for the general public.

The quality of Israeli scientific publications, defined by the average number of citations per publication, has consistently increased over the years. Since the beginning of the twenty-first century, it is higher than the OECD average.

GENDER EQUALITY?

The authors of this book both knew that gender equality might be the most serious bone of contention in this whole project of writing a joint book.

He wrote: "Full equality is won by the women of Israel."

She corrected: "There is no equality, surely no full equality."

He wrote: "The obligation to military service is the manifestation of full equality."

She corrected: "Only 6 percent of CEOs are women, only 4 percent of chairpersons, a wage gap of more than 30 percent, a few Knesset members and less of the government ministers."

He wrote: "Bank of Israel governor, CEO of three large banks, former prime minister and general accountant, former director general of the Ministry of Finance and president of the Supreme Court."

She corrected: "And parties without any female representation, and sexual harassment, and the murder of women in the family."

But finally, we were able to reach certain understandings.

According to World Bank figures, the percentage of women in the Knesset is rising steadily. According to the percentage of seats in the Parliament occupied by women, Israel is in a relatively good place in the world but needs improvement compared with OECD countries.

There is no doubt that the good results are particularly damaged by the ultra-Orthodox and Arab parties, where there is little or no representation by women. The ultra-Orthodox sector in Israel is often rightly accused of discriminatory positions on religious, ethnic, and gender grounds. But even among the ultra-Orthodox, we see the beginning of a new approach. Ultra-Orthodox women set up an ultra-Orthodox women's party, and others established the movement against denial of representation against women.

As for the Arab sector in Israel, it can be argued that the minority of women in the Arab parties are from Muslim culture, which views the man as the ruler, but still, the representation of Arab women in the Israeli Parliament is lower than the average of the Arab parliaments in the countries of the region. In 2015, Arab-women Knesset members constituted only 9.3 percent of Arab representatives compared with 17.9 percent in Arab countries. Arab women are also working to increase their representation in the Knesset, claiming that "a party or list that does not have equality does not make sense."

We would like to see legislation in Israel that requires proper representation of women in all key positions. Only such legislation will succeed in instilling this just change in all the sectors. It is not a naïve thought in a state based on a declaration of independence that guarantees gender equality, human dignity, and liberty.

If these two extremes can be neutralized, the ultra-Orthodox and Arab parties, the percentage of women's seats in the Knesset is higher than OECD average, even higher than the average of high-income OECD countries. The ratio between women's and men's MPs is improving continuously, from 12 percent in 1995 to 27 percent in 2017, a trend that is consistent with what is happening in the world as well.

Israel ranks third in Europe, after Norway and Sweden, in the number of women serving as council members in local authorities in the central regions, with a high rate of 44 percent.

In Israel, as well as in all of the countries in the study, in lower socioeconomic municipalities, there are fewer women serving as council members.

The senior women in the Israeli economy leave a strong impression of success. They are the leaders in the economic public sector—Dr. Karnit Flug, Bank of Israel governor; Dorit Salinger, supervisor of Capital Market, Savings and Insurance; Dr. Hedva Bar, banking system supervisor; Dr. Nadine Baudot-Trajtenberg, deputy governor of the Bank of Israel, and many others. Strong women are leaders in the business sector, but the percentage of women directors in large companies in Israel is relatively low and is ranked thirteenth among the countries surveyed. Following the amendment to the Government Companies Law, the percentage of women on boards of directors in governmental companies rose to 42 percent, although it should be noted that the rate has never reached 50 percent.

"When I was chosen to light a torch at the Independence Day ceremony, as the symbol of breakthrough women, I was full of doubts," says the first IDF female major general, Orna Barbivay. "Why do women need a ceremony devoted entirely to their achievements? But when I met the women who were chosen and their impressive achievements, I welcomed the choice. I hope that we will reach a situation where there will be gender equality everywhere and at every level. We have not yet completed the amendment, and until the time we get there, it is incumbent on us, men and women, to join the struggle for this important amendment to individuals and society in Israel."

In recent decades, there has been a huge jump in the participation rate of women in the labor force, but there is a high wage gap between men's and women's wages. According to the Adva Center, "Wage gaps between men and women in the labor force—in terms of monthly wages and hourly wages—are a universal phenomenon, reflecting aspects of inequality in the distribution of gender work both at home and in the labor force." In 2014, the average monthly wage of a woman in Israel was 67 percent of a man's.

In recent decades, we have seen that there are more women with academic degrees than men. This is undoubtedly an impressive achievement. However, when the promotion of women at the top of the academic staff is on the agenda, the representation of women drops radically to the point that at the highest level—a full professor—only about 20 percent are women.

Among the prominent women in the higher education facilities are the biochemist and winner of the 2009 Nobel Prize in Chemistry, Prof. Ada Yonath, of the Weizmann Institute of Science; Prof. Ruth Arnon of the Weizmann Institute, the inventor of Copaxone; the president of the Israel Academy of Sciences and Humanities, Prof. Rivka Carmi; president of Ben-Gurion University, Dr. Kira Radinsky, a brilliant researcher in the field of information mining whose name has caused waves in the technological-scientific world; and two hospital directors, Dr. Orna Blondheim and Dr. Chen Shapira.

But women also have a dramatic presence in other areas important to the state and society in Israel: Esther Hayut, chief justice of the Supreme Court; Ofra Klinger, prison service commissioner; Gila Gaziel, head of the human resources department of the Israel Police; Sigal Bar Zvi, First District Command of the Israel Police; and leading journalists and TV presenters, former and current Knesset members and singers, writers, poets, and artists.

May there be more like them.

III

DEMOGRAPHICS

EXISTENTIAL ANXIETIES

Prof. David Passig presents the three existential fears that govern Jews and Israelis. The first is the fear of plagiarism of its origin, its identity, and its future by Muslims and Palestinians. The Muslims identify themselves with Abraham, the father of the Jewish nation, as their father, too, and the Palestinians regard themselves as primordial to the land of Israel, while historically they are relatively new in the land.

The second existential fear of Jewish Israelis is fear of annihilation. Jewish existential anxiety finds its expression in the Haggadic[42] phrase "in every generation they stand up against us to destroy us."

The third anxiety is border dread. Passig relates only to the anxiety of the physical boundaries, and we also wish to add to this the anxieties of the metaphysical boundaries of: Who is Jewish? Only those whose mother was Jewish, like the Halacha defines, or all who have Jewish origin? Who is Israeli? Who belongs to the people, and who does not?

On the basis of these three fears, we can understand the demographic demonization that persecutes Israeli society, the fear of an Arab or ultra-Orthodox majority that might bring destruction to the country and its character.

However, birth trends since 2000 show that the secular and traditional Jewish sectors have birth rates of about 10 percent more than in the past, the ultra-Orthodox Jewish sector has about 15 percent less, and in the Arab sector, birth rates are 16 percent less.

The main explanations for this are the dramatic increase in the fertility of women among immigrants from the former Soviet Union, a marked increase in fertility among middle-class and especially the highest deciles in Israel, and the increase in the number of single mothers and same-sex parents.

THERE IS NO ARAB DEMOGRAPHIC THREAT

The demographic demon, which has been threatening Israeli society since the establishment of the state, says: "The Arabs are having more children and eventually will constitute a majority." The fear of this demographic demon led to the first prime minister, David Ben-Gurion, making a decision to encourage the Jewish birth rate by granting the "birth prize," a grant of one hundred Israeli pounds (the currency at the time), to mothers who gave birth to ten or more children.

In a memorandum written by Prof. Roberto Becky, who later founded the Israeli Central Bureau of Statistics (ICBS), the following scenario appears: "Jewish fertility will increase to 3 births per woman and Arab fertility will drop from 7 to 6 births per woman. Therefore, according to the optimistic scenario, there will be 2.3 million Jews in 2001, alongside 4.4 million Arabs—a Jewish minority of 34 percent." Of course, something went wrong with the forecast.

Even after the establishment of the State of Israel, the CBS continued to err in their forecasts, saying that in 2000, fertility fell to two births per woman in the Jewish sector, and that in 2015, the fertility rate would be 4.3 in the Muslim population. In practice, the trend was reversed. The fertility rate of Jews as well as the Muslim population in 2017 were equal: 3.2 children per woman.

The total closure of the gap between the fertility rate of Jewish and Arab women in Israel is also related to the Muslim phenomenon. The data indicate that there has been dramatic erosion in the number of births per woman throughout the Muslim Middle East and not necessarily in Israel. The number of births per woman has dropped in all Muslim countries at double or even triple the rate of decline in global fertility rates.

In this context, it is worth quoting Hania Zlotnik, head of the UN Population Division (2009): "It is amazing to follow the drop in Muslim fertility in the world." Dr. Nicholas Eberstadt, a leading demographer in the United States, said in June 2012: "The collapse of the fertility rate in Muslim countries is the strongest demographic phenomenon of this era… Six out of ten of the sharp declines in fertility rates in the world happened in Muslims countries." A study by the Population Reference Bureau in Washington, DC, shows a high percentage of Muslim women seeking to avoid pregnancy.

Demographers attribute this phenomenon first and foremost to literacy, especially among women, due to the past expansion of educational systems in the Arab countries and the desire to integrate into academic studies and also to urbanization, the reduction of teenage pregnancy, the fertility process that begins later and ends earlier, the peak divorce rate, the integration of women in the labor force, and family planning.

The fertility rate among Arab Muslims in Israel is 3.2 births per woman, higher than any Arab country except Sudan, Yemen, and Iraq, but it is also in a rapid decline. In Israel, Druze and Christian women have fewer births than Jews.

All of these indicate that Israeli Arabs pose no threat to the Jewish majority in the state, neither in the present nor in the future. On the contrary, their increasing integration into education and the labor force, as we shall see later in this book, is one of the relative advantages of the Israeli economy.

THERE IS NO ULTRA-ORTHODOX DEMOGRAPHIC THREAT

As we shall see below, the ultra-Orthodox Jews, Haredi[43], are a tremendous opportunity for the Israeli economy as they try to take their first steps into integration. There was a significant leap in the participation rate of ultra-Orthodox women in the labor force over the past ten years from 40 percent to 72 percent. Among ultra-Orthodox men, the jump was from 32 percent to 50 percent at the time, and the trend continues. There is also a significant leap in the number of ultra-Orthodox men and women studying in the higher education system. A small part of them, too small, also began to serve in the IDF.

In some ways, many Israelis see ultra-Orthodoxy as a cultural threat, especially a threat to the moderate secular or religious nature of the state. But to what extent will they really constitute a cultural threat?

The ultra-Orthodox are changing at an ever-increasing rate: at the beginning of the twenty-first century, the proportion of Internet users among the ultra-Orthodox was negligible. "The Internet is the greatest threat to ultra-Orthodox society," they say explicitly. The threat was so great that in 2010, rabbis banned surfing online. But it did not help at all. A survey conducted by the Israel Internet Association in January 2017 found that 49 percent of the ultra-Orthodox use the Internet.

The assumption that the number of ultra-Orthodox will rise dramatically relative to the rest of the population is also incorrect. Since the beginning of the century, and especially since the reduction of child allowances in 2003, and as noted above, birth rates have declined.

In recent years, a huge wave of secularization has been taking place in the ultra-Orthodox sector, which has attracted more than 10 percent of the younger generation. When it comes to the second generation of those who were secular and became ultra-Orthodox, the numbers are already jumping to 30 percent or more. In a series of TV interviews conducted by Channel 10 reporter Avishai Ben-Haim, Rabbi Yosef (Yossi) Mizrahi, one of the most prominent religious figures in the Jewish community, says: "The number of religious people in the world is not growing. Many of the ultra-Orthodox are leaving the path."

The ultra-Orthodox city of Elad is at the top of the list of cities in percentage of young people joining combat units in the IDF. In Elad, 56.6

percent are recruited to a combat unit. Taking into consideration that ultra-Orthodox girls do not enlist at all, it is quite a high rate.

Ultra-Orthodox associations that encourage the acquisition of a profession are leading the growing participation in the labor force. For more than a decade, awareness of the need to create special training frameworks and special tracks for academic studies has increased for members of the ultra-Orthodox community. In addition, the need for most of the young ultra-Orthodox to provide financial support for professional or academic studies was evident. In cooperation with government agencies and philanthropic organizations, various institutions and tracks were established, and economic assistance is provided to thousands of ultra-Orthodox students who acquire a profession or an academic degree. The economic distress of many families led to the creation of various programs to encourage employment by providing information about the world of work, tools for the labor world, and direct mediation between ultra-Orthodox job seekers and employers.

In recent years, high-tech entrepreneurs from the ultra-Orthodox community have been encouraged, and they have developed to be partners in the great success of the State of Israel in the field. Since 2010, a unique program has been in place to develop an intra-Haredi public leadership with a vision and a broad worldview that will deal with the challenges facing the community in a systematic manner and provide an appropriate response. This activity is based on visionary philanthropists who believe in the power of quality internal leadership to deal with the challenges of time. The common denominator of these new activities is that they deal with empowerment of the Haredi community in order to improve their economic and social situation and enable them to cope with the challenges they face.

In conclusion, the Haredi sector in general is changing and starting to integrate. A demographic demon does not exist here, either.

The demographics of Israel, as the youngest country in the OECD, with a median age of thirty compared with an average of forty-two in the OECD, are an advantage for the state, both socially and economically. The wisdom of the state, as well as the wisdom of the leaders of the various sectors, will be the long-term vision of the common good, along with the ability of Israelis to integrate and contain one another. The process of mutual containment, by its very nature, provokes extreme rhetoric and actions but also deep streams of integration. The challenge is to deal with the former in a specific and decisive way and to nurture the latter.

IV

A WINNING DEMOCRACY

Israel is commonly called the only democracy in the Middle East, but this is a misleading statement. Israel is an impressive democracy, not only in terms of the Middle East, whose regimes can be defined between stable democratic dictatorships at best or chaotic dictatorships and tribal wars in all other cases. The Middle East is also not the comparison point to which the State of Israel relates.

The *Freedom in the World* report presents a quantitative measure of the level of democracy and political freedom in various countries and territories in the world. Israel is defined in this report as a free electoral democracy with high esteem.[44]

"Today's Israel is an impressive democratic state, that in a short period built itself a vibrant political culture, lively media and impressive public involvement," writes Noah Efron, Nazir Majali, and Amitai Shaharit.[45] Dr. Nicholas Eberstadt adds that relative to the size of the population, there are more nonprofit organizations in Israel than in any country, and most of them advance in their activity political change and action.

All this is not obvious. Many of today's Israelis were not born into a democratic political regime, and if we look back two generations, only a small minority of their grandparents lived in democratic regimes. Israel's success in assimilating democratic values among its citizens is impressive, the researchers say.

In contrast, Prof. Sammy Smooha of Haifa University defines Israel as an "ethnic democracy" and views it as a flawed democracy. Smooha defines four "legitimate" democracies: liberal democracy, as seen in the Anglo-Saxon and Scandinavian countries, which view the country as a civic "package" of people who maintain absolute equality, irrespective of their ethnic and cultural affiliation; Republican democracy like in France, which is deeply involved in safeguarding and protecting the people's culture while attempting to give full equality to all its citizens; the cantonal democracy of Switzerland or Belgium, which recognizes the various cultural groups and takes care of equal treatment while promoting the autonomy of each of them. Like multicultural Britain and the Netherlands, multicultural democracy accepts the diversity and cultural diversity of its citizens and refrains from imposing one culture on another.

Yet almost all of these European democracies, which exemplify Prof. Smooha's ideas, failed only seventy years ago when they murdered or collaborated with the murdering of their Jewish citizens; these include France, Germany, Belgium, the Netherlands, and others. The murder of their Jewish citizens not only casts doubt on their abilities to serve as a model for democracy but also weakens them today as they confront the current reality in which there is an Islamic threat to their very cultural, national, and democratic existence.

The immigration of the Muslim refugees to Europe and their determination to preserve their cultural perception and ceremonies in their new homeland and even to impose them on their democratic environment is a challenging process that is still far from complete, and its consequences are still unknown. Will the Muslims succeed in establishing Sharia in Europe? Do the values of freedom of expression exist in France after the terrorist attacks, among them on the satirical magazine *Charlie Hebdo*?[46] Is the legislation known in France as a "veil law" that prohibits the display of religious symbols in schools legitimate? Will the right-wing initiative last in Switzerland—which won a majority in the referendum—to ban the construction of mosque's minarets on the grounds that this is a subversive political statement? And what about the demand in Germany to compel the imams in the mosques to speak their sermons in the local language?

Nondemocratic Islam, which does not respect human rights in general and women's equality in particular, and which acts violently against heretics, Muslims or not, challenges Western democracies. Israel has learned to contain the Muslim challenge early on and is most advanced in its multicultural perception.

LEXUS AND JIHAD

On Tuesday morning, September 11, 2001, with the fall of the twin towers in New York and the attack on the Pentagon in Washington, the paradigm that defined the way the world thinks also fell. This paradigm, coined by the American Jewish economist Thomas Friedman in his book, *The Lexus and the Olive Tree*,[47] and Uri Ram in his book, *McWorld in Tel Aviv, Jihad in Jerusalem*,[48] argued that there is a dichotomy between global trends—civil, capitalist, modern, democratic, and secular (the Lexus in the first and the McWorld in the other) in contrast to the local, militant, religious-nationalistic tendencies (the olive tree in the first and the jihad in the second).

Israeli interpretation of this situation places the global Tel Aviv against the local periphery, the global high techiest versus the local religious, the left versus the right, and the "winners of globalization" against its victims. According to this paradigm, social gaps and political differences are all explained.

Globalization and localism were perceived as conflicting trends that required a choice between them. The argument against the Israeli governments was that they do not choose, and "try to square the circle…and in the end, there will have to be a decision—one way or the other."

However, it seems that in the end, the Israeli decision not to choose between the trends is the right choice. As in many other cases, it was found that defining reality as a "zero-sum" game that paints the world in black and white is a simplistic and populist approach that closes possibilities in a sweeping manner.

The new paradigm, announced by the events of September 11, created the "third way," according to which the global Western world is committed to maintaining its existence against militant Islam by the same "circle square" and not choosing one way unequivocally.

The Islamic jihad is as global as it is local, and the preservation of democracy in its Western sense necessitates the implementation of an integrated approach of globalization on one hand while maintaining the state and local needs on the other.

A DEMOCRATIC NATIONAL STATE

According to Prof. Asa Kasher,[49] a democratic national state is not problematic or exceptional. "In Spain there are Basques, there are Parisians in the Netherlands, and in France there are Corsicans...In this respect, Israel has about 20 percent of another people is not exceptional." These statements, made in 2000, prior to the outbreak of the Islamic threat in Europe, are even more valid today. Israeli democracy is not a "defective democracy" but rather a model for other democracies. There is no prohibition in Israel on the construction of minarets of mosques, on the wearing of headscarves for women, or on the use of Arabic in mosques. Israeli democracy has managed to contain all of these.

The status quo, which is constantly under construction in Israeli democracy, is broad cultural autonomy for its Jewish and non-Jewish citizens: ultra-Orthodox, religious, traditional and secular, LGBT and heterosexuals, Arab Muslim, Christian, Druze, Circassian, and Bedouin.

The range of personal-cultural legitimacy in Israel is very broad. As in other countries, it is constantly being challenged by those who want to impose their positions and preferences as well as their ideologies, but so far, the Israeli democracy has been successful. The most striking evidence of this is the overwhelming desire of its Arab citizens to remain there and not to subject themselves or their villages to the sovereignty of the PA.[50]

Among the Jews themselves, the lines of confrontation over civil marriage, civil burial, public transportation, and commerce on the Sabbath and holidays constantly create a dialogue about the nature of the young state. But religious liberalism is winning in Israel. According to the annual *Index of Religion and State*,[51] 84 percent of Israelis support religious freedom, but more than half prefer to get married according to the Halacha. Sixty-six percent are in favor of a compromise at the Western Wall, but most will prefer to pray in the traditional square, with separation of men and women. The index reveals that most Israeli citizens think liberally but prefer a traditional life.

Are Austria, where all shops are closed on Sunday by law, and France, which keeps its Christian holidays, less democratic because of that? Is Israel?

A NATION OF REBELS

The success of rooting democracy in the State of Israel, a country that was formed by people who were not necessarily raised in a democratic environment, seems to be an outcome of the national character traits of rebellion against authority, pluralism, and opinion.

Throughout the Bible, we hear of a nation that strives against its God from the statue placed at the very beginning of accepting God on Mount Sinai to idolatry that continues throughout the entire Bible. The foreign gods were worshipped by all—kings and commoners, men and women, in the periphery and in the center. The prophets blasphemed them and repeatedly threatened them with the maximum punishment of the loss of the kingdom, the denial of freedom, and death—all in vain.

The tendency is to read this biblical text and to think that its purpose is to warn against worshipping foreign gods, but perhaps the purpose of the biblical writer is the opposite. Perhaps his goal is to educate about rebelliousness as a value. Not to follow, to debate, to doubt constant learning from an argumentativeness stand—all are the DNA of Judaism.

Shimon Peres said that the great invention that the Jews brought to the world is not monotheism and one God but rather the Talmud, which reflects the constant debate over everything that is accepted. Thus, a nation was created that in modern times brought out the greatest communists alongside the fathers of the capitalists; leading scientists as well as leaders in philosophy, literature, and arts; inventors and financiers; and technologists and scientists. A nation of rebellious people.

"That's how it is with us. Two Jews have three opinions," writes Dr. Gabi Barzilai on his Facebook page.

> Everyone has an opinion on almost every subject, and everyone is sure that their opinion is the absolute and indisputable truth. That's how it looks at every time a new storm breaks out in the local cup of tea…On the other hand, I also have an opinion on almost every subject…On the third hand, in Bible study I understand very well, and write about it quite a bit, criticism of people who think they know better what God meant by the Torah, so maybe we should do some order…Judaism's soul is the dispute: Judaism, like the Bible, does not espouse absolute truths but freedom of choice and the right to personal opinion. The Bible presents various possibilities and divergent opinions on almost every issue, and it is the responsibility of each person to find the right path for him and to follow it, provided that he does so out of integrity and consistency, and not for the accumulation of power, honor, or money. The term "heresy" is not a Jewish concept. "These and these are the words of the living God."[52]

In addition, immediately Barzilai adds examples of the differences that built Judaism: Hillel and Shammai, Rabbi Judah and Rabbi Shimon, Rabbi Yochanan and "Resh Lakish," Rabbi Yehuda Halevy and the Rambam, the Lubavitcher Rebbe and Rabbi Soloveitchik—they all disagreed with one another.

Prof. Gad Yair presents in his book, *The Code of Israeliness*,[53] the ten commandments of "being Israeli." For the purpose of our case here, we will mention the sixth commandment: "I speak, therefore I am—about the battle of circumcision and the war of opinion," and the eighth commandment: "They will not decide on you—anti-hierarchy and for equality."

Under such conditions, only a democratic regime can exist in which everyone can express his or her opinions and struggles for his or her path.

It is not clear whether the origin of the Jewish people is in the slave revolt in Egypt, as evidenced by the Bible, or in the rebellion of the lower Canaanite socioeconomic strata of power and authority, as the historians claim. It may be both. However, a nation that sanctified generation after generation the myth of a group of slaves who rebelled against their Egyptian masters is a nation that sanctifies the rebellion against the kingdom and the nonacceptance of authority. To this very day, these character traits exist in the Jews in general and in the Israeli democratic entity in particular.

But the individual's right to freedom of expression and rebellious character traits are but one side of democracy. The other side, argues Prof. Gideon Dror,[54] is the existence of all that is required to preserve it, including protecting it against external and internal threats. The Israelis' willingness to sacrifice their lives, their families, and their personal safety for the sake of the state may have no parallel in the world.

Sebastian Junger, the author of the best-selling book *Tribe*,[55] writes that in the distant past,

> people used to do everything in groups, including sleep, because it's safer. Our psychological needs have evolved in these circumstances, we feel best in groups, even when tensions arise from being with others. Modern society brings together people who do not need each other and are not dependent on one another for basic subsistence needs, do not need them, do not know them—to put food on the table or for your safety.

The feelings that "a people that shall dwell alone"[56] and "a state surrounded by enemies," are perhaps part of the explanation for the strong belonging of the Israeli tribe.

PARTNERS AND INFLUENCERS

In recent years, representative democracy in Israel has changed its character.[57] From civil involvement, which is characterized mainly by party activity and participation in the election process, it has changed to constant cooperation. It seems like representative democracy does not require civic participation in decision-making processes, since with the existence of a parliament with its various committees, the existence of parties and of free media, the freedom to strike and demonstrate, and a court that assumes "everything is justiciable," the need for additional civilian cooperation seems redundant. But in fact, we are undergoing a fundamental change—the participation of citizens in government decision-making processes. Citizens in all developed countries demand more transparency and accountability from their governments and seek opportunities to take an active part in designing policies that affect their lives. As a result, governments in OECD countries are looking for new ways to include citizens and civic organizations in policy-making processes.

Government offices and governing bodies are changing the way decisions were made in the past. Wherever the model of the "state that cares for its citizens" continues, there is a structural failure, and the governments do not receive public legitimacy. In the entire Western world, the rise of the wisdom of the masses on one hand and the technological ability to gather and analyze on the other all lead to a system of civic cooperation.

In such a relationship, the administration ostensibly gives up control but can have unprecedented achievements. The civil sector brings to the government institutions what they lack: power, public legitimacy, economic backing, and continuity over time—even when the government is replaced.

In almost every discussion of a committee of the Parliament (Knesset), the chairman asks the government officials if they consulted with the relevant civil bodies. Government sites publish future legislative plans and ask for public comments before they bring them to the legislation. Discussions between government officials and citizens are conducted through round tables, with civil representatives on government committees, and so on. It seems that the administration understood the change that has taken place in contemporary democracy and makes room for constant cooperation.

THE WATCHDOG OF DEMOCRACY

A report by the Israel Democracy Institute[58] claims; "According to international standards, freedom of the press exists in Israel on medium-high level," but the level of public trust in the media, as in the rest of the developed world, is low and even decreases from year to year. "The lack of trust in the media among the Israeli population is higher than in any other institution examined in the survey, including the Knesset and the Chief Rabbinate, who have also received low levels of trust." This contradiction is explained by the Israel Democracy Institute: "The media is seen as biased for a certain political position or interest groups."

This phenomenon of public mistrust in the media is undoubtedly damaging democracy, but it is neither temporary nor local. The media, closed in a bubble, believes in itself, does not commit itself to objectivity, and is not exposed to the public's feelings. Thus, it is unable to predict or understand democratic processes, as the countries of the world have observed one by one.

As soon as the media gave up its obligation to try to give facts and it mixed them with opinions, and with the rise of social networks that are faster than the media, the public's desire to get up from the newspaper, radio, or going to bed with television news declined.

The moment the media sacrificed its ethical commitment to truth on the altar of its will to influence, it lost public trust. Prof. Yuval Noah Harari explained the ethics of scientific-research,[59] saying that a distinction should be made between two questions: "What is important?" (which is the choice of scientists, according to their subjective opinion) and "What is true?" (in which the reporters are committed to truth, also contradicting their initial position and hypothesis). You can expect the press to go the same way. Every journalist can choose the issues he covers as much as he likes, but he cannot ignore, divert, or whitewash facts that contradict his personal views.

Thus, a journalist who supports someone can also be expected to note his mistakes, just as one might expect a journalist who opposes him to note some of the good things he did. A "social" journalist can be expected to praise some of the achievements of the capitalists and vice versa.

In general, we suggest that a courageous journalist is not the one who attacks the positions of power but rather the one who looks at the facts and does not fear to present them, even when they contradict his positions.

In addition, the media must leave its own bubble, alienate its inherent elitist power, and accept the wisdom of the masses. This is always true, but certainly it is true in a democratic society where the masses are ultimately choosing the leadership. It seems that democracy's watchdog has drowned in its own pride, in hubris, at a time when democracy needs it most.

———

Like other Western democracies, Israeli democracy is in a struggle between democratic principles and security needs. For example, most of the Israeli public opposes restricting freedom of expression by prohibiting harsh and public criticism of the state, while the opposition crosses all political camps, although it is more strongly felt on the left than in the center or on the right. In contrast to freedom of expression, the picture changes, and most of the public believes that the state should be allowed to monitor what its citizens write and publish on the Internet, and it should demand the arrest of suicide bombers before their crime is committed.

The democratic approach of the Israeli public is expressed, among other things, in the position presented in the report that, despite the high trust that the Supreme Court enjoys, the public is not comfortable with allowing the Supreme Court to annul Knesset laws. The Knesset is seen as a more basic democratic institution than the Supreme Court, which is not an elected body or one representing the public.

The Economist's "Democracy Index" report includes, among other studies, the political involvement of Israeli citizens, including voter turnout, voting rights, organizing for minorities, the proportion of women in

Parliament, membership in parties, expressions of interest in the state, and political involvement of citizens. Citizens must participate in legal demonstrations and encourage political participation by the authorities, and in this respect, Israel is ahead of most of the established Western democracies.

Democracy in Israel, despite its success, requires constant cultivation. The democratic consciousness of its citizens is not self-evident. We have already said at the outset: Israelis are the first or second generation of democracy.

V

BUILDING A FUTURE

Palestine was a remote and forsaken province of the Ottoman Empire. Desert desolation dominated everything. It was a neglected country, dotted with malignant marshes, without water and without cover. Its inhabitants were numbered: a few Arab fellahin, mostly tenant farmers and nomadic Bedouins and a small number of settlement outposts.

American author Mark Twain visited it in 1867 and described his impressions in gloomy colors. He found Jerusalem desolate and lifeless. "We did not see a soul throughout the journey,"[60] he wrote. British consul James Finn testified: "The country is empty of residents, and its most urgent need is people who will live there."[61] Charles William Eliot, president of Harvard University, wrote in 1867: "The land is very sparsely populated."[62] Reverend Samuel Manning wrote in his 1890 book, "But where are the inhabitants? This fertile land, capable of sustaining a vast population, is almost deserted."[63]

The landscape of the country in the middle of the nineteenth century is described by the German traveler A. G. Schultz (1851):

> The Holy Land became almost a desert. The tertiary fields are not properly cultivated, poorly formed and full of weeds, the saplings small and varied. The pastures were dried up, the forests destroyed, and even the few trees were cut down for the most part, and on our journey we often had to search for hours for a shaded

place. Many springs had dried up, the waterworks and the ancient pools had collapsed—and only their ruins had survived. The land of Israel has become a wasteland, where destruction and gloom reigns over all Turkmans, Kurds and Bedouin Arabs, with their flocks and black tents seen wandering from place to place, taking advantage of the grazing fields and crushing the permanent inhabitants…Under enlightened rule, The Land of Israel is nothing more than a huge pile of waste and a heap of ruins.[64]

The most famous among the robbers was Abu Jilda. He was born in 1902 in a village near Jenin, and he was named Ahmad Hamad Mahmoud. Later, his name changed to Abu Jilda because of a patch that covered a missing eye. He was a particularly cruel bandit whose victims, usually rural Arabs, were brutally slaughtered. He used to call his robberies "customs collection."

In May 1933, in the valley of the Jerusalem hills, Abu Jilda and his gang ambushed a convoy of Arab villagers who had returned from the market. They imprisoned them in the cave and took their property. But they did not stop there. Abu Jilda brutally abused and killed Hussein al-Asali, an Arab who served in the British police, who encountered the scene. British rule was rattled; extensive searches were conducted for Abu Jilda and his assistant, Salah Ahmed Mustafa, known as al-Armit.

Some say that Abu Jilda's hiding place was discovered after a member of his gang betrayed him, and some say that he was removed by one of his girls. In any event, Abu Jilda and his deputy surrendered and were tried and executed in the British prison in Jerusalem. An Arab lawyer represented him, and two Arabs were among the judges who sentenced him, yet he became a myth among the Arabs of Israel as if he were a freedom fighter and not a violent thief whose main victims were Arabs.

The fear of the bandits was enormous. Most of the land was either fields or used for grazing. Traditional agriculture was primitive and based on the labor of man and beast. The cultivation of the land was done using archaic methods in terms of that period. Large areas became swamps, and the areas near them were not cultivated, despite their fertility, due to the danger of malaria. Forests and grazing areas were abandoned, and constant and uncontrolled grazing flocks and cattle, without thought and without supervision, led to the destruction of extensive areas.

Only with the first Jewish immigration did the process begin of rehabilitation of the land. This included drying swamps, paving roads, and extensive afforestation aimed at turning the wilderness areas green and blooming. The desolation was turned into a place where people could live. Cultivating wasteland became the symbol of Zionism.

A GREEN COUNTRY IN THE MIDDLE OF THE DESERT

Israel is one of very few countries where the number of trees in its territory has increased during the twentieth century.

The mathematician, Prof. Zvi Hermann Schapira, came to the stage on the last day of the Zionist Congress at 1884 and read to the audience the purpose of a unique fund he wanted to establish that would collect money from all the Jews in the world. Two-thirds of the money was earmarked for the purchase of land, and a third was designated for preservation and development. The nineteenth-century Lithuanian scholar, rabbi, and mathematician is the man who, in his imagination, painted the barren land of Israel green. KKL-JNF was founded forty-one years before the establishment of the State of Israel and created a huge project of planting trees, which grew from only thirty-five hundred acres of forests then to 250,000 acres in 2017, with more than 120 million trees planted.

The reasons for planting were many and varied: the preservation of the land and the prevention of erosion, the occupation of the wilderness, the employment of new immigrants, security needs, the economic use of trees, a romantic attempt to bring the forests of Europe to the land of Israel, and to create a green landscape.

Trees and forests contribute greatly to air quality by absorbing dust and reducing radiation by creating shade. KKL-JNF forests each year deduct about half a million tons of greenhouse gases, equivalent to the annual carbon emissions of about seventy-five thousand private cars; planting them close to agricultural areas makes them a natural barrier that absorbs excess chemicals from fertilizer and pesticides. During the years, the afforestation project was so successful that Israel became an international example of a process that goes against the global trend of deforestation.

The "security planting," which was reinforced with the establishment of the State of Israel, stemmed from the need to create a barrier that would conceal the houses and roads from direct fire of the Arabs. There are those who say that this planting order was given by the first prime minister, and from there on it was called "Ben-Gurion Boulevard." To this day, in areas where Palestinian terror organizations have fired from Gaza, trees are planted to hide people from killing and destruction.

Israel's armistice line with its neighbors after the War of Independence was painted with a green pencil, hence its name: The Green Line. This fact does not lead many to believe that the name refers to Israel's forest line bordering the deserts of its neighbors. This belief is not really divorced from the geographical reality. The Google Earth map shows Israel's border with Egypt along the landline. On the Israeli side, the green is covered with vegetation, and on the Egyptian side, the land is exposed due to excess grazing sheep and not preventing desertification. Also, the line between the old Israel (before the Six-Day War) and Judea and Samaria, which were in the hands of the Jordanians, can be easily identified according to the colors: the green side and yellow side.

The "barren line" is defined as a field that separates two hundred millimeters of rain a year from one side and less than that on the other side. The barren line also serves as the border with the desert. Its move toward fertile land is the process of desertification. All of Israel is marked red on the global map of danger zones for desertification. Red marks symbolize the highest risk.

For over a decade, the desert line in the southern part of Israel (the Negev) has been fought by planting large quantities of citrus groves, following the development of Dr. Raveh of the Volcani Center, who adapted citrus to desert conditions. Another method was a system for capturing floodwater created by an artificial earth embankment that is built in a creek.

The sentimental attitude of the Israelis to their forests is expressed in their response to severe fires raging in them, whether it is an act of nature or the actions of human beings, either negligently or deliberately. The forests are the triumph of those who love this land.

THE FLOWING STREAMS

Only the flowing streams compare to the Zionists' forests. In this desert state, running water is not only life itself but also the people's soul. There are many stories of heroism from the time of the first Zionist pioneers in efforts to dry the swamps and clean the outlet of the streams to the sea. The swamps were dried and the riverbeds cleared, and the water flowed to the sea.

However, the massive increase in population density and needs caused rivers to be destroyed again. The living water was pumped from the streams for drinking and irrigation purposes. Sewage and industrial waste flowed through the creeks. The animals and vegetation disappeared, and poisons flowed into toxins that damaged the ecosystem. The Maccabiah disaster[65] and the diseases that were diagnosed with the Kishon underwater commando[66] were the culmination of the rift and led to the beginning of a correction.

One of the most difficult problems of rehabilitating the streams in the coastal area in general and the Alexander River in particular is their starting point in the PA territories and their use as a source of sewage. As much as the State of Israel is trying to rehabilitate the rivers, it depends greatly on the goodwill of the Palestinians as well.

However, in 2003, as part of the River Festival in Australia, the Israeli-Palestinian project to restore the Alexander River won first place in the Thiess International River prize. Israelis and Palestinians cooperated successfully to clean the stream from the sewage that flowed from the water system of the Palestinian city of Nablus. Despite the ongoing political security conflict, the parties signed a cooperation agreement, and it has continued since then. The plan led to the planning of the sewage treatment system in the city of Nablus, strengthening the banks of the river, supporting the restoration of the ecological system, and protecting the rare turtles that inhabit it.

In 1993, the Israel National Rivers Administration was established. Since then, pollutant quantities have been reduced in the main streams by 60 percent to 70 percent, master plans have been prepared to rehabilitate a large part of the streams, and the Water Law has changed, according to which nature is a legitimate consumer of water in this thirsty land.

The quantity and quality of water in nature are an inseparable part of the ecosystem and conservation of species diversity. The establishment of desalination plants (as described later in this book) further reduced the pressure on the water sources.

Dr. Orit Skutelsky, coordinator of water and streams in the Environmental Preservation Division of the Society for the Protection of Nature in Israel, is one of those people who gets excited from seeing streams flowing in a river. The story of the return of an extinct species of frogs in the Hula Lake causes her to tear up.

"Throughout the world, during the twentieth century, agriculture and development came at the expense of the natural streams and wetlands," says Dr. Skutelsky. "So in Israel too—wet habitats and streams were dried up, drained and polluted by sewage. But traumas also create opportunities. The drying up of Hula Lake and the swamp next to it was a formative event that led to the establishment of the Society for the Protection of Nature in Israel (SPNI), as well as the promotion of laws aimed at preserving the natural values and establishing a governmental authority for nature conservation. It also led to the establishment of the first nature reserve in Israel—the Hula Nature Reserve."

The goal of the Hula drying project was to increase the agricultural areas for the Upper Galilee kibbutzim and cooperative villages, reduce water evaporation and thus increase the water reaching the Sea of Galilee, and exploit the peat soil in the swamp as raw material for the chemical industry and organic waste.

This large engineering project, in which 15,500 acres were dried up, lasted for eight years. It ran under fire of the Syrians, who opposed it. Forty Israelis were killed, and about a hundred were wounded in the bombing, although the drying did not cause any damage to the Syrians. In the new agricultural areas that were added as a result of the drying, people grew peanuts, corn, cotton, and alfalfa.

Over the years, it became clear that drying damage exceeded its usefulness. The soil of the peat was often lit and burned for weeks. The eastern winds transported a large amount of peat dust and left it elsewhere. Nitrate compounds from the soil drifted into the Sea of Galilee and caused an increase in algae and damage to fish and water quality. The nitrates in the soil increased during the drought years and were absorbed in agricultural crops, causing the death of cows fed with the alfalfa.

Thus, in the 1990s, a project began, which was to flood about three hundred acres of peat land and to prepare about twelve hundred acres of park. In addition to tourism and conservation values, the flood has also allowed for control over the level of groundwater in a way that it will be drained in the winter and prevent dehydration and massive fires of peat soil in the summer. The flooding area is also used to prevent the flow of nitrogen-rich water to the Sea of Galilee preventing its destruction.

The flooding project does not detract from the importance of the project of the 1950s to dry the Hula, since the large area of the swamps and the ancient lake, some fourteen thousand acres, continues to be cultivated by kibbutzim and moshavim of the north.

In 2009, Agamon Hula was chosen by British magazine *BBC Wildlife* as one of the ten most important animal-sighting sites in the world, and Skutelsky excitedly recounted the reappearance of the Hula painted frog (*Latonia nigriventer*). "The return of the lost species is a great promise," says Dr. Skutelsky. "The promise of roundabout is that if we improve the quality of water and the stability of the flow in wet habitats and streams, the natural values that disappeared from the streams may reappear and be restored."

Skutelsky pursued snakes in the Arava and probed the behavior of scorpions on full-moon nights, and now her heart and mind are on the issue of the restoration of streams and natural wetlands. In 2015, she lit a torch at the central ceremony of Independence Day in the name of the Society for the Protection of Nature in Israel and in honor of the country's rivers.

GLOBAL BIODIVERSITY

According to the journal *Nature*, Israel is one of the twenty-five most important points for the conservation of global biodiversity. Despite its small area, only twenty-two thousand square kilometers, it is included in the map of the important areas of nature conservation, which includes less than 2 percent of the world's land surface.

Israel is rich in this wealth thanks to its geographic location, the intersection of three continents, and its topographical, geological, and climatic diversity in relation to the size of the land. For example, the amount of wild plants in Israel is one and a half times that of Britain, which is nine times larger than Israel.

The world's largest bird migration occurs in the skies over Israel, with about five hundred million birds of different species passing through it twice a year during their migratory route. For some of them, Israel is a critical bottleneck for the safe passage of entire populations, as in the case of the white pelican, whose entire global population passes over the country. What a spectacular sight!

FROM A DEAD LANGUAGE TO VIVID ARTS

One of the most common expressions in Israel today is *sababa*. Some say that the source of this expression is from the immigration of the French-speaking Jews of North Africa; the French expression *ça va bien* became *sababa*. Some say that the real source is Arabic: *sababa*, meaning longing, passionate love as an interpretation of the spoken language: beauty, excellent. The word *balagan* comes from Farsi, as does *ishpuz*. The *kibinimat* and the *katyusha* came from Russia. *Kiosk* is a word in Turkish. *Ahbal*, a*hla*, and *bassa* are Arabic words. Hebrew is a living language of an immigrant state.

But the language was dead for a long time. It was the language of the Holy Torah, which had almost disappeared from the world when it came to day-to-day life. Hebrew was preserved in writing and was used primarily for prayer and Torah study for nearly eighty generations. Jews in various countries spoke the local languages.

In an almost unique move, Eliezer Ben-Yehuda succeeded in instilling in the Jews who returned to the land of their forefathers the need to return to their common language. In a monumental life work, he renewed the ancient language and invented hundreds of new words, some of which are similar to or based on those written in the Bible, to suit the modern age. In 1919, Ben-Yehuda convinced the British high commissioner, Herbert Samuel, to declare Hebrew as one of the three official languages of the British mandate in the land of Israel. Hebrew, naturally, became the first official language of the young state. The Hebrew language is a powerful basis for the consolidation of the Israeli collective right.[67]

Globalization has long been leading a process in which most languages in the world disappear. Ethnologists agree that nearly half of the world's existing languages will disappear by the end of the century. Hebrew is a phenomenon that swims against the current.

Talking, reading, and writing—Israel is among the world's leading places in the number of books published per capita. The vast majority of famous books in Israel are originally published in Hebrew, which places it in the world's first place for producing original literature.[68]

The revival of Hebrew as a language of speech and creativity was accompanied by an extensive theatrical scene, with most of the performances being Israeli originals, and more than a third of the plays each year are new plays. About five million people visit the Israeli theater every year.[69] This is an exceptional number.

In contrast to what is accepted in the world, theaters and musical concerts in Israel, see themselves as committed not only to their audience in the big cities but also to the geographic and cultural peripheries of the State of Israel. About half of the plays for adults were performed outside Tel Aviv and its surroundings, and a third of them were held in localities with low socioeconomic status.[70] Israeli theater took upon itself an international mission as well; the theaters regularly travel abroad, where there are performances for thousands of foreign viewers.[71]

Israel has about two hundred active museums, making it number one in the number of museums per capita. In some cases, these are large and monumental museums, some of which are of global importance, such as the three museums in Jerusalem, including Yad Vashem, the Israel Museum, and the Bible Lands Museum, as well as the Diaspora Museum in Tel Aviv.

There are impressive achievements in many other fields of art and creativity in Israel. One of them is creating television programs. This industry is one of the largest in the world. The players of this field are huge companies. The industry is in the process of continuous consolidation, where the big companies grow even larger. The little ones do not survive.

Therefore, it is hard not to be impressed by the success of the small Israeli company Dori Media Group Ltd. in these huge markets, especially in the sale of formats. The first format that was successfully distributed was the series *In Treatment*, and then *Traffic Light*, which became a big success and won the American Emmy Award. Others include *The A Word*, purchased by BBC One, the *Who's Still Standing?* gameshow, *Shtissel*, *The Game of Chefs*, *Prime Minister's Children*, and *Touch Away*, *Heroes*, and *The Greenhouse*; these are all Israeli formats sold to the international entertainment industry.

"We were *Noch-shleppers* who toured world conferences and the most important conference in Cannes," says Nadav Palti, CEO of Dori Media Group Ltd. "Suddenly, it's us who make the cocktail for others. The way was long and rewarding," he says, noting that "the only way for Israeli creators to earn is to sell in the world. They have no other choice. The market here is too small."

When Sony bought part of Dori's company, it was the first time a large media company recognized the existence of business and creativity in Israel. Since then, other Israeli companies have been working in the field of producing and selling formats on television, computers, and the gaming world.

WINNING THE DESERT

On his way back from a military exercise in the Negev, Prime Minister David Ben-Gurion saw a hut and several tents. The year was 1952, and these were the first pioneers in Kibbutz Sde Boker—among them an American volunteer who fought in the War of Independence and some of his friends. They imagined a Texan cattle ranch that would realize their ideology that it was not enough to fight for the Negev, but it is possible and necessary to maintain a settlement in the desert area, which is so remote, sun filled, and uninhabited.

Prime Minister Ben-Gurion wrote to them the very next day, "Excuse me if I say that I have never seen a pioneering enterprise like Sde Boker…I never envied anything or anyone, not in property and not in qualities and attributes of people…I have a feeling of jealousy in my heart: Why did not I get to participate in such an act?" Ben-Gurion joined the kibbutz and even lived there in a wooden hut until his death after resigning from the post of prime minister.

Over the years, Ben-Gurion called for the flourishing of the Negev and saw this mission as of supreme importance. He called for action and didn't get to see the success. About a decade ago, the Israeli government adopted a strategic decision of great importance in the spirit of Ben-Gurion's vision: the decision to relocate many of the IDF bases from the areas of demand in the center of the country to the Negev. This decision has a significant economic rationale on both ends; the evacuated IDF bases from high-demand areas in the center of the country will become available for construction of cities and residential neighborhoods, and for the Negev to absorb many new residents, with all the socioeconomic implications. This is mostly due to the sale of the IDF's expensive real estate in the center of the country, which resulted in a one-time addition to the GDP of tens of billions of shekels after the construction of new neighborhoods in areas with peak demand.

The IDF's transition to the Negev is in the midst of dramatic changes in the Negev as well as in the country as a whole. The Negev will not be the same in 2030.

The first stage of the process has already been completed with the transfer of the air force base to the Nevatim. In this framework, the long runway was paved, an additional control tower was built, and maintenance and residential buildings were constructed along with all that was necessary for housing solutions for career soldiers who had moved south to places of employment for their spouses and to educational institutions for children.

At the opening ceremony of the new base, the pilots said, "We are proud to take part in turning the vision into reality, and we pledge to make the desert bloom and protect the State of Israel from the Negev."

"It is hard to believe, but the vision has become a reality, the wilderness has become an advanced operational infrastructure, the desert is full of people," said Ido Nehushtan, the commander of the air force at the time.

The second stage was completed with the opening of the IDF training center, which is called Major General Ariel Sharon Training School, and it includes diners, comfortable barracks, simulators, a sports center, and a banquet hall. The camp also includes five thousand housing units for career soldiers and their families, a technological college, a commercial area, a motel for visitors, schools, and more. The training center is designed for the training of all IDF combat supporters while improving the quality of training and assimilation of the most innovative technologies and learning methodologies available.

The training center was built with an innovative concept of cooperation of the business sector. The tender included planning, financing, construction, operation, and maintenance of the training base for a period of twenty-five years. The tender was won by a consortium of the Minrav company, Electra, and Rad-Bynet Group, which together established the Mabat Negev Group. The business sector was efficient and cost-effective while maintaining a very tight schedule.

Michael Biton, mayor of the nearby town Yeruham, summed up the contribution of the training base to his city, saying that "people do not understand, but it has tremendous implications; we have issued tenders that will quadruple our commercial areas." This is unprecedented growth in the region.

The teleprocessing campus, located near Ben-Gurion University and a civilian high-tech park, is the third stage of the IDF's transition to the Negev, creating a powerful triangle of academia, military technological units, and a high-tech civilian industrial park that will bring value to each of its vertices. There is no doubt that in addition to the employment advantages detailed above, there is an expectation that this project will increase the level of education in general and technological education in particular in the Negev and Beer Sheva.

The last, largest, and most complex stage is the establishment of an intelligence base east of Beer Sheva. The base is planned to accommodate ten thousand soldiers and officers, including the famous Unit 8200. The Defense Ministry notes that the relocation of the IDF bases will draw a significant number of technological industries from the center of the country, as these are attached to the intelligence units by their structure of operating.

The IDF moved southward in Israel, which was learned from the United States, where large military bases from across the country were transferred to five bases in the state of Maryland. The goal of the US Military Forces was to save about $7 billion a year in military spending. The cost of the move was estimated at $21 billion, but it actually totaled $35 billion.

A study conducted by the consulting firm Trigger Foresight for the Israeli Ministry of Defense, the Ministry of Finance, and the Ministry for the Development of the Negev and the Galilee tried to examine the feasibility of the move in Israel, where the transfer of some twenty-seven thousand soldiers to the south is planned. Also, the model for the coordination body that will connect the local businesses, mostly small ones, to a client as large as the military, Israel learned from the passage of US military bases to Maryland.

The Ministry of Finance's Budget Division forecasts a significant increase in employment in the Negev, with more than thirty-three thousand new jobs, mainly due to the privatization of services and the relocation of permanent employees. The hope is to reduce the relatively high unemployment in the Negev settlements and to raise the level of education and quality of life in the southern periphery.

Ben-Gurion predicted the prosperity and settlement of the Negev. It took time, but the State of Israel of now fulfills his vision.

AIR FULL OF PRAYERS AND DREAMS

The results of the votes in the UN and its institutions will not determine the affinity of the Jews to Jerusalem and its holy sites. The name of Jerusalem appears in the Bible 667 times (and does not appear even once in the Muslim Koran). Jerusalem is full of holy sites as well as government institutions. It is where the three monotheistic religions cling to one another, embracing and suffocating one another, and are sanctified and bestialized. In Jerusalem and its environs, everyone's exposed nerve endings are open to pain and touch.

There are many stories about Jerusalem, but we chose to bring here a story of an unimportant, unholy, and not very old place: Julian Street in Jerusalem, later renamed King David Street.

In the seven years after 1926, the Jews built the King David Hotel, the Christians the YMCA, and the Muslims the Palace Hotel (today's Waldorf Astoria). These three respected institutions stand not far from each other and tell about the special but also common history of the three and their physical and economic manifestations.

The first was the construction of the YMCA Christian Center in Jerusalem in order to provide service to the many British soldiers there during the mandate. The YMCA was inaugurated by Gen. Allenby during his visit there. The building, considered one of the most beautiful of the YMCA buildings worldwide, was designed by Arthur Loomis Harmon, who was among the planners of the Empire State Building in New York City. It was built by Albina, Katinka, and Dunya—a fascinating partnership among businessman Joseph Pascal Albina, a Christian Arab from Haifa; Jewish building engineer Baruch Katinka, who came from Bialystok to live in Jerusalem; and Tuvia Dunya, a Jew who immigrated to Israel from Lithuania and lived in Haifa. They built not only the YMCA, but also the Muslims' Palace Hotel, and many other buildings initiated by the British, the Jews, and the Arabs—including the home of Mufti Haj Amin al-Husseini himself. Among the craftsmen employed in the construction of the YMCA building were Jews from the Bezalel Academy of Art and Design.

Thus, from this national/ethnic/religious entanglement, the building combines Christian religious motifs with Jewish and Islamic ones. It contains the engraving of the Jewish phrase "the Lord our God is one" from the *Shema* prayer, as well as the Muslim "There is no God but Allah." In the yard are twelve cypress trees that symbolize the twelve tribes of Israel, twelve messengers of Jesus, twelve followers of Muhammad, and so on. The building has been used for residential purposes, committees, meetings, cultural events, and sports.

———

The second institution is the Jewish King David Hotel. The Mosseri family was a well-to-do Jewish family of Egyptian businessmen. In 1929, they invited their partners and friends to join in the construction of a luxury hotel in Jerusalem. They were all the leaders of the Jewish congregation: Joseph de Picciotto Bey, the Egyptian minister of finance, the de Picciotto family, and the Barons Alfred and Felix de Menasce. Under the British Mandate, which had just been applied to the land of Israel, along with the growing activity of the Zionist movement and the wealthy Christian pilgrims, they were all possible customers of the hotel.

Together they created Palestine Hotels Ltd., issuing shares on the Egyptian stock exchange, and they invested their personal wealth and bought a large lot for the hotel. Extra finance needed was taken from two Egyptian banks that were later nationalized by the Egyptian authorities.

The King David Hotel was inaugurated in 1930 as a luxury hotel that made sure to bring daily food supplies from Cairo, chefs from Italy, Sudanese waiters, and Swiss management staff.

A series of violent riots and acts of Arab terrorism against the Jewish community, the economic depression, and the Arab revolt caused great economic damage to the hotel. About a decade after its opening, the British Mandate authorities leased the southern wing of the hotel, which raised it from loss to profit.

In July 1946, the British government wing of the hotel was blown up by the Irgun,[72] who had warned the British about the intention of the explosion and demanded its evacuation. According to one of the testimonies, the head of the British administration, Sir John Shaw, responded to this by saying, "I did not come here to take orders from the Jews," and he instructed not to send the message to the many workers who remained in their offices.

The bombed wing was not rehabilitated, and the British military took over the entire hotel and turned it into a closed military zone. When the British left Palestine, the abandoned hotel became the borderline between the Israeli positions and the Jordanian positions. At first, the Red Cross took up residence but later evacuated to the more protected YMCA building. The UN flag did not prevent the Jordanian shootings from continuing, and when the UN personnel left, the Haganah[73] took control of the hotel and set up stands opposite the Old City wall. After the fighting ended, the borderline moved a few meters between the hotel and the walls of the Old City.

In 1958, the Federman family, owners of the Dan hotel chain, purchased half of the shares of the Israel Hotels Company and renovated the hotel, incorporating modern elements that were not there before, but they were careful to preserve the original style and design. King David Hotel was to be what its original builders planned—a luxury hotel for government service. The official guests of the Israeli government were housed in it, and it was able to preserve its place as the flagship hotel of Israel and Jerusalem.

———

The Arabs were angry. The mufti of Jerusalem was personally insulted in the name of holy Islam. They saw the beginning of the construction of the YMCA building, heard about the Jews' intention to build a luxury hotel, and knew that they could not be left behind. The Supreme Muslim Council, headed by the Mufti al-Husseini, issued a tender for the establishment of a competing luxury hotel.

The Jewish contracting company Albina, Dunya, and Katinka also won this tender after replacing its Arab Christian director, Albina, with an Arab Muslim director named Awad. The goal set by al-Husseini was to complete the construction at a rapid pace and to advance the Jewish initiative.

About four hundred Muslim workers and about one hundred Jewish workers were employed at the construction site, and Jewish artist Shmuel Melnik painted murals and ceilings. Although the land was a waqf (a Muslim sanctuary for religious purposes), this did not bother al-Husseini, who also raised money from the Muslim world. The building was completed a year before the opening of the Jewish King David Hotel.

The hotel was beautiful. In the hall was a round staircase and marble pillars. The entire building was decorated with carved arabesques and had an Arabic inscription with different interpretations, ancient and contemporary: "We shall build and build as they did."

The ceremony was attended by Arab, Jewish, and British dignitaries. Haj Amin al-Husseini praised the Jewish contractors for the speed and quality of their work. For the operation of the hotel, the Arab Higher Council chose Jewish hotel businessman Zeev (later: George) Barsky.

The hotel closed not long after its opening because of the fierce competition from the King David Hotel, and the British leased it to serve as a government house. They blocked its beautiful bows and wrapped barbed wire around the eaves, and the government's neglecting of the building took over the grandeur.

With the establishment of the State of Israel, the building was Israeli government property. There were various offices in it. For most years, it was the Ministry of Industry and Trade and is now the Ministry of Economy, which were hosted in the neglected building that was once breathtaking.

In 2006, the Jewish Canadian Reichmann Brothers purchased the hotel, and after extensive renovations, it was reopened under the name Waldorf Astoria Jerusalem, with emphasis placed on preserving the facade of the building, the huge arches and stone carvings.

———

Who won at the end, Jews, Christians, or Muslims? All are invited to sit in the lobby of the three impressive buildings and enjoy the splendor of earthly Jerusalem. The view from their rooms overlooks the illuminated walls of the Old City. They can walk to the Western Wall and pray, or to the Al-Aqsa Mosque or the Church of the Nativity, or they can ride bicycles on the light rail route that does not operate on Saturday. It's just a street in the holy city to the three religions.

Is this a story about politics? Economy? War? Peace? Most incoming tourism to Israel is concentrated in Jerusalem. While the city of Eilat takes the lead in the number of Israeli tourists, Jerusalem is the queen of foreign tourists.

TLV—A GLOBAL CITY

"Tel Aviv will be Israel's New York." This was the vision of one of the city's founders, Akiva Aryeh Weiss, in 1909, as he talked at the founding meeting of Ahuzat Bayit.[74] They stood there, a group of dreamers, and dragged sand dunes and dreamed of establishing the first Hebrew city. More than a hundred years later, I (N.K.) am sitting in the office of the current mayor, Ron Huldai, and we are discussing the realization of this vision as well as the realization of Herzl's vision. "Tel Aviv is the closest model to Herzl's vision of the Jewish state," says Huldai. "Tel Aviv is the bastion of Israeli democracy and rational thinking, a home for every minority and open to the world. One of the world's most beautiful beaches and world-class architectural charms. According to the *Traveler's Digest*, Tel Aviv is one of the ten cities with the most beautiful women and men, a gay-friendly city, and a home for all its residents. It is the source and center for culture and quality of life in Israel. Tel Aviv is a social home front for the entire State of Israel. This city that is called a bubble is everyone's city. The city offers so much that its inhabitants are willing to bear all the disadvantages of density, noise, cost of living, etc., so long as they can live there."

On the same day we talk in the mayor's office, the security forces are busy chasing a terrorist who is hiding somewhere in the city, which does not prevent the city goers from wandering around, the children from going to the kindergartens and schools, and the mayor from talking about safety in the streets of Tel Aviv, where men, women, and children can walk day and night. "Terror incidents are part of today's life in every big city in the world, but in Tel Aviv, as in all of Israel, there are residents who are skilled and experienced in dealing with terrorists," says he.

As I venture out into its rainy streets and its sparkling lights like crystals, I think of the mayor's career. So typically Israeli—from a combat pilot and commander in the Israel Air Force to the management of the Hebrew Herzliya Gymnasium and his long-term success as mayor of the first Hebrew city—the Israeli New York.

Tel Aviv is a "global city." This term was coined by sociologist and economist Saskia Sassen and is designed to describe a city with economic, social, cultural, or political influence beyond its physical location in a particular country and region.

The consulting firm Globalization and World Cities Research Network (GaWC), which ranks global cities, lists Tel Aviv in the Beta Plus group, together with Copenhagen, Berlin, Stockholm, Rome, and Prague. Jerusalem and Haifa are rated at an adequate level. It is not easy for us to see these three Israeli cities in a ranking. Larger cities, bigger and stronger, such as Osaka, Rio de Janeiro, Las Vegas, and Munich, are not included at all.

Tel Aviv lacks many of the characteristics of global cities. There are no world-class government institutions like the UN in New York or the Vienna Atomic Energy Commission, and there are no world-class financial institutions such as the stock exchanges in New York, London, or Frankfurt. There is no concentration of international headquarters of global companies—but yet, there is something there.

In October 2012, the international consulting firm BAV published the international brands' rating. From musical bands to cars, newspapers to technological icons, everything was mixed together to bring out the glare of the brands that could sweep many. Tel Aviv is more attractive than 90 percent of the most popular brands in the United States. The Tel Aviv brand is more exciting than Twitter and the Rolling Stones, and Tel Aviv is perceived in the United States to be more innovative than 75 percent of the popular brands, including the *Wall Street Journal* and Audi vehicles. It is perceived as unique, bold, and independent like Apple, YouTube, and *National Geographic*.

In October 2015, the magazine *Living 360* described Tel Aviv as one of the ten hedonistic holiday destinations in the world alongside Amsterdam, Berlin, Rio de Janeiro, and more. "Tel Aviv attracts young people," writes the magazine, "and these young people mingle with the culture, nightlife, and fashion of the city." Tel Aviv is known as the "Miami of the Middle East," and after seeing its beautiful beaches and sexy celebrants, it is not hard to understand why, the magazine concludes.

The *Wall Street Journal* announced in 2012 that Tel Aviv is one of the twenty-five most innovative cities in the world. Lonely Planet has set Tel

Aviv as one of the cities that are always celebrating. *Conde Nast*, a top travel magazine, listed Tel Aviv in the top ten cities for architecture lovers, and UNESCO has declared parts of Tel Aviv as a World Heritage Site because of the "white city" neighborhoods, with more than four thousand structures associated with the architecture of the Bauhaus buildings.

The Global Startup Ecosystem ranks the top twenty startup ecosystems[75] in the world, with five key components: performance, finance, talent, markets, and startup experience. Tel Aviv is ranked as the first startup city in the world outside of the United States, fifth in the world, followed by London in sixth place, Berlin in ninth, and Singapore in tenth.

The two subjects for which Tel Aviv is carrying the flags of success are that it is the city of entertainment on one hand and the city of technological innovation on the other. Some claim that the city should choose between the two and decide on one identity. Or perhaps it should stay in this connection. Maybe startups, technology, and innovation are sexy and cool in the day and in the night. Maybe the geeks of the day are also the bon vivant of the night.

PART II
SECURITY NECESSITY
AS A SOCIOECONOMIC FACTOR

VI

MILITARY AND CIVILIAN STRENGTH

The large budgetary expenditure of Israel's defense needs—about 5 percent of the annual GDP—consumes considerable resources that could have been devoted to education, welfare, and health. However, the military also has significant indirect contributions to the economy and the society, including imparting professional knowledge and developing qualities of leadership and excellence, training skilled workers, contributing to technological development and the defense industries. which are a source of growth in GDP and exports, and contributing to social integration, education, medicine, employment, settlement, and more.

"Blood" in Hebrew is a word that contains two meanings: blood and money; human life and wealth. We shall not deal in this book with the military aspects of security necessity. Israel is a military power aimed solely at self-defense, but solutions need to be found for the security necessity and the money it costs. An industry of military solutions for air, ground, and sea defense to prevent terrorism and cyber dangers brings to Israel, in addition to a high security level, revenues coming from broad export. This was evident at the Fourth International Conference on Homeland Security and Cyberterrorism in Israel, where over 150 Israeli companies were present in the field, and some fifteen hundred guests from abroad, buyers and professionals, participated.

Israel's military power allows the economy to operate as usual in the course of fighting or terrorist attacks. During the second intifada, 460 murderous terrorist attacks took place in the streets. In a fascinating study[76] examining the impact of the major terror attacks on the Israeli capital market, there was a certain decline in share prices after the attack, and immediately thereafter, a correction of the rates. Share prices were also unaffected by the targeted killings in response to the attacks.

Another study[77] conducted on the subject states that although sensitivity for each attack during this period has risen, no general change was found. That is, the market adapted itself to life alongside terror, and investors continued to trust the Israeli market. The Protective Edge operation, for example, lasted for fifty days, during which some Israelis were drafted, and yet the Israeli economy ended that year with real growth of 2.3 percent. The behavior of the capital market during Protective Edge attests to the security of the business community from Israel and abroad in the stability of the country and the Israeli economy.

Israel is no exception today in the Western world with the phenomenon of terrorism in its territory. We see terrorist activity throughout the world, in developed as well as undeveloped countries, in rich and poor countries, in those who are involved in conflicts in the Middle East and those who are cut off from it. This deployment of terrorism turns Israel into a "normal" state that successfully contends with a problem faced by the entire world.

Israel's economy knows how to contain terror and war, and therefore, investment in military strength can be seen as an investment that reduces casualties and economic risks.

INSIDE THE JUNGLE

The last decades reveal that the Arab world remained divided between loyalties and groups of belonging: clan, tribe, ethnic group, and religion— not just the states. The local nationalism of the modern Arab states has failed to create a "Syrian people," "Iraqi people," "Libyans," "Yemenite people," and so on.

The Arab world is also experiencing significant processes in the demographic field. David Goldman, an analyst with senior positions on Wall Street, a columnist for *Forbes* magazine, and the well-known Spengler columnist, is read by political leaders, investors, and intelligence organizations. In his book, *How Civilizations Die,*[78] Goldman analyzes the mood leading to the demise of civilizations and offers the free world new ways to prepare for the threats of the Muslim world. Goldman carefully analyzes the demographic trends prevailing in the Arab world, first and foremost the dramatic drop in birth rates in most Arab countries, particularly in Iran. Goldman concluded, ahead of the time before the Arab Spring and the rise of *Da'ash* (the Islamic State), that many Arab countries are moving toward cultural and economic disintegration as a result of a dramatic decline in the birth rate and because Arab culture is having trouble aligning itself with the modern world.

Goldman believes that the real strength of a nation is exposed in its encounters with the modern age, globalization, and an open and changing set of perceptions and ideas. The Islamic hierarchical and inflexible social structure finds it difficult to adapt to processes such as education, urbanization, changes in the status of women, and the weakening of tradition. Islam does not know compromises; its perceptions are total—all or nothing, belief or heresy, or total surrender or absolute victory.

The distinction between Muslims and radical Islamists is a distinction that the West makes to reconcile between human openness and acceptance, which is necessitated by Western thinking and its consequences: the growing conflict between Islam and the West. The diagnosis is intended to allow the West to persecute the Islamists without persecuting the Muslims. However, this distinction does not necessarily exist in reality. Muslims impose on Western culture customs and traditions alien to its spirit. What was intended to exist as multiple cultures is developing into a war of cultures.

Russian president Vladimir Putin leads a firm and unequivocal line with regard to the intra-Russian Islamic threat. In a speech delivered in August 2015 to Duma, the Russian parliament, Putin stressed:

> In Russia, people must live like Russians. Every Russian minority, if wants to live in Russia, to work and eat in Russia, must speak Russian and to respect Russian law. If they prefer Sharia over the law, and live life according to the Muslims' rules, we advise them to go to places where this is the law in the country. Russia does not need Muslim minorities. Minorities need Russia. We will not grant them special rights, and we will not try to change our laws to suit their desires, no matter how strong they shout "discrimination."

The West, on the other hand, and especially Europe, is polarizing between human-global-democratic perceptions on one hand and the rise of nationalist-separatist perceptions on the other. The aggressive Islamic conduct in the West, which includes terrorist activity and an unwillingness to integrate, strengthens nationalist perceptions and harms the Muslims themselves.

In Chancellor Angela Merkel's speech in 2017, she said that Islamic terrorism was Germany's greatest danger, and she and expressed her disgust: "It is particularly disgusting when terrorist acts are carried out by those who claim to be seeking protection in our country." The lack of determination and denial of facts are causing fermentation that could result in an explosion.

In any event, Israel is no longer the only "frontal outpost" of the Western world bordering on Islam. The lines of struggle have bypassed Israel and are currently taking place in France, Belgium, Germany, the United States, and other Western countries.

Israel is no longer the "thorn in the flesh" of the monolithic Islamic region in the Middle East. The vicious wars between the Shiite Arabs and the Sunni Arabs, among Persians, Kurds, Turks, Turkomans, Alawites, and Houthi, are shedding Muslim blood by Muslims in unspeakable cruelty and unnumbered dead, thirty times more than were killed in all the wars against Israel. Israel today is seen as the strongest and most stable entity in the Middle East.

Egypt and Jordan both have peace agreements with Israel, and these have survived despite the changes of governments there. These peace agreements have also become strategic collaborations in light of the current Middle East tumult, and in some ways, they expanded also to unwritten understandings with Saudi Arabia and the Gulf states.

The Islamic wars are not in a hurry to end, and these internal conflicts reduce the risk to Israel. Geopolitical commentator Dr. Guy Bechor notes that "what was once perceived as our greatest disadvantage—being 'foreigners'—has now become our great advantage. We are neither Sunnis nor Shiites, we are not radical Islam, nor are Arab swaying regimes."[79]

As of 2017, apart from the Iranian threat that is called a "beyond the horizon" threat, there is one other threat: a tactical, nonstrategic one called "asymmetric war." This is a situation in which an organized military force of a country confronts guerilla warfare. The characteristic of the terrorist forces guerilla warfare is the desire to win by killing civilians and harming civilian population. These terror guerilla organizations confronts the IDF, a humanistic defense force of the State of Israel, which seeks to minimize civilian casualties. The IDF is trained for these situations, but this is a different kind of war that requires rethinking.

IS IT DANGEROUS TO LIVE IN ISRAEL?

Former US president Barack Obama tweeted on June 21, 2015: "Here are the stats: Per population, we [Americans] kill each other with guns at a rate of 297 times more than Japan, 49 times more than France and 33 times more than Israel." Regarding Israel, Obama noted that the data also include those hurt by terror attacks.

Despite the repeated acts of terror by the Palestinian terrorists, the probability of being murdered on the street in Israel is only 3 percent compared with the probability of being murdered on the street in the United States.

An international marathon took place in Jerusalem in March 2016, about six months after the start of a new wave of Palestinian terrorism. Jerusalem's mayor, Nir Barkat, referred to the 2,615 runners from abroad who came from 64 countries and said: "The fact that in the very year that Jerusalem suffers a wave of terror, the marathon broke the record of those registering abroad. This is a testament to the strength of Jerusalem and the world's confidence in the capital of Israel."

There is a huge difference between the perceptions made by the announcements in the media about a Palestinian attacking Israelis with a knife, which creates a sense of constant daily and existential threat to the citizens of Israel, and the reality on the ground, which is relatively calm.

In the United States, with the exception of the September 11 attacks, most of the murders and attacks are not of a terrorist origin. Europe is different. Suicide bombings have occurred in Nice, Brussels, Berlin, Istanbul, London, Barcelona, Madrid, and many other well-established cities. The *Global Terrorism Index*[80] notes that the main terrorist victims are the countries that have absorbed the largest number of Muslim refugees.

The large Muslim minority living in Israel is involved in a negligible number of attacks, almost nonexistent. The Israel Security Agency report[81] notes that "the involvement of Israeli Arabs in terror attacks is on the rise this year but continues to be minor."

In fact, Israel is experiencing the calmest period since its establishment. In recent years, the number of fatalities, soldiers and civilians, as a result of wars, hostilities, and terrorism, has averaged two deaths per hundred thousand residents.

For a family that has lost its loved ones in a war or a terrorist act, there is no consolation in statistics, but at the level of the state's strength and stability, the rate of fatalities relative to the size of the population is extremely important.

In the Middle East, things change, and everything is fluid, but it seems that Israel's geopolitical situation has never been better.

THE PALESTINIAN ISSUE

We believe that every group is entitled to define itself, and it is not our place as Israelis to prevent or promote this. The Palestinian future depends on them alone.

However, facing the Western world, they present themselves as descendants of the ancient Canaanites, a freedom-fighter nation entitled to a state of its own. In contrast, to the Muslim world, they see themselves as natives of the Arab countries who have moved to Palestine in recent generations and are jihad fighters who continue the Pan-Islam war against the Jewish infidels in the Holy Land. It seems as if the Palestinians conduct two narratives simultaneously.

Since the seventh century, there have been Muslim Arabs in the land of Israel but not in the quantity or the perception that exists today. The large part of the current Palestinian population originates from migrant workers who arrived in Israel at the beginning of Zionism, when many jobs were created during the establishment of the Jewish community.

"Every Palestinian can prove his Arab roots, whether from Egypt, Saudi Arabia, Yemen, or any other place," said Fathi Hamad, the Hamas interior minister in Gaza, while talking in great emotion to his brothers in a live broadcast on Al Jazeera. "Some are from Saudi Arabia or Yemen or other countries...I am half Egyptian. There are thirty clans in the name of al-Massari...They are Arabs who came from Egypt, Alexandria, Cairo, Masawan, Deir Sid. They all came for the Jihad war."[82]

Walid Shoebat, a former terror Fatah activist, said in a television interview,[83] "Everyone I knew in Palestine knew how to trace his roots to the country from which its great-grandfather came, and we knew well that our origins were not Canaanite, even though that was what they were trying to teach us."

The economic prosperity that was brought by the Zionists to the land of Israel caused mass migration of Arabs in the region to it. In 1930, the British Hope Simpson Commission[84] recommended a stop to the massive immigration of Arabs to Palestine: "The Chief Immigration Officer has brought to notice that illicit immigration through Syria and across the northern frontier of Palestine is material. This question has already been discussed. It may be a difficult matter to ensure against this illicit immigration, but steps to this end must be taken if the suggested policy is adopted, as also to prevent unemployment lists being swollen by immigrants from TransJordania." [85]

Similar testimony was given by Winston Churchill in 1939 when he was the British colonial secretary in charge of the land of Israel and by Tawfik Bey Al-Hourani, who was governor of Hawran province, and others.

There is no doubt that there have been Arabs in the land of Israel since the beginning of the Muslim period, some of them Jews who converted to Islam, some nomads who came from Arabia, and some Egyptians who came while Egypt conquered the land from the Turks at the beginning of the nineteenth century. However, they were few, and according to the evidence we presented at the beginning of chapter five, "Building a Future," the land was largely desolate until the beginning of the Zionist enterprise.

The chances of a peace or even permanent agreement with the Palestinians seem to be further than ever before, but there is hope.

It seems that where politicians on both sides have no more solutions, the economy is the bridge in which both sides have a clear interest. Economic growth is a de facto solution that is often more effective than any political solution.

According to Eyal Waldman, Mellanox's CEO, the private sector will better solve the problems that politicians cannot. This might happen by creating common interests. Waldman not only speaks but also does; Mellanox employs sixty Palestinian high-tech professionals in Ramallah and Nablus. It also began recruiting high-tech personnel to its development center in Gaza. "Those who recruit for us in Gaza are our people from Ramallah and Nablus; they create the connection, interview and locate the workers," Waldman explains.

He hopes that other high-tech Israeli companies will follow. "That's what will bring peace...The Palestinian workers of Mellanox also worked during the operations in the Gaza Strip...they do not like us, but we get along. True, there's a cultural problem and we have to bridge the gaps, but it's solvable. I hope that in the future they will be able to implement the experience they acquired with us and build their own startups and high-tech companies."

There are many Palestinian settlements at strategic points in Judea and Samaria. A new Palestinian city, Rawabi, was built next to Ramallah for the young middle class, manifesting the hope for lives of prosperity and lasting peace.

Let's hope.

VII

SOCIAL VALUES IN THE PEOPLE'S MILITARY FORCES

SCHOOL OF LIFE

It seems that there is no more suitable way to open this chapter than with a letter written by Lia Tamir, a young female soldier who wishes to take a combat officers' course instead of serving as an officer in the Home Front Command: "Our future lies in our actions, faith, and the desire to grow and improve, everyone to himself and all of us as a nation," writes the nineteen-year-old girl. "In most of the situations in our lives, we can only influence our immediate surroundings, but there are some times and places where we get to do something bigger than ourselves. I find the IDF a place like this. A place where you get up in the morning and have to worry about more people around you, whether you like it or not, whether you are a soldier or a commander, whether you are religious or secular, poor or rich, Jewish or not. We all give in order to be part of something that we have and it is really not taken for granted."

The word "service" has a negative connotation in Hebrew. It is perceived as degrading to human dignity. Officials in the Israeli government do not "serve for the pleasure of the president"; shopkeepers and even telephone operators in service centers do not "serve." They are "service providers" or are required to "focus on customer needs." The only place where the word "service" is used in Israel today is in the context of military service. This is the only place where the pride of the individual is in subordinating his or her desires to the demands and needs of the system. This is the only place where the modern, rebellious, and individualist Israelis are prepared to stop the rush to a career, independence, and self-sufficiency to serve the country.

"I think that the contribution of military service to the uniqueness of Israel is far deeper and broader than security and technology," says Kobi Altman, CFO of Israel Chemicals. "I joined the military as a religious boy from a kibbutz, who knew only the narrow world of the society in which he was born into. I left after serving in the Paratroopers Brigade as a person who knows most parts of Israeli society. I learned the tremendous strength of teamwork. I was experienced in managing and carrying out daring missions. I learned in the military 'not to be afraid of the dark' which later, in business life became 'not to be afraid of difficulties.' The military plays a crucial role in training the Israeli youth and in providing the country with an advantage that does not exist to any other. Serving in the military is the Israeli substitute, and, in my opinion preferred, to studying for free in universities like in European countries. Three years of military service is a gift; we have to find ways to give it even to minorities. This will give them the latest tools for the future."

"We have the best leadership school in the world," said Eyal Desheh, chairman of the credit card company Isracard. "The IDF is one of the best and most significant things that exists here, in every sense, including in the social and economic aspects...Young children, on whose shoulders there is tremendous responsibility, learn how to lead. The IDF's ability, or necessity, to give very young people to express themselves, both in technologies and in field leadership, is a powerful engine. They learn values there. They learn how to take an idea and develop it into something. They learn leadership. I attribute my personal success to training in the youth movement and to my command in Golani brigade."

"The people's military is the largest placement project in the world, from recruitment, training, placement, and human development," says Maj. Res. Orna Barbivay. "It is a placement enterprise focused on maximum utilization of capabilities. This is a global patent registered in the name of the IDF," she emphasizes and adds that "the combination of the message conveyed to young people that they are responsible for the security of the country, and the intergenerational integration of regular soldiers with professional soldiers and reservists is the basis for success."

The military is also a gateway for advancement and integration in society for unprivileged and the disabled. There are special schools and training for that purpose. The military has even understood the relative advantages that people possess on the autism continuum—both in image interpretation and in software quality control—and adapted them to a service suited to their special needs. Thus, the idea of a "people's military" that is committed to all its citizens and opens opportunities to all has been realized. The encounter of the "specials" with the "standard" serving in those units combines the emotional ability and the practical knowledge to recognize and reach out to others.

MORE THAN SIXTY DAYS A YEAR

According to IDF publications, only 5 percent of the population that can perform reserve duty by law, age, and health status does participate in meaningful service. With heavy loads, commanders like reservists can do seventy or even eighty days in an average year while working in the civilian market; combat paramedics, divers, heavy-engineering-equipment drivers, special-unit fighters, and so on are also among the heavy contributors.

The demands of both worlds are well emphasized by Tal Atsmon, who serves as a senior attorney at the firm of Goldfarb-Seligman. Atsmon is a combat helicopter pilot in the reserves. After his discharge and completion of his legal studies, Atsmon lived a triangular life: he is a lawyer in the most demanding place, and he is measured in terms of customer charges per hour, competing with other talented and equally ambitious people.

At the same time, he led a team of four combat helicopters in the squadron, doing an average of sixty days reserve duty per year, which include border alert and fitness training, and he is measured each year on the number of flights he does. "I have to stand up for excellence in both activities," Atsmon says. "I'm measured constantly and the price of compromise on excellence is impossible on both worlds."

He would come to work in the morning and go to the squadron for a night flight. Family life, marriage, and fatherhood to his daughters are his other life, perhaps the first one.

"I do not have an out-of-office message on my office computer," Atsmon says. "I sit with my overalls on the border, taking care of my customers on my laptop. Suddenly a siren of alarm. I'm running to the helicopter, attack, shoot, and go back for my other obligations. It is possible. All is possible. Having a family, being a father, taking the role of managing partner in the largest law firm in Israel, and also leading a quadruplet of combat helicopters in the squadron."

"But there is also synergy," he says. "Because I was a pilot and a flight instructor, I earned leadership qualities. The squadron is an incubator for grazing, support, leadership, and contribution to the group. It is where I practiced cold-heartedness, decision making, to be a visionary, to think outside the box, and holding up pressure. Legal situations cannot stress me. I learned from the air force the wonderful ability of interrogating every mission. Even if it succeeded, especially if it failed."

WOMEN WARRIORS AND COMMANDERS

"During the Yom Kippur War, I was at the command base in the Golan Heights" (N.K.). "At exactly two o'clock in the afternoon, I saw the Syrian planes flying over the base and firing bullets in the bunkers. In the bunker I ran into, sat the GOC Northern Command at the head of the table with all the senior commanders on both sides. I helped there by answering the communications system and passed messages to a chief operations officer who, with a blue marker, marked our retreating forces and with a red marker the Syrian tanks advancing from all directions.

"There was a pause in the fighting at about seven p.m., and immediately trucks arrived to take all the girls back from the fight line. Until that moment, I did not know that I was a 'girl.' I thought I was a soldier. I was not ready to withdraw in the middle of the war. My repeated requests to allow me to remain in my position were answered negatively by the commander, who said: 'No girl stays, not even girls whose jobs are essential.'

"This was the doctrine for women at war. Not for women. I went under the green-tablecloth-covered general's table and hid there for a long time, waiting for the girls' truck to leave, so I would be able to continue my job. By midnight, we all lined up in a convoy of white cars rushed between the tank shells to Safed, where we were building a new war room all night for the general and his senior commanders.

"At seven in the morning, the girls came back, all cleaned and smelling good, reminding everyone of their home, wife, mother, sister, and beloved ones. I did not understand those girls then. I do not understand them still. Thankfully, over the years this doctrine has changed."

Beginning with Deborah, the ancient prophet of the Bible, through the Amazons who, according to the legend, cut off the right breast so that it would not interfere with their shooting, even the French virgin Joan of Arc, and Hannah Szenes—the participation of women in military in general and in combat forces in particular was marginal and only episodic in the past.

In the First World War, there were few women, almost all of them nurses. In the Second World War, there were already more women in the fighting forces on both sides. But women in the British military were not allowed to pull the trigger because it was too manly. Gender equality in the military began to seep in the early 1970s. In the US military, almost all women's roles are now open, whether among the combat forces or supporters of the fighting. In the Kurdish autonomous military, in the fights against the Islamic State, there are seven thousand to ten thousand female combatants operating under the Kurdish gender-equality vision to defeat the Islamic State's fighters, who fear being killed by a women, which would prevent them, according to their faith, from the seventy-two virgins waiting for them in the Muslim paradise.

The State of Israel is one of the only countries in the world where women have compulsory military service. The duty of service expresses first and foremost the concept of the IDF as a "people's military" that sees equality in carrying the burden of security. Even the reserve system of Israel, which has been based and is still based almost entirely on men, has increased the number of women serving in it eightfold in the last seven years.

Over the years, the IDF has gone a long way in promoting and integrating women into combat and command positions. For many years, there was a great reluctance against it. It took a dramatic turn in the wake of the Alice Miller case. Miller immigrated to Israel from South Africa, where she studied aviation and aeronautics and received a civilian pilot's license. She wanted to be admitted to the Israeli Air Force pilot course, but her request was rejected because she was a woman. In 1994, she petitioned the High Court of Justice against the Ministry of Defense and against the IDF for nonacceptance and gender discrimination.

The Supreme Court completely rejected the chauvinistic argument that men cannot bear to have the enemy rape a woman from their own and therefore, women should not be able to serve equally. The men's primitive need to protect their females, who were perceived as their property and even to preserve their superiority, was completely rejected.

The amendment to the Defense Service Law of January 2000 supplemented the High Court of Justice ruling on the right of a female soldier to volunteer for combat professions set by the Minister of Defense, and in 2001, Roni Zuckerman became the first combat pilot in the IDF.

Additional combat roles have been opened to women in the IDF over the years, including naval officers, infantry battalions, and fighters in the Artillery Corps, the Air Defense Force, the military police, and the Engineering Corps.

"Even before I enlisted, it was clear to me that I was going to do something very significant in the military," says the IDF's first combat battalion commander, Lt. Col. Oshrat Bachar. "It's hard to leave a child and a husband who is also in the military. I lose because I'm not with my little girl, to experience the little things she is going through, but to do it with love and a smile and a sense of self-fulfillment and inner happiness—make the difference...I think it also gives a personal example of the young girls who see it possible."

"Only when I reached the military I understood the values on which I was raised upon: teamwork, not giving up when it is difficult, knowing that you were capable for more...At the beginning of the week, I could be in classified activity with submarines in the northern arena, and at the end, in field security operations in the south. My obligation is to give more," says Sgt. Noa Keren, a sapper in the underwater task force. Lt. Col. Ido Kaufman, commander of the underwater missions unit at the Haifa base, notes the success of the fighting women: "Without them, we would simply be weaker."

The struggle for the place of women in the IDF has not ended. Since then, we have been hearing contradicting opinions, masquerading as medical, social, religious, and so on. These recommendations are attributed to the religious atmosphere that is gaining ground in the IDF command and to old chauvinism that raises its head.

The opposite evidence of these chauvinist attitudes is the proven successes of the Caracal Battalion, a combined battalion in which one-third of soldiers are men and two-thirds women. The main task of the Caracal Battalion is ongoing security on the Egyptian border. Its successes include the capture of infiltrators, the arrest of terrorists, the prevention of real-time infiltration, and the seizure of a large quantity of drugs. In September 2012, a battalion force killed three terrorists. In October 2014, in a clash with a large force of twenty-three terrorists affiliated with al-Qaeda and during the firing of antitank missiles and heavy machine-gun fire at the Caracal force, Capt. Or Ben-Yehuda and her liaison were injured. Second Lieutenant Rachel, commander of a platoon in the battalion, silenced the terrorists by ordering fire with a machine gun, which killed six terrorists, two of them by Capt. Ben-Yehuda.

The current revolution in recruiting for the IDF is the enthusiastic participation of religious women; their numbers have doubled as they have enlisted in intelligence, pilot training, and combat units. Within three years, the number of religious women soldiers rose by 71 percent, and the number of religious officers in compulsory service increased by 30 percent. This is done despite the rabbis' desperate attempts to fight the phenomenon.

Capt. Tamar Ariel, the religious navigator who died in a snowstorm in Nepal in 2014, became a symbol for religious girls, and in her name, there is a prestigious project—Tamar Wings—designed to promote "ground-breaking young people" from all areas of the Israeli society.

Orna Barbivay, who was the first commander of a corps that is not a women's corps (adjutancy) and the IDF's first major general (head of the human resources division), relates that women are integrated into the military. "Today, ninety-two percent of service tracks are open to women, and I think we should open everything. The integration should be well planned, and the necessary adjustment should be done, but everything should be open for women in the military. For example, the combat vest should be adapted to the woman's body, but with a suitable vest they can fight together."

Equal military service has a tremendous contribution to gender equality in civil society as well. While Israel is advancing on this issue ahead of most of the countries of the world, the challenge of full gender integration has not yet been achieved.

HUMAN LIFE AS A MILITARY VALUE

Most of the citizens of Israel aged eighteen and over have served in the IDF; many of them have found themselves in extreme situations, stress, and challenges. Military service in Israel charges a price but is a tool for life. It provides skills that are used in civilian life: discipline, ability to withstand pressure, survival in a hierarchical environment, exceptional administrative abilities in operating teams under extreme conditions, intense study of human relations, functioning under constantly changing conditions, and exhaustion of personal abilities.

An example of this is the story of Col. (Res.) Dr. Salman Zarka. On February 16, 2013, seven Syrian wounded arrived at the border fence and requested medical help. "Our soldiers, whose job is to prevent the infiltration of terrorists, have realized that there is something else here; they did not fire but ordered a medical team," says Dr. Zarka. The team examined the wounded, and the doctor decided that they should be evacuated to the hospital. The injured arrived at the Ziv Medical Center in Safed, not too far from the border, were treated for several days and returned to their country. Dr. Zarka, who was then assistant director general of the Ministry of Health on leave from the military, received a phone call telling him to return to uniform and to help plan the project to provide humanitarian aid to the Syrians.

"For years, I worked in the North in planning the medical response for soldiers and residents against attacks from Syria. And suddenly, we are thinking about how to help the wounded Syrians who are coming to us," he says. "The humane considerations and the doctors' oath have won."

Under the leadership and command of Col. Zarka, a military emergency hospital was built on the border fence, which will enable the rescue of the wounded and prevent unnecessary jolts in emergency situations. He brought doctors, nurses, laboratory and X-ray workers, equipment and logistical systems, all from the IDF Medical Corps, and began to build a team. Within a month, the military hospital opened. Everyone who came to the fence received medical treatment and was never asked about his or her political and religious identity. When the wounded could not be adequately treated in the military hospital, they were evacuated to the civilian hospitals inside Israel.

The military hospital was transferred to Operation Protective Edge to help the patients and the wounded from Gaza, once again under the responsibility of Dr. Zarka. Only this time, Hamas, rulers of Gaza, prevented the civilians from receiving medical assistance, and therefore the hospital was unnecessary.

––––––

The tremendous importance that Israelis see in preserving and protecting the lives of civilians and soldiers can also be learned from the story of the

Merkava tank. The development began in 1970, led by Maj. Gen. Israel Tal (Talik). The working assumption was that the tank should be built around the person inside it, and this includes the maximum comfort and protection conditions.

The first revolutionary idea in this field was to place the engine at the front of the tank. It might be damaged, but it will protect those inside it. A front engine also allows for the installation of a back opening to serve as an escape door for the crew.

To further protect itself and the team, it was equipped with a unique active defense, one of a kind worldwide, an armored shield protection called the Windbreaker (or Armoured Shield Protection – Active). The Rafael system, developed in cooperation with Elta Group, detects and identifies real-time threats from antitank weapons, assesses its optimal intercept route, and destroys the threat away from the tank it defends.

During Operation Protective Edge in the Gaza Strip, the Merkava tanks had a significant involvement in the maneuver, thanks to the Windbreaker that successfully intercepted at least fifteen antitank rockets fired at them, saving the lives of the crews. During the fight, the 401st Armored Brigade commander, Col. Saar Tzur, was quoted on Channel 2: "The division is equipped with the Windbreaker system that has very high quality and saves lives. Everything that was fired at the tanks was stopped, and this system proves itself day by day, hour by hour. It is not a defensive system, but an offensive one. It allows us to run forward without thinking about whether the tanks will be harmed or not." The developers received the Israel Security Award in 2014.

FIGHTING FOR DEFENSE

"The noise is tremendous; it's almost inconceivable. I'm right under the explosion; the whole earth is shaking," said Yuval, a young officer in the Iron Dome battery, describing what he heard and saw when Tamir, the antimissile missile fired by his soldiers, had hit a Qassam rocket launched by Hamas from the depths of the Gaza Strip. The goal of the Qassam rocket was to kill innocent Israeli civilians in the small town of Netivot.

"It's amazing every time to see the incredible speed with which the missile flies in relation to the seemingly slow flight of the Qassam rocket, how it changes direction in the air until it reaches the target and explodes it," he added.

The launch was one of hundreds that the IDF carried out at that time to intercept Qassam and Grad rockets fired from the Gaza Strip. Many major cities suffered weeks of these attacks during the months of July and August 2014, and some of them were completely paralyzed. Iron Dome allowed Israel's leaders to make decisions during times of war without being under public pressure due to casualties.

Iron Dome is a brilliant and unique Israeli invention composed of search and guidance radar, a control center, and interception missiles developed by three high-tech security companies: Rafael, which manufactures launchers and missiles; Elta, which manufactures the radar; and MPrest, which developed the control system. It operates day and night in all weather conditions and is capable of dealing with a large number of threats simultaneously. The success rate was almost 90 percent.

"It's like striking a very small ball, moving at an incredible speed in high altitude with another small ball," said Yossi Druker,[86] head of Rafael's missile division. A delegation of senior American professionals who came to examine the system prior to its construction gave a 15 percent chance that the system would succeed in meeting its goals or that the project would meet the defined timetables. Unlike other projects, where development was done jointly by Israel and the United States, in this case the development was entirely Israeli, but the Americans were supposed to finance the production stage and perhaps use it later for US military bases.

At the height of the race to meet the deadlines, hundreds of people worked: engineers, technicians, draftsmen, and administrators. They came from all over the country, in quiet times and during the war,[87] abandoned their homes, families, and friends, and for three years gave all they had to save the state and its citizens.

In March 2011, the first two batteries of Iron Dome were transferred to the air force. Seven days later, there was the first successful interception of a Grad rocket in the skies of Ashkelon. In Operation Protective Edge, at 2014, Iron Dome marked its thousandth interception. A thousand rockets that, if not intercepted, would have killed and injured many civilians and caused extensive destruction of property, morale, and national strength.

We cannot finish the story about Iron Dome without the story of Adir Levy, a native of Sderot who grew up in the shadow of the harsh fears of the Color Red alarms from missile attacks from Gaza. He remembers, as a boy, running to hide in terror. In the enlistment application form, in which the recruits indicate their military service preferences, Levy wrote, as his first priority, that he wanted to serve in the Iron Dome battery. As a second priority, Iron Dome, and in third place he wrote: "Only Iron Dome, I was born in Sderot and I wish to defend my home and to serve in an iron dome battery, only iron dome."

In his first shootout during his military service at Iron Dome, Adir says that "the picture of the hysterical child that I was, looking for a safe place to hide from the Qassam does not leave me. I press the mouse harder, and I see the explosion of the rocket that protects the skies of Ashkelon."

Most secrets of Iron Dome are confidential. Hundreds of engineers from three companies worked on it in for more than three years. Eight of them received the Israel Security Prize for the development of the system, headed by Brig. Gen. Dr. Gold.

Israel has decided to dedicate the best efforts and brains of its best engineers to create active, revolutionary, and expensive defense systems that will provide citizens with protection. The operational Iron Dome is part of a whole system of interception missiles for active defense of five layers, developed by Israel against high-trajectory weapons.

ROBOTS ON THE BATTLEFIELD

Part of the solution to minimize the number of casualties during combat will come in the form of robots. The basic idea seems to be from a Hollywood movie, but most of the robots already operate in the field and are well integrated into the IDF's brigade exercises; these will include remote-controlled tanks and armored personnel carriers.

"When the threat is peripheral, 360 degrees, the military goal is to see what happens not only from on the surface, but also behind the wall and the in tunnels," says Maj. Gen. (Res.) Gadi Shamni, head of IAI's land division. This new concept came first from all from the desire to save lives of the other side's civilians. It is the IDF code of conduct. They are trying to minimize casual damage. Furthermore, there is an effort to bring back ammunition, already launched for targets, if orders are changed due to intelligence about civilians nearby or from any other reason.

The next phase of the new concept developed by the IDF in recent years is called the "smart trigger." It provides the division to open a sort of "fire tender"—which of the various fire systems available will hit the target most effectively.

VACCINATION AGAINST FALLOUT

Israel is also preparing for nuclear threats in case a ballistic missile carries an atom bomb exploding in the atmosphere and nuclear fallout falls on the population in the area of the explosion. The Israeli company Pluristem, which is listed on NASDAQ, has invented a solution: a vaccine against radiation. It sounds like science fiction, but on February 16, 2016, the Pentagon announced that they had decided to join the project and its funding. They probably know what they are doing.

Nuclear capability, if any exists in Israel, is for defensive capability only. "Israel has four hundred nuclear warheads capable of hitting Iran," Iran's foreign minister, Mohammad Javad Zarif, said in April 2015. Jimmy Carter estimated the figure at about three hundred in 2014. The *Bulletin of the Atomic Scientists* that year estimated a much lower figure, around eighty to a hundred nuclear warheads. In November 2015, the Institute for Science and International Security published an article estimating the number at 115. As for the means of launching, various estimates speak of two dozen Jericho III missiles, some with split heads, another twenty cruise missiles, in submarines of the Dolphin type, as well as several squadrons of bombers, capable of carrying and dropping nuclear bombs. Thus, according to foreign estimates, Israel is a member of a very limited group of countries with doomsday weapons and the ability to launch them great distances.

According to missile experts around the world, Israel is capable of covering all the Arab states and launching nuclear missiles from launch facilities in the dugouts as well as from mobile systems. More importantly, for deterrence, Israel has the ability to initiate a counterattack even if the nuclear bases on its soil are destroyed, for which it has five Dolphin submarines, each carrying four cruise missiles with a range of fifteen hundred kilometers.

If foreign publications are correct, Israel can defend itself by means of a vague threat without lifting a finger. No country with a normal leadership—a democracy, a dictatorship, or a radical Islamic state like Iran—would really want to try to destroy a nation that could respond in turn and completely destroy the aggressor state. It is true that this assessment can be counterproductive: Egypt and Syria attacked Israel in the 1973 Yom Kippur War. Did their leaders know then, or did they think that Israel had atomic bombs? Probably they did, but they did not believe it would use them. There is a claim that the Arab armies refrained from intensifying the attack, which began after they received a warning from the Soviet Union that it might end in a nuclear attack by Israel, but no Arab country has attacked Israel since 1991 except for Iraq with ballistic missiles, but its attacks did not constitute an existential threat to Israel.

TAKING CARE OF THEM

The phenomenon is very strange and unusual: the citizens of a foreign country contribute considerable money, time, and personal effort to the military forces of another country. Such is the American Friends of the IDF (FIDF). The organization's motto: "Their role is to care for the State of Israel; our job is to take care of them." The organization's mission is to support the education and welfare of IDF soldiers, "to ease the burden that the soldiers and their families carry on behalf of the Jewish communities throughout the world. The organization invests over $60 million a year and employs about two hundred people and volunteers worldwide.

Among the many activities of the organization are the programs for awarding academic scholarships to combat soldiers from needy families. In return, the scholarship recipients provide extensive community service. In this way, the value of the donation is strengthened, as not only did the soldiers from the families of distress receive opportunities to learn, but they themselves contributed to the community. In addition, the organization supports programs for education and enrichment of IDF soldiers in the fields of Judaism, Zionism, and Israeli identity, and it assists soldiers who have not completed high school, supports individual soldiers, and adopts bereaved families and wounded IDF soldiers. Another effort is the organization of battalions of fighters as part of the Adopt a Fighter project and contributions to the welfare of the battalions.

"I decided to donate my money and energy to the cause," said Sam Moshe, a senior executive at Morgan Stanley and president of the FIDF in Palm Beach, Florida. "I think it's really a holy work and the little that the American Jewish community can do." Maj. Gen. (Res.) Meir Klifi was appointed as FIDF's CEO in 2014 after serving in the IDF as the military secretary of the last two prime ministers, Ehud Olmert and Benjamin Netanyahu. His wife, Brig. Gen. (Res.) Gila Klifi-Amir, served in her last position as IDF chief of staff's advisor on women's affairs.

Arthur Stark, who serves as president and chief commercial officer of the prestigious Bed Bath and Beyond chain, and President Peter Weintraub, was chosen to be FIDF chairman. On his election day Meir Klifi said about Stark that he has a "deep love, commitment, and generosity to the State of Israel and its soldiers which constitutes a promising leadership for the organization."

Another organization, Adopt a Fighter, is a unique project of leading businesses in the Israeli economy, with the assistance of the FIDF, adopting battalions of fighters. The companies and the military units are adopted by reinforce the Israeli ethos of the People's Military. The companies assist the battalions' budgets for social activities and support the families of soldiers from low socioeconomic backgrounds.

"It is impossible to do what we do without a sense of mission and commitment to the people of Israel," says Lt. Col. Shachar Beck, Lahav battalion commander of the Combat Engineer Battalion, adding that the adoption of the battalion by Adopt a Fighter contributes to this sense of mission.

"It gives us a good feeling to just know that the house is behind us. It strengthens us," says Lt. Shenhar Rotner, deputy head of human resources at Rosh Hanikra.

"Nothing requires you to have a real smile, a warm word, a strong embrace, all of which come from your heart," said a soldier at the President's Excellence Ceremony. The IDF chief of staff said that the essence of the IDF's character is that it comes from the Israeli society and returns to it, hence the importance of the connection in material and spirit between the people and its military.

A good example is Ackerstein Industries, a private company whose entire donation is directly at the expense of the owners, and only on them. The company has, for two years, adopted two combat units: a school of military engineering and an air defense school. "In contrast to the many companies which prefer to adopt the IDF's prestige units, we preferred to choose the somewhat forgotten but multiaction battalions," says Giora Ackerstein, chairman of the company. "These are almost unknown soldiers who work hard far away and have very little glory; we are there for them." The Combat Engineering School trains the Engineering Corps fighters in mining, sabotage, bridging, and D9 operation, and it provides special training for those who continue to work in heavy mechanical engineering equipment. The School of Air Warfare trains the Patriot fighters and the Iron Dome soldiers.

"We are there because they are the constant reminder for us, owners, managers and employees, our Zionism, our past as IDF soldiers and the future of the country, which depends to a large extent on these soldiers. We are a company with Zionist values that built this country," says

Ackerstein. He held joint evenings for soldiers of the adopted units and employees of the company, hosted soldiers in the company, participated in unit events, helped to recruit workers from the soldiers to workplaces upon completion of their service, and so on. "Our profit is in the pride of the company's managers and employees for our contribution to the people and the state. In the end, the units are the ones who adopted us and not vice versa," concludes Ackerstein.

PART III
THE FOUR COMPARATIVE ADVANTAGES OF THE ISRAELI ECONOMY

VIII

Economic Success

Since joining the OECD in 2010
Israel is performing better
Than other members of this rich country club
The Economist, November 2014

Israel is a story of economic success in the present, but we argue that when the four advantages and the three revolutions described in this book reach their full effect, it will achieve even greater economic success, especially in comparison to the OECD countries that are losing their growth engines. Of course, it depends on Israel's conduct and the provision of adequate answers to its challenges.

Israel is one of the OECD countries, but none of the organization's other thirty-four countries have started with such a poor opening. Considering Israel's many challenges, these achievements can be perceived as miracles. Other than miracles, we found that the Israeli character, the Jewish genius, the military service, the immigration, the understanding of the huge opportunity, and knowing that "there are no alternatives" all are the reasons for this success.

Israel's population growth in the last twenty years is indeed the highest of all the developed countries and by a considerable gap, but this growth of about 50 percent does not explain economic growth of 140 percent in Israel at the same time. Since the 2008 crisis, the Israeli economy has grown by about 35 percent, faster than any other OECD economy (apart from Turkey).

The rate of unemployment in Israel, 4.2 percent as of the end of 2017, is one of the lowest in the developed world, and this fact is even more pronounced in light of the significant increase in the participation rate in the labor force, which rose dramatically.

The UN *Human Development Index*, which compares life expectancy, education, and income, ranked Israel before countries such as Belgium, Finland, Austria, and France in 2016.

In 2000, the Bank of Israel gave a comprehensive forecast of the growth rates that were allocated to the Israeli economy. "If we act correctly," the report states, "the Israeli economy will reach GDP at a real scale of NIS 750 billion within 15 years." In practice, fifteen years later, the Israeli economy beat this forecast, and the real GDP reached NIS 910 billion, 21 percent higher than the Bank of Israel forecast, despite the 2008 crisis in the middle.

Growth is important because it allows for expanding the budget pie. It is important for every country but mainly for countries that have challenges in all areas of life, like bringing the periphery closer to the center, which requires transportation infrastructure, railways, interchanges, and roads. This is a lot of money coming from growth.

"In the long-term view, we have something to be proud of," says Eldad Fresher, CEO of Mizrahi-Tefahot and former acting accountant general of the Ministry of Finance. "It is due to the master plan, created in the mid-1980s and is executed by all governments and parties since. The result is an economy with a vivid private sector that generates income, exports, profits, and jobs creation, which expands the state's revenue base from year to year and allows the government to give its citizens more.

"This master plan of economic policy determined that we would aspire to be: a liberal, open, and achievement-oriented state. The result was that GDP per capita increased dramatically during this period, the deficit reduced, inflation was conquered, and unemployment reached the lower level of today, while the population and labor force increased by more than

100 percent during this period. Even more so because of the geopolitical challenges, investors appreciate the Israeli economy. "

Fresher served in the Finance Ministry at the end of the 1980s and early 1990s, when the State of Israel received its international debt ratings for the first time, and therefore, he can testify: "We received a relatively low credit rating of BBB in 1995. On the eve of the first independent Israeli debt issuing our credit rating rose to BBB+. The loans expiry was for ten years, and we met with risk-averse foreign investors, including pension funds, provident funds, municipal funds, etc. Twenty years passed since then. Israel's rating today is A+. The economic changes were tremendous. The debt-to-GDP ratio fall sharply and is close to the best practice."

"In 1995, we said that one day, Israel's GDP per capita would cross the $25,000. We thought we were optimistic," recalls Fresher. "The reality in the end was much more optimistic than we were when GDP per capita crossed the $35,000 line.

"When you build economic resilience, you also build the state's ability to deal with very difficult situations, as they did. We experienced horrific terror attacks, with which the Israeli economy coped well, and we experienced missile strikes on population centers that did not cause economic regression. The most significant financial crisis in the world—and we passed it without having the government stick its hand into its pocket—while other countries are having difficulties.

"All this happened because we have abandoned the past policy of government control. We let the private sector 'take the country on its back.' We have enabled individuals to find their way in diverse industries and to utilize their abilities. It is true that those who led their initiatives also earned more, and the inequality increased. Now we need to cope with this inequality."

In his office on a high floor overlooking Tel Aviv's multilayered landscape and in a voice full of satisfaction, another senior manager shows us that we hardly see the sea from his office anymore, only an innovative urban landscape of a city that reflects impressive economic success. "I was at the Ministry of Finance at the time we first issued the state's bonds abroad," he says. "We prepared a presentation for Standard & Poor's who were supposed to determine the country's rating for the first time. We were young and highly motivated to get a good rating. We discussed our hope that within twenty years, Israel would be almost in the economic level of the secondary countries of Europe, such as Portugal and Greece… Every time I present today the Israeli macro presentation, which overtakes those countries, and many others too, I am filled with pride in the quality of this country that has fulfilled all of our hopes and dreams."

———

All countries were affected by the economic crisis of 2008, but relatively speaking, Israel emerged better than any other OECD nation in all the important economic parameters: the minimal damage to GDP, the debt-to-GDP ratio, unemployment rate, and so forth.

"Compared with 2007, Israel's situation improved significantly, relative to comparable countries, according to a series of key economic indicators: per capita GDP, the government deficit, the public debt, the stability of the financial markets and the banking system," according to Daniel Rosenman, director of the Information and Statistics Department at the Bank of Israel,[88] "Processes that last for a generation and affect the gaps between countries in the standard of living, as measured, for example, by GDP per capita, occurred relatively quickly. The standard of living in Israel rose during this period to the level of major countries such as Italy, Spain, and New Zealand."

Thus, for example, in 2008 through 2017, the change in the nonfinancial business sector's debt as a percentage of GDP not only did not increase but also declined significantly, and thus Israel became one of only two OECD countries that experienced this (the second country being Norway). The decline from the level of business-sector debt to GDP of 92 percent in 2008 to 69 percent (as of 2017) made it one of the lowest.

How did it happen? What made Israel an island that managed to isolate itself from the financial storm created in 2008?

The resilience of the banking system and the business sector in Israel play a significant role in this phenomenon. The Israeli banking system was not harmed and did not need any bailouts from its central bank at a time when such bailouts were becoming more common in the United States and Europe. The conservatism of the banks' management and the strong stance of the central bank were at the core of the matter. Senior executives of Israel's banks at that time were the graduates of the great banking crisis that took place in Israel in the early 1980s, and a few years later, they also experienced Israel's severe economic crisis.

As a result of being burned badly, most of these bankers were more conservative and reluctant to run after subprime and similar ideas. There was also considerable vigilance by the Bank of Israel. The governor of the Bank of Israel at that time, Stanley Fischer, and the supervisor of banks at the time, Rony Hizkiyahu, acted with force and firmness and dealt with those bankers who nevertheless insisted on tasting the cup of poisoning of the subprime and its like. The Israeli economy also has an advantage: its banking system is actually composed of seven banking groups, and so few bank managements are easier to monitor. However, because of the small number of banks in Israel, each is probably "too big to fall" and therefore requires close monitoring by the central bank in order to ensure high financial stability.

Another factor that explains the Israeli economy's resilience during the period of economic collapse is the fact that at the end of 2008, there was no real estate bubble in Israel as in many other OECD countries. The absence of a real estate bubble was due to the drop in property prices during the second intifada. The conservatism of the mortgage market in Israel has helped.

Another unique reason is that the Israeli business sector is based on high-tech companies and receives capital financing from foreign and Israeli investors and therefore is almost irrelevant to bank credit.

Most of the economic threats came from a number of Israeli tycoons who raised bank credit and issued bonds on the Tel Aviv Stock Exchange. The funds were invested in real estate in the United States, Eastern

Europe, and Russia. Later, they came to the point of bankruptcy, or "hair-cuts," for investors. Still, the Israeli banking system has not experienced bad debts in the wake of the 2008 crisis at rates that have even approached those of other banking systems around the world.

In those years, nonbank credit began to develop in Israel; it was given mainly by institutional bodies such as insurance companies and provident funds, which entered the game being very strong financially. They helped the banking system to bear the burden of problematic debts and, in some cases, gave the finance needed to companies that the Israeli banks refrained from providing.

In conclusion, the conservatism of the bankers, the close supervision of the Bank of Israel, the absence of a real estate bubble, the development of a new nonbank sector of financially sound institutions, and a big high-tech sector that has no need for bank debt all were contributing to the absence of banking crises that so many countries experienced in 2008.

FINANCIAL STABILITY

At the end of the 1980s, a delegation from the American Fed landed in Israel. The experts came as guests of the Bank of Israel to explain to the locals how the state's debts should be managed. They stressed that the high debt-to-GDP ratio of that time, which exceeded 140 percent, was much too high, harmed growth, and above all, was dangerous to Israel's financial stability.

As of the end of 2017, Israel's debt-to-GDP ratio fell to a completely reasonable level of 60 percent. However, this ratio jumped to an average of 105 percent in the OECD, while in some southern European countries, there are already dangerous levels of 120 percent or more. So far, Israel has gone against the flow.

Israel's international credit rating of A+ is considered high and could have been even higher had it not been for a problematic geopolitical environment.

The State of Israel continues to record a surplus in the current account (balance of payments) every year from 2003 and in 2016 recorded a record with a surplus of 4.5 percent of GDP. On average, for the last seven years, Israel has enjoyed a surplus of some 3.2 percent in this account compared to only 1.2 percent in OECD countries. The Bank of Israel's foreign exchange reserves continued to climb to reach $110 billion at the end of 2017. The surplus in the current account is expected to be maintained in 2018 to 2019. It is expected that the international liquidity ratio of Israel will continue to improve.

STRONG CURRENCY

In July 2006, Israel's foreign currency markets were hit by the outbreak of the Second Lebanon War, which followed the attack by the Lebanese Hezbollah terrorist organization in which two IDF soldiers were kidnapped on the northern border of Israel and three were killed. Following the incident, Israel responded with a massive attack on Hezbollah military positions, first from the air and then with ground units.

In the wake of the panic, Israeli and foreign investors began selling large amounts of shekels and buying dollars, and the dollar exchange rate climbed within a few trading days more than 4 percent after a long period of steady trading. This process is well known; the currency is devalued for every country that enters a war, as people who start to fear for their property buy American dollars and sell the local money. Foreigners do so to avoid a weakening of the local currency.

But in Israel during the Second Lebanon War, the opposite happened. After a few days, the shekel began to strengthen again. It was strange because just then, massive rocket attacks began on Israel's densely populated industrial zone in Haifa Bay as well as on the residents of Haifa itself. The shekel was supposed to weaken further against the dollar, but instead it began to strengthen.

One of the senior managers of Financial Immunities[89] was asked to clarify, against all logic and economic experience, how the shekel was gaining strength. After several phone calls, he returned with a surprising answer: "It is the foreigners who are actually returning to Israel, while the Israelis continue to sell." In a phone call to one of the senior foreign exchange people of Barclays Bank of London, he discovered that the giant British bank was buying shekels.

"You're making a mistake," the Israeli said to his English interlocutor. "You do not seem to understand what it means that Hezbollah is bombing Haifa."

The Englishman replied calmly, "But you'll win in the end, will you not?"

The Israeli responded, "Of course we will win. We have no option to lose."

"So we buy the shekels again and sell the dollars. We trust you," the Englishman replied.

The results in the foreign exchange market are the cumulative weighting of actions carried out by countless investors and companies and thus constitute the largest concentration of wisdom on the planet. The wisdom of the global masses voted for Israel.

In 2017, the Israeli shekel was the most powerful currency against the dollar out of thirty major currencies traded worldwide. It was not the first year it had finished in this place. This also happened in 2013, 2015, and 2016.

The inflows of foreign investment to Israel, mainly for investment in the high-tech industry, are so large that they are central factors in the strength of the shekel, thereby harming other export sectors in the country. The discovery of the gas deposits in the Tamar and Leviathan drills also contributed to the State of Israel's transformation from an energy-intensive importer to an energy-independent, energy-efficient nation that needs a lot fewer dollars to finance its energy consumption.

FROM A DEVELOPING TO A DEVELOPED COUNTRY

Few analysts would bet on the Jewish state in 1948. Even fewer would bet on it if they knew what its very existence was about. Even those individuals who would have continued to gamble on that crazy card would not have believed that not only did this isolated state survive, but it flourishes, thrives, and overshadows all its rivals in the region and many more.

In comparing Israel's per capita GDP relative to countries that have undermined its very existence since its establishment, it appears that while per capita GDP in Israel grew by 2,400 percent between 1950 and 2015, its hostile neighbors grew by only a few hundred percent. Per capita GDP in Iraq grew at the same time by 800 percent, Egypt by 640 percent, Jordan by 490 percent, Lebanon by 340 percent, and Syria—there is no way to determine; we are all full of hope for better days.

There is no doubt that part of Israel's success is related to the fact that in many cases, it had no choice; either it would succeed or cease to exist. This is a threatening situation that created opportunities.

In 1985, after a dramatic economic stabilization program, Israel emerged from hyperinflation and huge deficits. It was the beginning of a process in which Israel transformed itself from a developing country into a developed one. In a time frame of thirty years, from 1985 to 2015, the number of residents grew by 100 percent; the product increased ten times more. Israel's total exports rose by 860 percent; high-tech exports rose from a few billion dollars to about forty billion. The government sector's share of the economy dropped from 74 percent to 42 percent, defense expenditure as a percentage of GDP fell by 75 percent, government debt as a percentage of GDP declined by 78 percent, and American aid dropped from 10 percent to 1 percent of GDP. Foreign exchange reserves jumped from $4 billion to $110 billion at the end of 2017. Many other indicators can be presented, but the conclusion is clear: the Israeli economy is a success story.

The positive prominence of Israel happened mainly after the global economic crisis of 2008. It is not only because Israel succeeded in achieving good economic results, but also because most of the OECD countries have since achieved poor economic results.

We argue that Israel will be able to continue to stand out in the future because it is experiencing extraordinary trends, from demographic trends that will leave it as a young state while almost all OECD countries are aging through energy independence as a result of discoveries of huge gas fields in the sea. This is a result of the construction of some of the world's largest desalination plants and sophisticated wastewater treatment plants, its continued status as a "startup nation," the increase in labor force participation rates, the phenomenon of continuous entrepreneurship among its youth, its highly educated population, and the continued immigration of Jews.

We also argue that Israel will stand out favorably because the world, especially the developed world, is in serious trouble due to the end of most economic growth engines, and its growth will be minor and staggered.

There is broad consensus among economists that the best way to improve the quality of life of nations is to generate economic growth. However, when analyzing the history of the economic growth of the world, a surprising fact is revealed: throughout most of human history, until the Industrial Revolution, global growth was negligible. Until the beginning of the Industrial Revolution, the world grew at an estimated rate of about 0.2 percent per year. With the beginning of the Industrial Revolution, the growth rates (especially in the Western world) increased significantly and reached about 1 percent per year. Today, we are all living in a world where we have been accustomed, for several generations, to growth at the rate of several percent a year, but these are exceptionally high rates for what humanity has been accustomed to in all generations since the dawn of humanity. A situation of positive growth is not necessarily a law of nature.

According to Stephen D. King,[90] who served for many years as HSBC's chief economist, the rapid growth of Western economies in the twentieth century was the result of a combination of five one-time processes during this period. The first factor is the rapid development of world trade after World War II.

The second factor is the entry of women into the labor force. From a time when less than 40 percent of women worked, we have moved to a situation in which 70 percent of the women are in the labor force. Countries that did not do so, such as Japan, had lower growth rates.

The third factor is education. In 1950, only 15 percent of young men and 4 percent of young women in the United States studied in universities. After World War II, university studies became more and more common. The creation of an educated workforce of engineers, technicians, and researchers accelerated growth.

The fourth factor is consumer credit. Its increase gave Western companies the opportunity to benefit from the advantage of size and was an important driver of growth.

The fifth factor is population growth. In the United States, the baby boomer generation increased both labor and consumer power.

According to King, all these factors worked together with technology to accelerate economic growth in the West. Today, these growth factors, apart from technology, are no longer available, so King predicts that economic growth in Western countries will be much slower during the twenty-first century.

In his opinion, the predictions of many governments are based on optimistic forecasts that what was in the twentieth century is likely to continue. King argues that this is dangerous because these exaggerated assumptions may create overly optimistic forecasts, excessive government promises to the public, and, as a result, will eventually be a disappointment and lead to an increase of extremist elements.

In addition, it can be noted that the OECD countries will not be able to move forward with a "Keynesian push," meaning increasing government demand to encourage growth, because many of them are drowning in high public debt.

THE DEMOGRAPHIC DIVIDEND

There are many indications that demographic trends are of greatest importance to economic growth. The significance of young people joining in the labor force is reflected in what is known as the "demographic dividend," which, according to researchers like Bloom[91] and his partners, accounts for up to a third of East Asia's impressive growth between 1960 and 1990. All researchers agree that the opposite happens in an aging population—growth decreases. A young population is a key factor in the economic forecast of each country, which sometimes contributes 25 to 40 percent of growth. When this trend is reversed and the labor force decreases, there are fewer working young people and more older people who do not work; the impact on growth is also clear.

In a study produced for the G20 Summit, it was written that the world population is characterized by decreased fertility and increased life expectancy. The main result of both trends is an aging population. The proportion of the population aged sixty and over will rise in the developed countries from 22 percent in 2010 to 33 percent in 2050. The working-age population will decrease from 49 percent to 41 percent at the same time. The significance of the data is a dramatic increase in the number of elderly people and a dramatic reduction in the number of people working and producing. The report does not mention this, but there are demographic studies showing that there will be a significant decrease of about 14 percent among young people aged twenty to thirty-four of the total labor force in developed countries by 2030. This is already a problem that affects other economic issues, since this age group is characterized by the highest labor productivity as well as the highest consumer demand.

In April 2014, the *Economist* reported that by 2035, more than 1.1 billion people, or 13 percent of the population, would be over age sixty-five. This is a natural consequence of the reduction in birth rates and slowing of the general population. That means there will be fewer young people around. The famous dependency ratio, which is the number of elderly people dependent on working young people, will grow even faster. The UN predicts that in 2035, in the rich countries, the numbers will be fifty-four elderly people for every one hundred people of working age; about one out of three will be "dependent."

A striking example of this problem is Japan, which is aging and has the oldest population in the world. Japan has a median age of forty-eight and has been unable to produce growth for almost twenty-five years. Germany also has a serious problem, with the second-oldest population: the median age is 47.5.

The aging of the OECD population has a dramatic impact on economic growth in the member countries of this league, and the demographic forecast, as stated, is very pessimistic. In the same *Economist* article, a study by Amlan Roy, an economist at Credit Suisse, calculated that the labor-force population contraction dragged down Japan's GDP growth by an average of just over 0.6 percentage points per year between 2000 and 2013, By 2017, this rate will increase to 1.0 percentage points a year, and the shrinking labor force in Germany will offset GDP growth by nearly 0.5 percentage points a year. In the United States, the retirement of the baby boomer generation will offset the economy's growth by 0.7 percentage points.

In Europe, the ratio between the working and nonworking population (the dependency ratio) has fallen from a peak of 2.2 people working to every person who does not work in 2010 to a predicted low of 1.65 in 2030. From there, the ratio will continue to deteriorate, albeit at a slower pace.

In the short term, the waves of immigrants to Europe will probably have a certain positive effect, encouraging growth due to the flow of government budgets to social services and the construction of shelters and rehabilitation centers; immigrants' demand for housing, education, and consumption; the addition of cheap labor to basic industries; and an increase in the profitability of these industries. But already in basic industries, there is no shortage of working hands in Europe because waves of immigrants, mainly from North Africa, have been arriving for a long time, and they have filled the quotas. Paradoxically, the new illegal immigrants threaten the jobs of the legal immigrants who arrived in the past. In the long term, they will have a negative impact: a constant burden on social and security budgets, a decline in per capita GDP, social gaps and cultural gaps, lack of identification with the state, gaps in education, declined in work ethic, political changes, and terror.

SOURCES OF GROWTH

The great growth engines that enabled the developed countries to grow in the twentieth century are disappearing. The growth rates expected in the future will be similar to those achieved since the 2008 crisis, and they may serve as a wake-up call to a new phase that the OECD countries are currently in. Since the 2008 crisis, the developed world has relied on three main growth engines: quantitative expansion, cost reduction, and technological innovation. While it is possible to add the elusive factor called productivity increase, in any case, it is combined with efficiency based on technological improvements—and technological improvements, as we shall see immediately, constitute a solution on one hand, but on the other, a problem.

In terms of "quantitative expansion"—meaning interest rate cuts—central banks in most developed countries admit that they have more or less exhausted quantitative tools, and solutions will have to be found elsewhere. It is interesting to note that in the United States, the administration is trying a different way of fiscal stimulus, which will lead to greater demand on the part of the government itself, but at the same time, the budget deficit and the huge external debt will grow.

The United States brought to the world new energy production technologies: Oil and gas and shale gas production gained momentum in the first decade of the twenty-first century with the introduction of two technologies required for commercial production; fracking and horizontal drilling. Indeed, these technologies fulfilled all the hopes. The price drop was also caused by the economic slowdown in China and by the Saudi price war aimed at harming the young shale industry and, at the same time, its bitter rival, Iran. A drop in oil prices is a double-edged sword; it is very helpful to the countries that import this resource, but it harms countries that export it. Still, since most of the world's countries, certainly the most developed ones, are oil and gas importers; overall, the benefit is far greater than the damage.

Some see renewable energy as a source of optimism. But at least according to the published data, which track the progress of these sectors (solar, wind, water, and biodiesel), there is little reason for optimism. The world needs more energy, and the relative weight of all the green energies in the world supply does not rise relative to the energy produced by burning fossil fuels (gas, coal); it remains at about 7 percent (although they both grow, of course, in absolute terms).

We are therefore left with accelerated technological innovation based on developments in biotech, biomed, high tech, genetics, and nanotechnology. Indeed, these are manufacturers of growth, but all the developments in these fields come with robotics, smart software, artificial intelligence, and automation that improve the profits of companies but omit people from the workforce. The United States and other developed countries have lost tens of millions of blue-collar workers in the past twenty-five years as a result of the introduction of robotics and innovative manufacturing technologies, and they have assumed that new professions will be created all the time. The majority of experts, from the beginning of the twenty-first century, are convinced that technological change is so rapid that many more jobs will be eliminated than new ones will be created.

While jobs are removed, companies and/or production lines of "older" technologies are eradicated as well. As cassette tapes destroyed records, compact discs destroyed tapes. MP3 players destroyed the discs and the Walkman. The smartphone replaces the MP3 players. All praise the Apple company for the iPhone, but after the iPhone has eliminated some of the manufacturers of MP3 players, the smartphones also eliminate the digital camera manufacturers, which, in turn, severely damaged the makers of old film cameras such as Kodak, Minolta, Canon, and others.

THE LABOR MARKET SHRINKS

What happens to employees? Are the companies with the new technologies producing enough jobs for all those who have been ejected by technology? MegaResearch claims that labor markets in the world's fifteen largest economies (both developed and developing countries) will lose five million net jobs as a result of technological changes by 2020. The study calls it the Fourth Industrial Revolution, which includes developments in previously unrelated fields such as artificial intelligence and computer science, robotics, nanotechnology, 3-D printing, genetics, and biotechnology, and it will cause widespread "disturbances," not only to business models but to job markets as well. The researchers assume that a huge change in skillsets required by workers will be needed to thrive in this new and changing landscape.

According to a Merrill Lynch and Bank of America study, the rise of intelligent machines becomes an integral part of our daily lives. According to their forecasts, robots are expected to take up to 45 percent of the production tasks by 2025. Simply put, they expect mass layoffs on a scale that the world has not yet experienced: rapid growth in the areas of artificial intelligence, robots for agriculture and mining, industrial manufacturing automation, no human beings on production lines, UAVs (civilian and military), FinTech (financial technologies) that mainly change the banking system, industrial robots, medical robots and computer-assisted surgical procedures, self-driving cars, robotic service help at home and in stores, software-based financial and medical advice, and more. This analysis concluded that we are facing a paradigm shift in the way we live and work.

According to a recent study by two Oxford University researchers, 47 percent of the existing professions in the United States will disappear within ten to twenty years as a result of the introduction of software and robots. Today we know that you will be successful if you can create a code, design computer screens, work in digital promotion, create a "user experience" for costumers, locate leads through the Internet, engage in computer-integrated clothing, promote websites, program computer games, robots or industrial products that can be connected to the Internet. But for too many parts of the middle class in the world, "smart" instruments are a wake-up call. The moment when the world's population will be divided into two parts is coming closer; one part of the world will be those who breathe, live, and swim in the digital world will be able to earn a living, share it well, and share it with dignity. The others? Their future is not certain. In a short period of time, there will be professions, some of them surprising, that will simply disappear. In these areas, wages will lower.

The next wave will be the introduction of "smart agents" known as BOTs that will allow anyone to get help with simple tasks on the Internet. So more professions will be at risk. The greater the understanding of the algorithm regarding application of emotional intelligence features in the BOTs, the greater the number of human workers in many fields who will be at risk. In fact, the types of professions at highest risk belong to the middle class. The most exposed are white-collar workers and administration. On the other hand, the professions that will flourish will, of course, be in the fields of computers and digitization.

In general, workers at the top of the salary scales or people with expertise in personal service are not threatened. The professions of the lower deciles who deal with physical areas, such as gardeners, hair dressers, nurses, physiotherapists, plumbers, and electricians are relatively protected because robots that replace human capabilities that have physical complexity are not really yet on the horizon.

The McKinsey consulting firm claims that "the rate of change that human society is undergoing today is 10 times higher, 300 times as large, and 3,000 times as much as what humanity experienced in the Industrial Revolution."

Jacob Kotlitzki, one of the most prominent high-tech professionals in Israel who has been in technology for five decades, is very concerned about the global trends of creating a smaller number of new jobs than those that are being waived and that the situation is only getting worse. The solution, he believes, is the growth of academic education to support the new professions. In his assessment, there is an understanding in Israel among some of the younger generation of the need for advanced technological studies—and even advanced ones. "I see this on my side in the preoccupation and the tremendous interest in all the subjects of robotics. The Faculty of Machines at the Technion, which until a few years ago was the least popular among the new students, has become one of the most desirable faculties in recent years, mainly thanks to robotics. Even in the pre-academic center at the Technion, where I donated a robotics laboratory for children and youth, the demand has grown tremendously. The three laboratories are filled with children and youth from all the schools in the north (Arabs and Jews) who come for a whole day to experience the building of robots. There is no doubt that mechanical technology, computerization, and artificial intelligence have reached a place where man is becoming increasingly redundant, and we are already deep in the process. The problem that I see is the huge employment problem of young people who already exist but will get worse, and I do not see how it is reversed and what governments will do with all these unemployed people and what the unemployed will do themselves."

Kotlitzki also notices another problem. "I see that we have come to quite a state of saturation in our ability to make a real change, a breakthrough in technological innovation, much of what is renewed is at the level of 'nice to have' and a relatively small amount of real needs that masses of people will begin to consume. Get more, consume more, along with the inability to make a living and earn; really scary things like this have led to revolutions in the past. The problem is that there seems to be no solution."

Economist Thomas Friedman also describes how globalization and technology are among the causes of the flattening of the world, and the world's predisposition to a paradigm shift similar to the revolution of the printing press and the Industrial Revolution: a world that alienates professions and jobs at a higher rate than it can produce and a world in which the disparities between the flat and dynamic world dwellers and those of the old world are swelling into serious economic, social, and political problems that may translate into escalating wars and terrorism.

———

In conclusion, as we can see, the economic benefits of technological innovation will be offset by a shrinking middle class, an increase in unemployment, and social unrest. The net loss of jobs will reduce consumer demand worldwide and increase the resentment and discontent of large parts of the population. The risk, especially for young people who have not yet accumulated work experience, will increase serious social and economic dangers and belief in the ability of technological progress to extricate the world economy from the mud.

ISRAEL HAS ANSWERS

The greatest risk to the Israeli economy stems from the fact that about 30 percent of Israeli products are exported. Damage to economies around the world also affects Israeli exporters. In fact, the Israeli economy has felt this damage for a long time, since 2008.

However, Israel has good answers to the problems presented above, more than most of the developed world. As a result of the relatively low impact of the global economic crisis on the Israeli economy, the government can increase its demand. But much more importantly, Israel has significant relative advantages that are unrelated to any other government decisions, which we will touch upon later.

In 2010, the US Central Bureau of Statistics (CBS) defined 840 different completely new types of professions in the US economy, mainly in high tech, biotech, biomed, genetics, and nanotechnology. All these fields are very common in Israel, and they generate a lot of new jobs.

Another major advantage of Israel is the centrality of the defense industries. Large inventions in the twentieth century were born in a leak of knowledge from the military industries to the civilian market—satellite communications, the Internet, digital cameras, some miniaturization technologies, and more. Therefore, the expectation is that military technologies will continue to infiltrate the civilian economy and create new positions in the labor market. Some of the Israelis who are exposed or serve in technological units in the IDF develop civilian assimilation of the things they have been exposed to after their military service. Indeed, in Israel, many military technologies go into civilian life, and there is constant cooperation between technological units in the IDF and civilian high-tech companies.

The population of Israel is one of the most educated populations—third in the world—and is young and entrepreneurial by nature. Many young people in Israel are able to move quickly from profession to profession and from field to field and are very open to innovation. It's a cultural matter.

———

Another help comes from a completely different direction, a kind of economic miracle. Israel has been able to discover large-scale offshore gas reservoirs that have led to an energy independence it has never experienced before while enjoying a dramatic decline in energy costs for its industrial and urban sectors. At the same time, it enjoys a tailwind as a result of the decline in world oil prices. These trends block economic risks from other directions.

———

The Atlas of Economic Complexity of Harvard University in the United States brings interesting insights. The atlas tracks the global trade of more than one hundred countries and the dynamics that change with time and their growth opportunities in order to highlight ways countries can improve their situations over time and encourage optimal growth. The atlas attempts to measure the amount of "productive knowledge" that each country holds to explain the enormous differences in income among the nations of the world and especially to try to predict their future economic growth.

The atlas, which consistently examines 128 countries, marks Israel together with only two other OECD countries as having significant economic growth over the next ten years.

IX

THE GLOBAL ADVANTAGE

SMALL-WORLD NETWORK

A global people in a global world have a built-in advantage. An interconnected society in a networked world has a similar advantage. The strength of the Israeli economy is based on the density of the network within Israeli society as well as outside connection to the global world.

The internal links are based on Israel being a small and crowded place where everyone studied together, were in the youth movement together, and served in the military together. Global links can be on a scientific or technological basis, such as research and development relationships with other scientists, researchers, or R & D centers around the world or on a business basis with companies, markets, and global investors. Global links sometimes have a national basis to Jewish or Israeli communities around the world. The Israeli Jewish network is warm and available for the development of business, economic, and other opportunities.

The modern information economy sees the flow of information as the manifestation of everything,[92] economic growth in particular. The denser a network is, the more information flows through it. Under this terminology that economic power is based on the efficiency of information processing, Israel has an advantage stemming from its global connections and citizens.

Israel has a global advantage that comes from being an immigrant society with extensive knowledge of cultures and languages, openness, and curiosity to the world and the temperament of nomads who know how to feel at home—everywhere.

We dealt with the internal connections of Israelis in previous chapters. This chapter will discuss Israel's global connectivity. In global connectivity, we should distinguish between two levels. Macroconnectivity, the state is responsible for, and its purpose is to enable the conditions required for the flourishing of microconnectivity, which is the responsibility of businesses. We will discuss them both in this chapter, starting with the macro level.

AMERICA, MY LOVE

It is impossible to talk about Israel's global advantage without mentioning its strong ties with the United States—relations that are expressed in economic, cultural, political, and military terms. In the United States lives and flourishes the biggest Jewish and Israeli communities, the second largest in size after Israel.

The United States is Israel's largest trading partner. The Free Trade Agreement between the two countries constitutes the basis for the development of trade relations but also is an advantage to Israel as one of the few countries to sign such Free Trade Agreement both with the United States and the European Union.

There is a dramatic prominence of Israeli companies traded on the two major exchanges in New York. Many American are very active in Israel as investors, strategic or financial, in high-tech or traditional industry, building or buying Israeli companies.

Steve Ballmer, Microsoft's second CEO after Bill Gates, called Microsoft "as much an Israeli company as it is an American company."[93] Many large and successful Israeli companies are listed as American; businesses are managed both from Israel and the United States.

A study published by the US-Israel Science and Technology Foundation placed Israel's technological ties with the United States in third place in the world after Switzerland because of the pharmaceutical industry and Canada because of its geographic proximity.

The study showed that the technological relationship between the United States and Israel is stable in all the indices compared with sixteen major countries examined; these indices include government relations, academia, innovation and patents, investments, business cooperation, R & D, and so on. In the business relations category, Israel is ranked second and ranked as a leader in the private investment index in R & D.

———

Large populations in the United States are especially favoring of Israel, as evidenced by various surveys published there for decades. According to the Gallup Poll,[94] Israel is one of the most popular countries, with 71 percent of Americans feeling sympathy or great sympathy toward it. That is far more numerous than the number of American Jews and tens of millions of Christian believers living in the Bible Belt. Broad American populations have a special emotional and religious connection to Israel.

For Israelis, the United States is, by far, the most beloved country in world. It is expressed in Israelis' desire to resemble the United States, both on a national and personal level. The United States is frequently called by Israeli politicians "our greatest friend." Israelis feel at home in the United States like nowhere else in the world.

"For the United States, Israel is a stable, loyal, and militarily skilled asset," writes Michael Oren, the former Israeli ambassador to the United States and author of the book *Ally*[95] about his life between the two countries. "For the United States, Israel is a stable, loyal and militarily competent asset—a source of scientific and technological power—and a pro-American island in a stormy and often poisonous sea...There is an ideological, strategic, and natural alliance between them."

The fact that Israel is the only democracy in the Middle East is undoubtedly one of the keys to understanding the special relations, but these have developed over many years and are built in many layers. The strong ties that exist between the two countries are exceptional by any measure.

Judaism has been an integral part of the history, morality, culture, and values of the United States since the beginning of the seventeenth century. Israeli-US relations are based on four hundred years of tradition and values, with the anchorage of the first settlers who arrived in the modern "Promised Land" (United States) after the "crossing of the modern Red Sea" (the Atlantic Ocean), and they made the "modern Exodus." Under the same way of thinking, the United States was founded in the eighteenth century.

"I really wish the Jews an independent state in Judea," said John Adams, the second president of the United States, 148 years before the establishment of Israel. At the height of the American Civil War, Abraham Lincoln promised to work for the return of the Jews to their land once America was united again. His wife, Mary, said that on the last day of his life, he talked of his desire to see Jerusalem before his death.[96]

It is a spiritual affinity that has no parallel between other nations with a different language and a considerable geographical distance. Thus, only eleven minutes after the establishment of the State of Israel, the United States was the first country to recognize the young Jewish state.

Today, too, quotations from the Bible are featured in the public, political, and legal discourse in the United States. Only in the United States will you find streets named for David Ben-Gurion, Golda Meir, and Yitzhak Rabin, and Israel is the only Middle Eastern country to commemorate leading Americans such as La Guardia, Kennedy, Martin Luther King, and the victims of September 11. The Israelis and the Americans are also similar in their willingness to fight for their ideals; they defend the same values and deal with the same threats, from Soviet communism to Saddam Hussein and jihadist terrorism, says Oren.

Israel's relationship with the United States has been regarded by Israel as its most important international relations since the end of the 1960s. Israel regards its associations with the United States as paramount, and the United States defines them as "special relations."

Even President Obama, who, in Israeli eyes, may have been the most problematic in his preferred relations with the Muslim world on one hand and misunderstanding Israel on the other, said that "unity with Israel is a fundamental interest of our national security...Therefore...our alliance with Israel will last forever."[97]

In addition to international political support, Israel received approximately $3.4 billion annually in military aid. This aid represents less than 1 percent of Israel's annual GDP. Eighty-four percent of the money was earmarked for military purchases in the United States alone; therefore, in a circular motion, the agreement actually increases job creation in the United States. The new aid agreement signed in September 2016 increased the sum to $3.8 billion per year but also increased the percentage of buying in the United States to 100 percent, and thus, it expands job creation even further in the United States. Still, it's very important aid for Israel, saving it the need to finance some of the IDF's equipment. But in addition to creating jobs, does this support bring additional value to the United States?

"Israel is the largest American aircraft carrier in the world that cannot be sunk," stated US Secretary of State Alexander Haig in 1981.[98] In 1986, Gen. George Keegan, who was the head of intelligence for the US Air Force, claimed that the contribution of Israeli intelligence to US security is equivalent to five CIAs.[99]

According to Senator Daniel Inouye, chairman of the Senate Intelligence Committee and the Senate Appropriations Committee: "The scope of intelligence received by the United States, from Israel, exceeds the scope of intelligence received from all NATO countries combined."[100] Israel's intelligence services provide it with counterterrorism intelligence, which saves billions of dollars each year.

In 2014, former commandant of the marine corps Chuck C. Krulak said, "In Iraq in 1991, I implemented the lessons of Israel's armored warfare in Sinai."

The US Army Corps of Engineers has built airports and military camps for the IDF as well as installations for American forces to use in

Israeli territory. The two militaries conduct joint maneuvers and training and have ongoing dialogues that determine policy and military collaboration. American forces are training in Israel's military base in the Negev for fighting in urban surroundings according to the methods and models developed by the IDF. As a result of the military aid funds, most of the equipment and weapons in the IDF are manufactured in the United States. The IDF provides a huge field of testing for innovative technologies of the US military, and the United States has also been stockpiling its military equipment in Israel since the 1990s.

It is important to remember that the United States provides aid to the only democracy in the Middle East and helps a partner who is probably the best it has ever had, especially given the fact that the United States is losing its geopolitical influence in the region, particularly against the backdrop of renewed Russian influence.

According to Yoram Ettinger, who served as the US ambassador to Washington and is currently a senior US affairs columnist and president of US-Israel Opportunities consulting firm for US and Israeli business and policy makers, "Israel extends the strategic arm of the United States."

———

American Jews have come a long and admirable way since their status did not allow them to enlist the United States to help save their brothers, Europe's Jews, during the Holocaust. They contributed to the uprising and the establishment of the State of Israel, which helped them to consolidate their status. It was Louis Brandeis, the first Jew on the bench of the US Supreme Court, who said, "Every American Jew who supported Zionism was a better American because of it."

Members of AIPAC, the most powerful Jewish lobby organization in the United States, see themselves as Americans working to strengthen the country through its ties with a strong Israel. Israel is strong in maintaining the US position in the technological, military, and economic fields,

AIPAC claims, and it is incumbent upon all of us to maintain and preserve this strong and basic alliance between the two countries.

History shows that reality does not usually allow the powers to shrink back in. Empires withdrawing from their position of influence in the world are weakening their country of origin. That was the case of ancient Persia, Macedonia, Greece, Rome, and the Austro-Hungarian, British, and Ottoman empires.

In the coming decades, the Americans will have to decide whether they want to lose their global, military, political, and economic power and whether they really want to remain global. Internal seclusion will not bring economic value to the United States; on the contrary, it will only reduce its impact on the global economic organizations that regulate the world economy in its favor.

WHEN TWO ANCIENT NATIONS MEET

China today is a global superpower, competing for its place in the world arena. It is the second-largest economy after the United States and may be the first by 2050. China is the world's largest exporter and second-largest importer and is the number one destination for foreign direct investment. "The twenty-first century is our century," the Chinese say—and comply.

It is important to remember that the Chinese have a history of xenophobia and have good reasons for it. Until the middle of the nineteenth century, it was the world's largest economy, and most Chinese believed that the aggression of foreign nations had caused many years of decline from which they are only now emerging. Although China's fundamental xenophobia is so deeply ingrained, Jews and Israelis are actually loved and appreciated.

As an ancient nation with such a rich culture, the Chinese cherish Jewish history and culture, and they view it as a common denominator for both nations, in contrast to the way they see the other "new and young" nations that have not yet developed a worthy culture and heritage. For the

Chinese, this is first and foremost the brotherhood between two of the oldest nations on the globe.

The Chinese have feelings of superiority toward many countries whose inhabitants still roamed like wild peoples in the forests when China developed a profound culture more than two thousand years ago. The Jews are a similar case, as British prime minister Disraeli responded in the nineteenth century when he was attacked by a member of Parliament for being Jewish: "Yes, I am a Jew, and on the days when the honorable gentleman's forebears were cruel savages on a remote island, my forefathers served as priests in the Temple of Solomon."

In China, there is an instinctive sympathy for Jews because both peoples share the central values of the importance of family, learning, and making money. The Chinese view the Jews as a very wise people, and they are aware of the enormous number of genius Jews, including many Nobel Prize winners who have left their mark on the exact sciences, a topic the Chinese greatly respect. Albert Einstein is probably the most admired (non-Chinese) historical figure for them. They also greatly appreciate Israel as a country that has had tremendous achievements in a short time.

China contributed to saving the lives of Jews who fled Nazi Germany. Shanghai had more than thirty thousand Jews who had fled from Europe. In fact, Shanghai absorbed more Jewish refugees than Canada, Australia, India, South Africa, and New Zealand combined.

Although the State of Israel was the first in the Middle East and one of the first in the world to recognize the new regime in the People's Republic of China after the Mao Cultural Revolution, the two countries found it difficult to establish friendly relations until 1992. The reasons for these difficulties lie in China's dependence on Arab oil as well as the Chinese desire to create an opposition to the United States, which supported Israel, and Russia, which supported Arab countries. Thus, the Chinese developed a prominent pro-Palestinian position.

Today, China is Israel's second-largest trading partner, with a significant surplus of imports from China to Israel over Israeli exports to China.

Israel has expertise and knowledge in subjects of interest to the Chinese: agriculture, environment, science, and technology. The amount of real investment by the Chinese in the Israeli economy was second only to investments by American companies. These investments certainly reflected the way the Chinese see Israel's potential.

Israel is also supposed to join the initiative of the "New Silk Road." Israel can indeed serve as a logistical and industrial transit station for China, being a geopolitical link among Africa, Europe, and perhaps even West Asia. The interests of China in the ports of Haifa and Ashdod and the possibility of a significant footing on the Ashdod-Eilat Red-Med railway are one step in this broad Chinese strategic plan.

The scientific ties and academic cooperation between China and Israel culminated when Tel Aviv University and the prestigious Tsinghua University in Beijing signed a strategic cooperation agreement in May 2014 in innovative research for the mutual benefit of both institutions and the two countries. The two universities have decided to invest $300 million to establish a joint center, which will serve as an international hub for scientific and technological innovation. The center will be named Shin, which means "new" in Chinese, and will initially focus on scientific fields in accelerated development, both in Israel and in China, such as the field of nanotechnology.

The agreement was preceded by a donation of $130 million by the billionaire Li Ka-shing to the Technion for the establishment of a branch in China. He donated to the Technion with the money that he got from the exit of the Israeli company Waze, which was sold to Google for $1.1 billion. Ka-shing invested in Waze through the Horizon Fund in his ownership. "Today there are more than one thousand Israeli companies operating in China," Shimon Peres said at the launching ceremony, and he added that both countries have a lot to share and learn from each other.

Some of China's important ties with Israel are in the field of environmental industry. Israel, as a global leader Water and Cleantech present many innovative technologies that can help the Chinese deal with pollution problems they suffer. Uri Starkman, president of Veolia Israel, says that in light of Israel's success in recycling sewage with a utilization of almost 90 percent, the Chinese mayors at the meeting he attended began to calculate the critical significance of whether Beijing or Shanghai or even Guilin will recycle the same percentage of their sewage.

At the micro level of companies, the experience in the Chinese market has not always been successful. It is easier for Israelis to work with the familiar American or European business world. However, the strength and growth of the Chinese market cannot help but tempt Israeli companies from trying again and again.

At the macro level of interstate relations, one must take into account the influence of global forces' values. The political and economic system developing between the two countries is far from being exhausted, but it also has reservations. Israel has no more important friend than the United States. The alignment of forces between China and the United States influences and will continue to affect the relations between Israel and China, especially in view of China's ties with Iran and its support for the Palestinians. Israel, for its part, maintains close relations with Taiwan—all of which may delay the development of this relationship further.

When an Israeli company sends its product to Europe, it minimizes the fact that it was produced in Israel. More than seventy-five years have passed since the Jews were massacred in the death camps, and for some Europeans, this anti-Semitic demon is coming back—as if it is OK to hate Jews again throughout Europe. Therefore, it is better to sell Israeli products in Europe without "incriminating" signs, some Israeli exporters claim. For the Chinese, this is the opposite; they specifically want to mark Israeli products with a Star of David. "It will sell better this way," they noted to a senior official at Ahava, which distributes cosmetics made out of natural minerals from the Dead Sea. In the eyes of the Chinese, Jews are considered wise and successful, and for some, the Star of David is a symbol of quality.

Ben Bernanke told me (N.K.) more about the Chinese perception of Israel when he was governor of the US Central Bank. At a meeting with the Chinese minister of commerce, the minister said, "And as far as Israel is concerned, I wanted to tell you that although we cannot always support you politically, we, more than any other country, appreciate your abilities in terms of economics, science, and technology." The Chinese minister, intentionally or unintentionally, did not make the distinction between the Jewish governor of the American bank, and Israel. By his choice of words he expressed his deep appreciation of Israel.

THE INDIAN CONNECTION

A country of great importance, which is expected to get even stronger in the coming decades, is India. An overwhelming majority of Indians express great sympathy for Israel and regard it as a country with something to learn from.

The relations between India and Israel began in the years following the collapse of the USSR after a long period of coolness between the two countries that began the day they were established. Today, relations between them are flourishing and include extensive military and intelligence cooperation and ever-increasing trade.

India has apparently become the largest export destination of Israeli military equipment due to its anxiety about the Muslim minority within it as well as the constant threat of its longstanding enemy, Pakistan and, more recently, its concern regarding China.

In the last few years, India has probably become the leading export destination of Israeli military equipment. Israel has also trained soldiers from India, especially in counterterrorism activity. There is also fruitful nonmilitary cooperation between Israel and India, especially in the fields of agriculture and high tech, and a trend is being pushed from above by both ex-Prime Minister Ehud Olmert and Prime Minister Netanyahu to further strengthen these ties. More about the Israel-India connection will be described later in this book regarding the Indian mission for "more crops for drops" and the Israeli irrigation systems.

ISRAEL IN THE EYES OF THE EUROPEAN AMUSEMENT PARK

It was a dinner at our house (N.K.) where the Austrian ambassador Wolfgang Paul and his psychiatrist wife were invited. The ghosts of the memory of the Holocaust and the responsibility of the Austrians were hovering like black ravens over the white tablecloth. Riddle glasses—the Austrian manufacturer of the finest wine glasses—were filled with gourmet Israeli wine. The subject of the conversation was the attempts at European intervention in the Middle East peace process. "It's clear to me why the Israelis do not trust the Europeans; it would be amazing if it was different," said the psychiatrist.

"My parents were born here, my one grandmother was born here, the rest of my grandparents came to Israel as teenagers. I have no personal reason not to trust the Europeans," said foolish me. The conversation flowed here and there until we came to deal with issues of security and peace (or in their proper name: terrorism and war). "I must share with you my fantasy to cut Israel off the Middle East and drag it to another place, to connect it to another neighborhood," I said.

It took the psychiatrist only one moment to ask, "And where will you connect Israel?"

There was silence. I remember my thoughts, searching for the best place to put an anchor in. I considered here and there, but one thing was clear to me; the clever psychiatric was right. "Not to Europe; they cannot be trusted. We have been examined and burned with fire and blood."

The Israelis would not entrust the fate of Israel to the Europeans. Europeans do not know how to digest and understand the Israelis—kind of a distorted figure in the hall of crooked mirrors in the amusement park. Sometimes the Israelis are too thin, like *muselmanns*, and sometimes too fat due to the money they collect in their pockets. Sometimes they look tall and strong and heroic, like IDF soldiers "who should be prosecuted," and sometimes low and without color.

But despite all of the above, the European Union is Israel's leading trade partner. EU trade with Israel has been stable over the years, and it appears that the EU countries' confrontation with the absorption of millions of Muslims will probably open up new and hungry markets to Israeli homeland defense, cyber, and intelligence capabilities.

It is also possible that the Islamist struggle against Western Europe will improve Israel-Europe political and commercial relations. When Europeans change their naive desire to see the Israeli-Palestinian problem as the centerpiece of everything, and if the situation is solved, peace will endure in the West Islamic conflict.

———

Germany is Israel's largest trading partner among European countries. Israel is in second place in German trade cooperation and trade in the Middle East.

The two countries have cooperation in scientific and industrial research. Financing of industrial cooperation projects between Germany and Israel is an important pillar of trade relations between them. It is based on an intergovernmental agreement signed in January 2010 between the German Federal Ministry of Education and Research and the Office of the Chief Scientist of the Israeli Ministry of Economy. The ministries agreed to finance industrial R & D projects in selected fields. These projects focus mainly on biotechnology, water and environment technologies, security, and safety.

In addition, at the beginning of 2011, the Israeli Ministry of Economy and the German Federal Ministry of Economics and Technology launched a cooperation program that enables Israeli and German companies to jointly develop and support innovative products and services and create significant business ties. Since the launch of the program, dozens of joint projects have been funded and are considered to be particularly fruitful.

The two governments are also working on a program to encourage industrial R & D between Israel and international corporations, focusing on the periphery and traditional industries. It seems that these examples are sufficient to show that extensive economic cooperation has existed for a long time between the two economies and the companies operating in their framework. In terms of its trade with Israel, Germany is the third-largest partner after the United States and China.

———

Over the years, Great Britain and Israel have enjoyed good and extensive trade relations, which are attributed to the British heritage from the British Mandate period and especially to the English language, which is also well known to most Israelis.

The economic activity is reflected in the investments of British companies in Israel and the permanent presence of about 250 Israeli companies in the United Kingdom. There were also large numbers of acquisitions, mergers, and issues by Israeli companies in the United Kingdom. The United Kingdom and Israel have extensive commercial ties and cooperation in the field of science and technology. This is a result of the assessment by British private and public bodies of Israel's leadership in matters related to technological innovation, most of which are based on generic pharmaceuticals, but also rubber and plastic products, aircraft, and metals.

The political gaps do not affect relations between the two economies. For example, despite the sharp criticism of Israel at the height of Operation Protective Edge, the volume of trade between Britain and Israel rose by 28 percent.

Britain's military-industrial relations with Israel are anchored in a strategic alliance that has strengthened trade relations between the two countries. These are intensified by much interest shown by the British government in weapons that have been tried on the battlefield by Israeli companies. A lucrative field in this context is drones; the UK Ministry of Defence is working with Elbit Systems on a billion-pound program called Watchkeeper to develop the future *Hermes* aircraft, developed by Elbit.

———

To our detriment, we see that Europe, as a whole, is in a difficult situation. It seems to be in the process of demographic suicide due to the accelerated aging of its original population, and it is forced to choose between being a dying continent with the absence of manpower or accepting Muslim immigration at the expense of far-reaching concessions on Western European culture.

"Europe is in the process of polarization," says Prof. Dan Schueftan. "The left has allowed the massive entry of a Muslim population, and many Europeans are becoming the result of this extreme right wing and fascist." Where Europe is going is unknown at this stage.

A WORLD AID RESOURCE

It was 1999 in Turkey at three in the morning, and the ground shook. Over seventeen thousand were dead and tens of thousands wounded. Hundreds were trapped under collapsed buildings. Six hundred thousand people were without shelter. The smell of death was everywhere. People with hollow eyes looked at what had once been their homes. Next to the pile of rubble were people who were trying to rescue a mother, father, baby, or little boy. One found a doll. Another found an old blanket. As in other cases, the IDF sent a rescue force to evacuate buildings and set up a field hospital. The IDF rescue force saved eighteen trapped in a tremendous battle against time.

But the big story began long after everyone left Turkey. In September, the harsh winter was approaching. Hundreds of homeless people would die of cold that winter. The Israeli plan was to establish, until the winter, a village for the refugees. It was the most complex project ever done by the IDF, but within two months, 312 housing units were built along with three playgrounds, a school, a clinic, a police station, and shops.

The division of labor was for the Israelis to build, in Israel, the containers for living in and to transport them to Turkey. They would be responsible for moving and placing them on the ground. The Turks were responsible for the infrastructure: earthworks, electricity, and roads. The crews worked day and night. The harsh winter of that year struck fiercely, but extreme snow and cold did not harm the villagers.

Turkey's prime minister, Bülent Ecevit, declared, "We, the citizens of Turkey, will forever remember with sympathy the assistance and the hand of the people of Israel, and we would like to thank the prime minister, the Israeli government, and our Jewish brothers who live in the world."

———

Dozens of rescue and assistance activities by the Israeli government, the IDF, nongovernmental organizations (NGOs), and individual Israeli citizens have taken place in many areas throughout the world: a flood in Cambodia; earthquakes in Mexico and Armenia; victims of fighting in Bosnia; medical aid to Rwandan refugees; search and rescue in the US Embassy in Kenya; flood victims in Central America; Kosovar refugees; emergency aid in Ethiopia; earthquakes in El Salvador, India, and Peru; a flood in Sri Lanka; Hurricane Katrina; earthquake in Indonesia and flood in Romania; fire in Macedonia; storms in Mexico and the Dominican Republic; the earthquakes in Haiti and Japan; the tsunami in Thailand; the typhoon in the Philippines; and the earthquake in Nepal. This is only a partial list of the disasters in which Israel has contributed to the rescue operations, given medical help, and assisted with evacuation and search and assistance missions.

The earthquake in Haiti, measuring seven on the Richter Scale, lasted sixty seconds, leaving over eighty thousand dead and about 250,000 injured. More than a million were left homeless. Many countries, commercial companies, and private individuals have contributed money and sent rescue aid missions to those trapped under rubble, which also treated the wounded, brought humanitarian supplies into the areas, and fixed infrastructure. Israel also dispatched an emergency search-and-rescue team of 220 people and set up a field hospital capable of treating five hundred casualties a day (it actually treated about twelve hundred casualties a day).

"There's a mess here," said the report on MSNBC. "The Israelis are the exceptional. We watched their 747 plane landing at the airport, and they brought everything they needed to build a hospital of the highest standard, just as you would expect the Israelis to do. They arrived efficiently, thoroughly, and well-managed, and immediately started work."

The interviewer from the studio asked: "You are saying that the American delegation is organized less well than the Israeli one?"

The field reporter replied, "The Israelis simply arrived much more prepared than the other delegations, and within hours they set up operating rooms."

In a CNN story that was broadcast to more than ninety-three million viewers in the United States, the same reporter went to one of the American generals on the ground and asked him how a small country like Israel could have done what no other delegation in Haiti did.

The IDF delegation to Japan after the earthquake and tsunami was the first to receive permission to operate in the disaster area. Japanese law does not allow doctors who do not have government certification in Japan to operate in its territory, and emergency legislation was passed in order to allow the Israeli delegation to establish the clinic. The Medical Corps team consisted of specialists in the fields of surgery, orthopedics, gynecology, radiology, and more. The medical team was joined by rescue experts, IT and logistics personnel, and experts from the Atomic Energy Commission. It was a small, efficient, and smart delegation.

Israel had the largest rescue delegation to the earthquake in Nepal in April 2015 of all the countries participating in the aid operation. The purpose of the activity was to assist two thousand Israelis who were in Nepal at the time and to provide as much assistance as possible to the local population. Four planes, helicopters, jeeps, two hundred medical personnel, and ninety-five tons of medical equipment were sent, and a field hospital was set up. Other countries had citizens in Nepal at the time. For example, there were four thousand Chinese, seven thousand Americans, fourteen hundred French, one thousand Indians, and so on. Scandinavian travelers were amazed. "Our country would never send us such a bailout," they said.

The responsibility of the Israeli government to rescue its citizens was exceptional, but particularly touching is the participation of medical clowns in the delegation who tried to put a smile on the faces of the small survivors. Their goal was to relieve trauma and reduce pain and anxiety. They talked to the Nepali children in the clown language and sometimes had the small success of making someone smile. "There is no laughter here," said one of them. "We make do with a smile."

Israel's humanitarian activities are also carried out for Jews and other populations in distress and help them immigrate to Israel. The year was 1982. It was night, and the sea was infested with sharks off the coast of Sudan. The naval vessel disguised as a cargo ship anchored in front of an improvised resort village organized by the Mossad to confuse the Sudanese authorities. The goal: to gather a group of Jewish refugees from Ethiopia from the coast after a long journey of suffering; some of them did not survive.

Navy commando boats descended from the ship, landing on the shore, and taking refugees into the boats. Shuki Koriski was on board the ship as a young intelligence officer on behalf of the Israeli Air Force. "When the commando boats loaded with the refugees, used by the naval commandos, arrived at the ship and the passengers began to climb, I saw very young Ethiopian women there," Koriski said. "Some of them looked like small girls; they carried small babies, and one looked at me and asked 'Jerusalem?' I knew from the briefing that this was the code word they were familiar with. Immediately I replied 'Jerusalem! Jerusalem!' She handed me the baby that she was holding. I wrapped it up, reached out for her hand, and helped her down into the hold."

Thus the rescue of forty thousand Yemenite Jews in 1949 in Operation Magic Carpet, in which 280 flights were carried out. About seven thousand Ethiopian Jews were saved in 1984 in Operation Moses and about fourteen thousand Ethiopian Jews in Operation Solomon in 1991.

But rescue of Jews is not the only focus. In 1977, Israel saved four hundred refugees, "the shipmen," who fled from Vietnam. They were absorbed in the country in which they live to this day. In 1993, Israel was among the few countries that agreed to absorb Muslim war refugees from Yugoslavia. From 2002 to 2007, Israel absorbed war refugees from Sudan.

The UN recognized ZAKA[101] in 2003 as an NGO. ZAKA is a series of voluntary community emergency response teams in Israel. Yehuda Meshi Zahav, chairman of ZAKA, testified that for two years, ZAKA wanted to upgrade its international standing, and always, Israel's enemies, Iran and others, intervened and prevented it. In an all-embracing effort, the ambassadors of Israel and the Americans acted for this recognition. "We are in all the disasters in the world: earthquakes, floods, terror, airplane crashes—anywhere, at any time, we have twenty-two units operating around the world. During the earthquake in Japan, for example, a delegation of Iranians joined us; we worked with them, we were photographed with them. There is no difference between the tears of a Palestinian, an Israeli or a Japanese," he concluded.

ZAKA has five units of minority members in the south of Israel, the commander of these units is sheikh Aqel Al-Atrash, whose children served in the security forces. At the ceremony commemorating the eighth anniversary of the Twin Towers, he was together with Meshi Zahav, who was in his ultra-Orthodox clothes, and the sheikh was in his traditional clothes. Thus, the sheikh participated in the Selichot[102] in the Great Synagogue.

Save a Child's Heart is an international organization based in Israel. Over the past eighteen years, Israel has treated more than twenty-eight hundred children suffering from heart disease; they were from thirty countries where local treatment was inadequate and included children from the Gaza Strip and even children of senior terrorist organizations operating against Israel. Since the organization's establishment in 1996, six thousand children have been examined by doctors on its behalf.

About ten years ago, a girl named Katya, who was then four years old, was brought from Moldova for treatment in Israel. Katya suffered from very serious heart defects and was close to death. After five months and four highly complicated operations and dedicated teamwork, Katya was ready to go home. A few days before she left, she drew a picture of a hand holding a little girl with a heart. When she was asked to explain her painting, she told the following story: "I had a dream, there were many colors above my bed, and suddenly a very big hand arrived in the middle of the night." This painting of Katya is the logo of the association.

There are many more anonymous Israelis who fly to every disaster-stricken place in the world to offer help. We cannot count them all. For example, Shachar Zahavi is a member of Moshav Hadar Am and the initiator and chairman of IsraAID, Gal Lusky, of Kibbutz Hukuk, founded Israeli Flying Aid, an organization that operates only in countries with no diplomatic ties with Israel. This is for the benefit of people in situations of territorial or disaster conflict or countries that are hostile to minorities and prevent the entry of international aid that saves lives. In most cases, these are areas where no one can enter, and they include areas of war in which fundamentalist Muslims are present.

Despite the great heroism of emergency assistance, an equally important value is constant assistance to the ongoing promotion of developing countries. In its early years, MASHAV (International Cooperation Center) was established in Israel to assist the efforts of developing countries to eradicate poverty and hunger and ensure food and education for all, health, and reduced infant mortality.

"The activity is based on the transfer of technological knowledge and its assimilation through training for professionals from the developing world, who will help them solve existential problems in their countries," said Gil Haskel, deputy director general of the Foreign Ministry. Israel helps in areas where it has proven capabilities and reputation: agriculture and water security—which accounts for about half of all training, food, green growth, health, education, community and rural development, empowerment of women, entrepreneurship, and coping with climate change. All of these issues are on the global agenda as part of the effort to eradicate poverty and hunger in the world.

MASHAV currently operates in 130 countries, from China and India to the tiny islands in the Pacific Ocean. Since its establishment, more than 280,000 people have participated in its professional training activities in Israel and abroad. Over the years, thousands of these graduates have reached key positions in their respective countries, including presidents such as Honduran president Juan Orlando Hernandez and five Guatemalan cabinet ministers, as well as members of parliament in many countries.

Israel also helps establish centers of excellence throughout the third world. Such a center of excellence can focus, for instance, on growing mangoes: from planting the nursery through all the cultivation processes to the shelf. The Israeli experts expose Israeli technologies to the locals, and in this way, Israeli export companies benefit from this exposure in places where the Israeli private sector would have had difficulty or had to invest considerable financial resources in order to get to them.

BUSINESS ON A MISSION

"When David Ben-Gurion founded the State of Israel, he knew very well that one of the most significant challenges facing the young state is to turn the arid deserts into green fields," says Saar Bracha, CEO of the Tahal Group. "From planning the water projects in the north and center, the drilling and the unique solutions to the Negev and the Arava, the master plans for the water and energy sector, and the desalination plants—the story of the State of Israel is Tahal's story, and vice versa."

Tahal, which was established as a government company and was privatized in 1995, is now owned by the Kardan NV Holding Company, which is listed on the Tel Aviv Stock Exchange and on the Euronext Stock Exchange in Amsterdam.

Since 2012, under the management of Bracha, Tahal has undergone strategic and structural change and operates in Israel in all areas of engineering, infrastructure, and project management. In 2016, it had its second consecutive year in which it was ranked first among the engineering companies and planning offices in Israel. In its international operations, Tahal focuses on four core areas: water and wastewater, agricultural development, natural gas, and the environment, and it is one of the largest one hundred engineering planning companies in the world in these fields.

"More than a third of the world's population suffers from water shortages or low-quality water," says Naama Zeldis, CFO of the Tahal Group.

"The UN forecast is that in 2025, this distress will increase twice as much. Nearly one billion people suffer from hunger and malnutrition, which account for 45 percent of the deaths of children up to age five in the world. These are three million children who literally die of starvation. Water and food security are the main areas in which the Tahal Group operates, to which it brings the best of Israeli technologies and daring, creativity and knowledge," adds Bracha.

Tahal completed the construction of the Kimina project in Angola in 2016 and entered into a seven-year, $370 million operation phase. The project, located about seventy kilometers east of the Luanda capital, is the first agricultural settlement in the country, in effect a replica of the Israeli cooperative village model, which was built from scratch on an area of some 12,500 acres. "The project includes three hundred residential and private farms, measuring 2.5 acres each, thousands of acres of field crops, a logistics and agricultural center with sorting and packaging facilities, poultry farms that will supply more than twenty-four million eggs a year, and of course all the accompanying infrastructure, starting with roads, transmission, and treatment of water, sewage, and electricity infrastructure. The expected crops in the project will reach about sixty thousand tons of agricultural produce a year and are planned to be sold in the local market," Bracha notes. "We are helping Angola dramatically reduce dependence on imports."

In Yakutsk, Russia, the coldest city in the world, Tahal is establishing a project to treat and supply drinking water to the residents. "Our teams operate in a freezing cold that reaches fifty degrees below zero," says Bracha. "Tahal has a unique expertise and rich experience that enables it to successfully cope with challenges and extreme conditions anywhere on Earth." Between the hydrology projects in the deserts of Dallol in Ethiopia and the water-treatment project in Yakutsk is a gap of more than eighty-five hundred kilometers and about one hundred degrees Celsius. "In both cases, the same engineers and professionals based in Or Yehuda,

Israel, find creative solutions that greatly improve the quality of life of hundreds of thousands of people all over the world."

In Serbia, Tahal is setting up a large-scale agricultural project on rocky terrain. The top of Israeli technology is integrated into the project: semiautonomous agricultural tools that are used by GPS; irrigation systems, fertilizers, and drips that are managed remotely in a computerized interface; and a clear and calculated agricultural plan, including a business plan for full utilization of the produce, both in the local market and in the orderly export of the country. "I feel fortunate to lead a leading company in its field," says Bracha. "A company which takes advantage of the unique expertise and experience it has accumulated in Israel to bring good to the world—in the form of clean drinking water and ending starvation in developing countries. We are exporting the essence of the essence of what is the State of Israel, and that is my pride."

———

Israel is considered an empire in the field of seed cultivation, thanks to academic research institutions such as the Faculty of Agriculture in Rehovot, the Volcani Center, and a number of veteran Israeli companies. Hazera is a global pioneer in the cultivation, production, and marketing of hybrid seeds of vegetables and field crops. A significant portion of its annual turnover is invested in R & D, and in this way, Hazera has succeeded in providing unique and innovative solutions while developing vegetables with improved taste and appearance that are healthier and have longer shelf-lives; at the same time, it meets the growers' demand for varieties that yield more crops, are resistant to diseases, and are more environmentally friendly. These hybrid seeds have established their position as a leading global brand and are constantly innovating to create innovative and high-quality-yielding varieties by applying advanced technologies in the field of plant genetics with traditional cultivation methods.

Hazera won international recognition in the 1990s with the development of a special tomato, Daniela, whose shelf-life was two to three weeks compared to three to five days for ordinary brands of tomato shelf-life, that were common then. One seed of the Daniela tomato produced a ton of tomatoes and came first in a comparative study conducted at Beijing University, where tomato varieties from leading seed companies around the world participated. Later, Hazera developed special and delicious melons and small, seedless watermelons.

Rami Dar, CEO of the company, tells of a huge investment of NIS 85 million that the company has made in order to build a new R & D center. The R & D center includes the most advanced laboratories in the world to examine genetic markers through which to know the characteristics of the vegetable, examining the properties on a full-size plant. For this purpose, the company employs geneticists and bioinformatics specialists who are experts in the task of optimizing the ability of examination of genetic databases, of monstrous proportions. Hazera also employs phytopathologists, who are experts in the field of plant diseases, as well as experts whose role is to examine the resistance of vegetables to insects and more.

ISRAELI GLOBAL COMPANIES

Global companies operate in the world as if it were one playground. They manufacture, market, and manage various sites around the world according to their economic considerations. They are often called "companies without a homeland." Hence, the title of this section is an oxymoron because if they are global companies, how will they be Israeli? If they are Israeli companies, how will they be global? But in fact, it is almost impossible to find purely global companies, and we can associate almost any company, despite its global structure, with any country.

It is not easy to maintain the national identity of a company in the wake of the dwindling Israeli holdings compared to global investments, and management is required to provide answers to shareholders who rightly oversee the welfare of the company and its stakeholders.

Israel's biggest challenge is to help the global Israeli companies keep their head offices, the beating hearts of the corporations, in Israel. The advantages of this are many, including the strengthening of Israeli sentiment and its long-term retention, the employment of managers and service providers such as lawyers and accountants, the empowerment of the Israeli capital market, and the development of real estate—while the market and investors are far from simple.

Teva is the largest global Israeli company. In 1955, Teva began to be listed as the first industrial company on the Tel Aviv Stock Exchange in a process of acquisitions and mergers that began in 1968 with a merger of three companies into Teva Pharmaceutical Industries; Eli Hurvitz was appointed CEO.

A long series of acquisitions of companies in Europe and the United States led Teva to become the world's largest generic pharmaceutical company, and the company entered into the development of original drugs and brought Copaxone, a treatment for multiple sclerosis, and Azilect, a treatment for Parkinson's disease.

In 1982, Teva was listed for trading in the United States, first on NASDAQ and then on the New York Stock Exchange, and Teva's sales in 2017 exceeded $20 billion; only a few percent of which were in Israel. Teva's worldwide workforce reached more than fifty thousand. Teva has succeeded in establishing its leadership position in the field and certainly as Israel's largest and leading global company. In spite of Teva's crisis in 2017[103], it is likely to continue to succeed and reestablish itself as a leading Israeli-global company.

Netafim resembles Teva, as it sees its future as a global Israeli company since its foudation. Netafim, which was created because of the water shortage in Israel, has become a world leader in drip-irrigation technology, which leads to higher crop yields, maximizing water savings, and reducing soil erosion. The company presents annual growth of more than 15 percent on average and is expected to continue to grow at a similar rate in the coming years. Netafim is a global company with four thousand employees, seventeen manufacturing plants in eleven countries, and over twenty-seven subsidiaries and representative offices in more than one hundred and ten countries. India, for example, is subsidizing the purchase of its drip irrigation instead of subsidizing the water itself with the Israeli businesses Netafim and NaanDan, the big drip companies there.

A company is considered global when it trades in at least one capital market that is not its home market and when more than 56 percent of its sales derive from countries other than its home market. As of the end of 2017, ninety-three Israeli companies are traded on NASDAQ; thus, Israel is the third country in the number of companies listed on the NASDAQ after the United States and China, with twenty-three global companies with an annual turnover of over $500 million each; these have more than 56 percent sales abroad. It seems that even if we leave the analysis of the number of global companies, there is no argument that the Israeli market is worldwide in nature.

Mobileye, which develops, manufactures, and markets advanced assistance systems for drivers and will do the same in the future in autonomous cars, issued on the NYSE at a value of $5.8 billion in 2014 and is considered the largest Israeli issue of all time. Mobileye was sold in March 2017 to Intel for $15.3 billion, which is considered the largest Israeli exit ever.

Mobileye began with a question directed at Prof. Shashua, a lecturer and researcher at the Hebrew University of Jerusalem, during one of his lectures in Japan. He was asked whether an artificial vision system can identify cars and pedestrians. Shashua not only answered positively but developed a product and established Mobileye, whose development center is located in Jerusalem. The device is currently installed in many vehicles in the world and is the most advanced of its kind for the prevention of road accidents. The success of Mobileye has led to the development of dozens of Israeli technology companies in the field of autonomous vehicles and machine learning.

Orbotech, one of the world's leading companies in the development, manufacture, and marketing of testing systems for the electronics industry, is more similar to the growth of a startup than an established company that has been around for a long time. It has a market cap of more than $2.5 billion and twenty-five hundred workers, of whom seventeen hundred are around the world, including about four hundred in China. What is there in this Israeli company? What can we learn?

Orbotech is taking full benefit of the country's technological advantage. The main knowledge and technological strength of Orbotech is the integration of diverse fields of knowledge and technologies into a range of market-leading products. The company employs hundreds of engineers, scientists, and technical personnel from a wide range of specialties, including software, algorithms, hardware, mechanics, optics, chemistry, and more.

"The leading companies in the world of electronics, both in consumer and industrial products, know Orbotech and its importance in providing innovative and unique manufacturing solutions that will be a critical component in the production of their future products," says Asher Levy, CEO of Orbotech. "It would be reasonable to say that the smartphone industry wouldn't have been able to take such an incredible technological leap without the direct imaging product we developed, as well as the products we developed for the flat-panel displays."

In each of the markets in which the company operates, there is competition, but over the years, Orbotech has built a leading position through constant investment in research and development and building a global infrastructure and a significant array of customer service.

The technology and electronics markets are characterized by volatility, which has affected many companies over the years. "We have contingency plans to be prepared for any event in the global markets," says Levy. But Orbotech does not stop there, and it strives to balance the volatility by increasing the range of products it offers in the markets in which it operates. Orbotech has thousands of installed machines and service agreements. It aims to reach 30 percent of its revenues through customer-service, as it is an excellent source of revenue in itself. Customer-service also stabilizes the volatility in the global equipment market. "We view our installation base as an asset, rather than as a commitment. This is an important basis for revenue generation, upgrades, and understanding of the market and customers," says Levy.

The contemporary dream of the generation of experienced Israeli technological entrepreneurs who have already "done so" is to establish a large company. Israeli entrepreneurs seem to have grown up. They learned to manage the risks and prospects of rejecting the fast money offered to them for long-term development. They believe in their managerial capabilities to expand their companies and manage them over time. This is not just another technological challenge. The new Israeli entrepreneurs also have challenges in management, joining Gil Shwed from Check Point, Eli Hurvitz from Teva, and others.

New Israeli companies have been created due to technological and business opportunities. The digital world has opened up a new country that is almost indifferent to the biggest Israeli obstacle: the geographical distance from the market. The Internet is a new platform for these Israeli companies to develop new products designed to meet new needs. Digital marketing now enables Israelis to reach the global consumer market with their fingertips while sitting on their chairs in Israel. They are all close and intimate with one another.

The regulation of Internet chaos in general and advertising in particular, the cyber threat and the need to protect against cyberattacks, hardware and software required in the future direction of 3-D printing, visualization and image decoding, and the Internet of things are all new hunting fields. So, too, the life sciences are a blue ocean, abundant in life. The Israelis, just like the explorers, are dwelling on the new horizons that are opening. New markets are being born.

An exceptional example of creating a market is Yaron Galai's Outbrain. Galai's previous company, Quigo, was sold for $63 million. On the day of its sale, Galai began setting up the new company. The motivation, he says, is to prove that the first success was not due to luck but rather to something inside. It is strange to him that people ask serial entrepreneurs why they are setting up another venture after the first one succeeds. A singer will not be asked why he is releasing his second album after the first one managed so well.

Outbrain, with five hundred employees in Israel, deals with content recommendations of the kind we have become accustomed to on many leading sites such as CNN, BBC, the New Yorker, Vogue, and WIRED. While reading articles on their website, you will see this sentence displayed: "If you read this article, you can also be interested in these articles"—with a reference to additional articles—some of these options contain content articles and some are for advertising. The content-based advertising market doubles in size each year. Galai invented the market and positioned Israel as a power on the subject. The main competitor, Taboola, is also Israeli.

Kenshoo, which has developed a prediction system designed to help optimize the allocation of advertising budgets, is also active in Internet advertising. It looks at the traffic on the web, which search keywords were the most commonly used in search engines, and what are the hottest topics on social networks. All this is done in real time in the present. Company advertising managers can, based on this, maximize campaign results and reduce costs. Kenshoo has 450 employees in Tel Aviv and Silicon Valley and competes with Marin, Adobe, and DoubleClick.

Wix also invented the market in which it operates, or rather it reinvented an existing market. The web-building industry was heavy, expensive, and cumbersome and intended only for experts who know how to design and write code. Wix has shortened processes. In 2006, Avishai and Nadav Abrahami sat with Giora Kaplan, known as Gig, and worked on a certain startup for which a website was required. Having learned the difficulty of setting up sites, they decided that there was a huge global market for this and looked for a solution. Two years later, Wix was launched. Five years later, after it had nearly fifty million users worldwide, it was listed on the NASDAQ. Wix is the world leader in its own market, with over one hundred million users in 190 countries, and the number is growing rapidly. Wix has over one thousand employees who are sitting in Israel, near the Tel Aviv port.

Another step taken by some of the companies is the construction of a growth strategy based on acquisitions, which indicates maturity and the desire to build a large and leading company in the market. For example, Imperva acquired three companies and merged their operations; Stratasys has also carried out a series of acquisitions designed to expand the markets in which it operates. NICE has also entered the market, thanks to its acquisitions in the cloud. In doing so, Israeli companies deepen their multinational quality.

Sometimes the structure of the market in which the company operates requires it to choose a certain path. If the company operates in markets where there are giants, selling is often the only chance for a small Israeli company to survive. Even when a company operates in markets where the source company is important, it is preferable for it to be sold to a local company or to become a public company controlled by the public. In markets where the competitive advantage is contingent on extensive investments, it is preferable for the company to be sold.

Many Israeli economists and businesspeople criticize the phenomenon of startups that are mainly sold while they are small companies rather than being developed into large companies. Eyal Waldman, founder and CEO of Mellanox, the Israeli high-tech giant, disagrees. "Israelis make money from sales, and they will make more money and build new startups all the time. It's hard to set up a company like Mellanox, so people sell companies at much earlier stages. But there will also be other large high-tech companies. People will do it, that's for sure."

These include Chromatis Networks, which was sold in 2000 to Lucent for $4.8 billion; Mercury Inc., which was sold to HP in 2006 for $4.5 billion; M-Systems, which was sold in 2006 to SanDisk for $1.6 billion; and NDS, which was sold to Cisco for $5 billion in 2012.

The *Exits Report* of IVC Research and the law firm of Meitar Liquornik Geva Leshem Tal states that in 2014, 104 high-tech exits were executed for $9 billion—the third-largest volume of transactions in the last decade. An average exit deal surged to $87 million, up $62 million from the previous ten-year average.

———

In the following case, the negotiations were conducted entirely in Silicon Valley. The Israeli entrepreneurs were not involved, leaving the venture capital funds in the company to take over the reins, the Blue run fund comprised of former entrepreneurs with extensive experience in developing, designing, and marketing mobile products. At the last minute, after most of the details of the agreement with Facebook were approved and the price tag was $870 million (40 percent of the amount in Facebook shares), Google placed an offer of $966 million dollars in cash on the table and bought Waze.

A part of Israel's globalization is a result of what happens in world, where investors from many countries knock on its doors and seek the "next big thing." The first exit that excited and ignited the imagination and coined the term in the Israeli consciousness was that of ICQ in 1998. Mirabilis developed software that was the first to provide an instant-messaging service on the Internet. The pronunciation of the name of the software's name sounds like "I seek you." The company, which was founded only two years earlier, was acquired by America Online for the amount of $407 million, which, until then, was the highest amount ever sold by an Israeli high-tech company. A shareholder in ICQ, Yossi Vardi, who led the negotiations, has since been considered the guru of the Israeli Internet.

Jacob Kotlitzki was already involved in advanced technological fields long before everyone started calling them high tech. In 1973, together with his brother Moshe, he established Visonic, which focused on home and business electronic security and was a pioneer in its field.

"My father came from a poor family and had only three years of schooling," says Kotlitzki, a member of a family of Holocaust survivors from Poland. "As I grew older, I realized that I had actually grown up in a development lab, and when you grow up in a place where the father constantly builds and creates, you learn to do it yourself, without asking anyone else to do it for you." The company's products include controls, switchboards, signs, and detectors. When Visonic was sold in 2010 to Tyco International, the electronic security products company, at a company value of about

$100 million, it employed about five hundred employees, and its products were sold in more than seventy countries around the world.

The second-largest Israeli exit ever was by ISCAR, an industrial company, the world's second-largest manufacturer of advanced cutting-edge metal cutting tools. ISCAR was founded in 1952 by Stef Wertheimer and was sold in two stages for a cumulative sum of $6 billion to Warren Buffett's Berkshire Hathaway in what the latter described as his first acquisition outside the United States. ISCAR and its subsidiaries employ about ten thousand workers. The fact that its management is located in the Tefen Industrial Zone, "in front of Hezbollah," did not prevent Buffett from executing the deal while he emphasized that with the company's operations in the United States, India, China, Germany, France, Italy, and South Korea, "Israel has a disproportionate amount of brains."

In Israel, Microsoft's first R & D center was established outside of the United States. It was founded in 1991 in Haifa and to this day is considered one of Microsoft's three leading centers in the world, with more than a thousand employees, alongside large R & D centers in India and China. Microsoft also has smaller development centers in other parts of the world, but the status of the three major R & D centers makes these locations preferable for Microsoft to investment in their academia, industry, and community.

A simple question is why Microsoft maintains the R & D center in Israel. The explanation for the centers in India and China is clear: these countries are characterized by relatively cheap engineers' labor costs relative to the United States and very large markets for Microsoft products. But Israel? The cost of labor here is almost equal to costs in the United States, and the market is minimal.

Yoram Yaacovi, Microsoft's director of R & D in Israel, explains the reasons for this, especially because of the high quality of Israeli manpower. "There are two leading faculties in computer science, two of which are the Weizmann Institute and the Technion, which are on the list of the top twenty faculties in the world, and Tel Aviv and Hebrew universities are only slightly behind."

Satya Nadella, Microsoft's third CEO after Bill Gates and Steve Ballmer, testified that his visit to Israel left a strong impression on him and helped him form his way of thinking about Microsoft and embrace a culture of daring.

"We managed to develop very significant products for the company in the areas we defined and to double the number of our employees from five hundred to a thousand in three years," says Jacoby, adding, "In the past year, we bought four companies in Israel—and we will continue to do so. The vision—ambitious as only Israelis are able to create—includes two challenging elements: one—to make the business leadership of one of the areas in which the global company focuses—from Israel, and the second is to develop the company's next big thing. Because we think differently and more dare."

More than 315 leading international companies have chosen Israel as their target for establishing their R & D centers; these include Facebook, Microsoft, IBM, Intel, GE, Oracle, Google, Apple, HP, Cisco, Motorola, Philips, Dell, Applied Materials, EMC, Hewlett Packard, ChemChina, Siemens, Syngenta, KLA-Tencor, and more.

The key to Israeli success in high tech, according to Oded Cohen, director of IBM's research lab in Israel, is a conjunction of three critical factors: high-level academia, venture capital investments, and the number of global companies operating in Israel. "The secret is not in any of the three, but rather that all three are together in a small geographic area and have high mobility," says Cohen.

"The Israeli ability is the willingness to take risks," he explains, "because it is a bit dangerous to live here, and also because the military trains very young people to take responsibility for the country as well as the team they lead. Part of Israel's 'island of success' stems from the high waves around it, from the challenging environment in which Israelis live, from their personal and national experience of overcoming crises."

IBM's research lab was founded in Israel in 1972. The reasons for its establishment in Israel were similar to the circumstances in which Intel was established in Israel. One of the reasons was similar in particular—a senior Israeli who wanted to return home. IBM's management has allowed Joe Raviv, who worked at IBM's research center in the United States, to set up a small research center, which has grown over the years because of its successes and is still IBM's largest research center outside the United States, despite the power of other such centers in Zurich and Tokyo, which opened together with the ones in Israel, India, China, Australia, and other countries. Over the years, IBM has made about twelve significant acquisitions in Israel, and this process is also growing.

Israel has advantages in various areas of research. For example, in the medical field, its benefit stems from the fact that medicine teaching is of a high standard, from good doctors oriented toward research and with international exposure who have studied in good universities, and Israel has strength and success in medical devices. This encourages a company like Philips Medical to place a large R & D center. The structure of the medical market in Israel gives benefits to research, since some health insurers are also the operators of health services and manage some of the hospitals. A small number of technology companies maintain their Israeli identities after being acquired by international businesses.

In addition to this, HP Indigo, which develops, manufactures, and markets digital printing machines, has also managed to remain an Israeli company with Israeli DNA, an Israeli CEO, separate information systems, and so on. There is no doubt that this success stems first and foremost from impressive business achievements and also from the personality of CEO Alon Bar-Shany.

In the six years from 2001 to 2007, when HP bought Indigo Israel, it also bought Scitex Vision, Nur Macroprinters Ltd., and Mercury. All of these companies, except for Indigo, were merged into HP's purchasing system. Only Indigo kept its identity. From these data, it can be concluded that the identity of the acquirer and the size of the acquired company affect the future of the business and its ability to preserve its unique identity.

With over $1 billion in exports, Indigo is one of the top ten exporters in Israel. "In 2015, it employed twenty-seven hundred direct workers, 40 percent of whom were engaged in development, 40 percent in production, and 20 percent in management," says Alon Bar-Shany. The fact that the production and the directors are in Israel, in addition to the R & D, is unique to Indigo. Another unique factor is "the very high loyalty of the managers and employees to the organization," says Bar-Shany, adding that almost all members of the current Indigo board were there twenty years ago.

"The advantages of Israel are that there is a young population here who can and wants to work, and the Israeli human diversity impresses all the visitors," says Bar-Shany. "Our big challenge is how not to lose Israeli identity in a multinational society, while keeping the order and the focus of the multinational company. And you have to know how to go through crises, because we went through a difficult crisis in 1995, we now know we can; we have raised the ability to survive."

In contrast to other multinational companies, KLA Tencor was not founded by a senior Israeli from an American company who wanted to return to Israel, but the opposite. In 1986, Dan Vilensky sought a strategic investor for a unique machine for the semiconductor industry. Vilensky developed the product with a group of ex officio members of the Haifa branch of the American company Kulicke & Soffa. Kenneth Levy, founder of KLA, which develops, manufactures, and services equipment for testing the quality of processes for the semiconductor industry, was happy to lift the gauntlet. KLA subsequently merged with Tencor and became KLA Tencor Israel and Vilensky served as the Vice President and General Manager. Israel is now the center of development of KLA Tencor outside of the United States.

"We are building the capabilities of Intel, Samsung, Toshiba, and all the other chip manufacturers in the world to produce more advanced chips for over thirty years," says Dr. Ami Appelbaum, president of KLA Tencor Israel.

The advanced machine, manufactured in Israel, measures the accuracy of laying the layers of the chips on top of each other while creating a multilayer, integrated circuit. During the test, the machine, which measures a few nanometers, moves the silicon wafers at high speeds, which requires very advanced vibration damping. In the mid-1990s, "the Swiss product combined with the KLA Tencor Israel machine was not accurate enough," says Dr. Appelbaum. "So I found myself, an Israeli manager, challenging the Swiss on the issue of precision. In addition, the German bearings that were integrated into the machine were not quality enough, and again an Israeli manager proves the Germans on quality issues. It was a formative experience for someone who grew up on a kibbutz in the south to stand in front of the world's largest and most admired icons of accuracy and quality. Yes, we Israelis can demand that the Swiss and the Germans meet their own image requirements. This testifies to the long way that the Israeli high-tech industry has passed since the 'hat and the sandals' to the technological and engineering leadership of the highest international level, which is also difficult for industry giants in the world to meet its challenges. A blue-and-white (colors of the Israeli flag) industry that is now highly regarded and revered by world icons to learn from us."

KLA Tencor produces in Israel not only the most advanced machines in Israel, but other machines developed in the United States were transferred to Israeli production on a purely economic basis. The Israeli advantage is supported by the government's policy of capital investment in general and in the periphery in particular. This is in addition to the highly skilled manpower, high-level subcontractors, and competitive prices, as well as subcontractor management capabilities, all of which have led to lower production in Israel relative to the United States and performance at higher levels than in East Asia.

In Israel, 60 to 70 percent of the world's products that measure the production efficiency of the semiconductor industry are being developed and manufactured. KLA Tencor, Applied Materials, Nova, and Jordan-Valley are creating worldwide leadership based on science and technology, but the location of Israel has to be fought for all the time. "When KLA Tencor transferred the production of machines from the US to Israel, we improved gross margins by more than 10 percent," Appelbaum says.

"Today, no leading scientific/technological company in the world will develop new technologies and applications without an Israeli presence," says Appelbaum, adding that despite the geopolitical situation and the first and second Lebanon wars, "we did not shut down the plant for one day. This is the commitment of the management and no less of the employees. Everyone is committed. Everyone understands why." Therefore, Rick Wallace, CEO of KLA Tencor, can talk about manufacturing in the United States, Israel, and Singapore—a third everywhere—as a given situation and future target.

Thus, the Israeli economy, which is so affected by the high-tech industry, is connected to the global world through thick cables. Whether this is for financing, cooperation, flotation, or marketing, the world is the playground of Israeli companies, and at the same time, Israel is a place where foreign companies are happy to operate.

X

THE ENTREPRENEURIAL ADVANTAGE

"In Israel there is exceptionally high entrepreneurial activity," writes GEM,[104] which focuses on analysis of entrepreneurial activity in sixty-seven countries. "The uniqueness of the Israeli initiatives is that they are export-oriented and technologically oriented."

The *National Report on Entrepreneurship in Israel* states[105] that Israel is a country characterized by social and cultural norms that support and encourage entrepreneurship in all fields, and Israeli culture supports and encourages personal success achieved through the investment of personal efforts. It emphasizes and appreciates independence, autonomy, and personal initiative; encourages creativity and innovation; and emphasizes the individual's responsibility to manage his or her life more than the collective responsibility.

In Israel, there is a clear and recognized entrepreneurial culture that is supported by the success of entrepreneurs and by the media, which reveals the entrepreneurs' achievements, their new status, the wealth that has been achieved, and the social acknowledgment accompanies it. The appreciation of entrepreneurial culture in Israel was and remains very high throughout the years. This is a stable cultural phenomenon whose roots lie deep in the Jewish and Israeli DNA of rebellion against all that is accepted, which views every difficulty as a personal challenge and does not punish for mistakes and failures.

The GEM[106] ranks Israel third in the world in the amount of entrepreneurs in their first steps per capita. Israeli companies tend to experiment with new technologies and innovative ways of doing business, and Israeli consumers are responding to the challenge. The authors of the report also believe that veteran companies are willing to accept new and innovative entrepreneurial companies as their suppliers, based on the assessment of the capabilities of the young companies and on the creation of familiarity and trust between them.

The study indicates that there is also an openness among Israeli consumers to purchase new products and services from young, entrepreneurial companies. However, this is limited by the sophistication and experience of consumers and the desire to avoid failure in purchasing a product or service that promises and does not fulfill. This finding indicates a conscious consumer population that uses innovation while, at the same time, is sophisticated and critical.

The extraordinary power of entrepreneurship in Israel can also be deduced from the fact that Tel Aviv University ranked ninth[107] in the world in universities that encourage entrepreneurs. The ranking examines universities whose graduates are most active in setting up venture capital start-ups. The Technion reached sixteenth place, and the Hebrew University was ranked thirty-third. Tel Aviv is the only non-American university that succeeded in being in the top ten. Only in twentieth place is a non-American, non-Israeli university—Waterloo University in Canada. In the top fifty, there is no representation of a non-North American university except for the three Israeli universities mentioned.

Tel Aviv University also placed eighth in the ranking of universities whose graduates initiated companies that made significant exits. These totaled more than $5 billion during the reporting period.

"There is infinite creativity in Israel that transforms the world," says Isracard chairman Eyal Desheh. "Fortunately, I got to work at several Israeli companies that created completely new fields and industries and completely changed the industry in which they operate, such as Scitex,

Check Point, Teva, Mobileye, Stratasys, and others. I was there. I saw Israeli power at its best and learned a few things about Israelis' ability to make a difference. Courage is one of the basic characteristics of business success. Fall, get up and continue. Israelis have a lot of it."

In many cases, it is difficult to draw the line between the entrepreneurial advantage discussed in this chapter and the technological advantage discussed in the next. Many of the Israeli entrepreneurs are technologists, and many of the companies are startups, some of which grow into medium and large companies that change the market and industries in which they operate.

———

Eyal Waldman grew up in a middle-class Israeli family, served in the IDF as a combat officer, participated in the first Lebanon War, and then graduated and studied at the Technion in Haifa for a bachelor's degree in computer science and a master's degree in electrical engineering. Waldman was one of the founders of the Galileo high-tech company, one of the most prominent successes of Israeli high tech in the 1990s. During his work at Galileo, Waldman moved to California, where he set up another high-tech company, but after three years, he returned to Israel and succeeded on a large scale when he founded Mellanox, one of the largest and best-known high-tech companies.

As of 2017, Mellanox is traded on NASDAQ at a value of $3.2 billion, with Waldman having served as CEO and president since its inception. Mellanox, headquartered in Yokne'am Illit, is a technology company specializing in the development and manufacture of electronic components for communication systems designed for rapid transfer of information between servers and storage systems. The company is a leading supplier of InfiniBand communications chips, an architecture that significantly improves the performance, reliability, and use of computer servers. Mellanox has 2,550 employees 1,860 of them are in Israel. Thus, the company is one of Israel's largest high-tech employers.

Another well-known Israeli entrepreneur is Benny Landa. "He is a technological genius, but also, and perhaps mainly, an indefatigable entrepreneur," says attorney Tal Atsmon, a partner at Goldfarb-Seligman who has been accompanying Landa for many years. "Benny Landa is a second generation of Holocaust survivors. Like many Israelis, Landa has a vision, an ability, an idea, but his uniqueness lies in his success in establishing a worldwide technology company and his continued commitment to new ventures. He is, in my view, the extreme example how you can explain Israelis," Atsmon continues. "There is an Israeli drive to create something that will bring fruit, value, and money. The motivation is not money; it is the desire to do something and leave a mark in the world. To create value. A European at the age and financial condition of Benny Landa was long sitting in the summer house he built near a lake from which he could look at the clouds. Landa employs hundreds of people who follow his dream and his drive. That's the difference."

Landa's initiatives helped create an entire industry in Israel that became a global leader, not only in 2-D printing, but also in 3-D printing. Since the end of the 1990s, a magnificent industry has developed in this exciting field with enormous potential. If expectations indeed materialize, the 3-D printing revolution will transform serial production into production on demand from which all sectors of society can benefit, from the largest industrialists or small businesses to private individuals. Every person can hold the power to create almost anything—to create objects, toys, electronic devices, and, in the future, even drugs and biological products.

Guy Menchik knows this industry and was one of its founders. For many years, he has served as VP of R & D and innovation at the Israeli company Objet, which has become Stratasys and is traded on the NASDAQ. Currently, he manages the company's product division, whose management is located at Rehovot Science Park in Israel. Stratasys is considered the world's largest company in the field of 3-D printers.

In trying to explain how Israel became a leading force in this new 3-D industry, Menchik goes back to Benny Landa and his success to make Israel a global leader in 2-D printers. "This accumulated knowledge has led retirees from the 2-D industries to take this step forward. Knowledge of how to design machines, manufacture and maintain those machines, and also knew marketing, distribution, and logistics in these industries, all of this existed," says Menchik. "Also, knowledge arrived from retirees of the military industries. They had knowledge and experience in artillery, missiles, and control systems."

Menchik, who has a lot of experience working with Americans and Japanese, reinforces the advantageous insights of Israelis: "They always look for a smart solution, create a different thinking outside the box; even if there is an existing solution, they think of a new one who might be better. Israelis are daring, creative, and improvisers." He also has criticism: "When everything becomes orderly and methodical, the Israelis lose interest, it is on that stage where the Americans are much better. Mass production is not for Israelis; it's boring."

The worlds of 2-D printing also leapfrogged through Israeli companies such as Kornit Digital, which specializes in digital printing systems for industrial textile applications; Scodix, which specializes in digital printing on glass using eco-resistant ceramic ink; as well as the empire Landa's new company, Landa Labs, which deals with nanographic printing machines.

Another initiative in a completely different field is One-Hour-Translation, or OHT, which was launched in 2009 and, within a few years, became the world's largest online translation agency. The company, whose management is located in Ness Ziona Science Park in Israel, employs twenty thousand professional translators in more than one hundred countries, and they translate seventy-five languages and handle over a hundred thousand translation projects every month. It employs two hundred people in software development, sales, customer service, marketing, management, and operation in nine branches worldwide.

The global translation market is estimated at $40 billion a year, and OHT is a leading pioneer in transforming it from traditional translation agencies that operate offline into an online model over the Internet.

Ofer Shoshan, CEO of OHT and one of its founders, is a unique figure who was recruited to a unit that is considered one of the most prestigious in the IDF: Haman-Talpiot, whose graduates fit into prestigious positions in the IDF Intelligence Directorate. After his military service, Shoshan established a medical equipment startup, and with a friend, Dr. Meir Marmor, he invented a lifesaving cardiology device. He then founded two other successful high-tech companies and was one of the only individuals who was accepted to the MBA studies at INSEAD, France, on a personal and professional background and without a first degree. Only later did he come across the idea of an online translation agency.

"As someone who travels a lot around the world and interviewed a lot of people in many countries, especially in the developed countries, I can say that Israelis are better entrepreneurs than the rest," says Shoshan. "The American system works very well when there are large, orderly, and preplanned systems, but this is usually not the case in growing companies. Israeli employees can criticize the boss, challenge him, offer ideas, and get a positive response from the boss and a true reflection on their proposals, including the implementation of these proposals if they are better than his own."

———

In 1798, Thomas Malthus published his famous book, *An Essay on the Principle of Population*,[108] arguing that while the world population doubles periodically, food production is growing more slowly, resulting in a significant reduction in the amount of food available to each person. Malthus predicted that this is going to lead to catastrophe and extreme hunger that will ultimately cause a population reduction. In practice, this catastrophic forecast did not materialize because of technological progress.

To further delay the Malthus forecast, a worldwide consortium of eleven hundred scientists in the relevant fields was gathered. This consortium tried, for ten years, to decode the genomic sequence of wheat, and they had an investment of more than $50 million. The effort resulted in the decoding of only 20 percent of the genome and not at high accuracy.

Decoding the genome of the most important and popular food in the world has significant economic and social implications because it will allow the development of wheat varieties with better nutritional values, high resistance to extreme climatic conditions, increased yield, and resistant strains.

The international consortium had at least four years left to complete the full genome required to improve the yield of new wheat varieties. Then a small Israeli company, NRGene, took the burden on its shoulders and succeeded in just one month in decoding the genome, with a financial investment of only half a million dollars.

NRGene is a big-data solution providing company in the genomic world; it develops advanced computational tools and innovative algorithmic models to facilitate the discovery of optimal gene properties for seed companies, animal breeders, and the academic world. The founder and CEO of NRGene, Dr. Gil Ronen, says, "We are giving huge international companies a huge leap forward by indicating which seeds are worth planting, from which there is a chance that the next big thing in the field of vegetables."

Another such underdog story is of an Israeli entrepreneur of the younger generation, Yariv Bash, whose story is particularly exciting. After military service in a special unit in the artillery corps, "where you learn about yourself and your physical and mental boundaries," he significantly shortened his trip after the military for only two months, a trip in which most Israelis after their military service travel to exotic countries for a very long period of time, and returned to Tel Aviv to study electrical engineering at the university. After graduating, he worked in the technological development unit at the Israel Security Agency, "where we manufactured everything that was needed."

During that time, he participated in Yossi Vardi's Kinnernet, and on this basis, he initiated, developed, and managed MachaNet for training the security R & D units in thinking outside the box. "The entry ticket was an idea of clever product with no value," said Bash. "The idea was to connect people in a creative way in different areas from their day-to-day work. The programmer welded, the commander screwed, and everyone went crazy as far as you could imagine, all with no uniforms, rank, and organizational affiliation. Years later, the air force is still using the question of how four F-16s approaching the landing can be disrupted by only paper and candle. The answer was given in a project group of us that blew Chinese paper lanterns on the runway."

"Towards the end of 2011, my idea for MachaNet was to build a rocket that would reach the tip of the atmosphere and land back with a parachute, just because I really like to fly things in the air," says Bash with a smile. "A friend of mine proposed to enlarge the project even more and join the competition to land a spacecraft on the moon announced by Google. Just a fantasy, I thought. I really did not have the $50,000 registration money, so I sent a letter of intent for $1,000. That very night, I put a post in Facebook about the planed project and asked a friend to meet on the weekend for beer and discuss the idea. We had nothing, but we were first of all the competitors who have signed a launch contract that will take the spacecraft out of Earth. We have set up SpaceIL organization for educational reasons, because in addition to winning the Google competition, we wanted to make the younger people interested in space. We have met more than 150 young people, talked to Arab children in the Galilee and some ultra-Orthodox in Bnei Brak, with students in Tel Aviv and the periphery. They are all interested in. They are all excited. They are our great hope."

In order to continue progressing they brought a professional CEO, and Bash went on to his new adventure. Together with a friend, they developed a black box that connects to a multicopter drone and communicates with it via a cellular application. They can fly drones from anywhere in the world to anywhere using the cellular network. "What Amazon plans for another four to five years, we know how to do today," he says.

Israeli entrepreneurship is also reflected in the fact that not only are people from the exact sciences setting up high-tech companies, but they often come from the social sciences and include MBA graduates, attorneys, accountants, and executives. FinTech is where many of the online trading platforms were founded by people from the Israeli capital market.

Udi Mokady, a lawyer by training, founded the successful cyber company CyberArk together with Alon Cohen and Amit Remez in 1999, and it was traded at the NASDAQ at the end of 2017 at a value of $1.55 billion.

Gett, formerly known as Get-Taxi, was launched in 2010 as an application for taxis via smartphone. It is a location-based service that allows taxi drivers and passengers to communicate directly with each other and coordinate collection, make a payment, and provide feedback on drivers. Gett has expanded rapidly outside of Israel and already reaches one hundred large cities, with more than sixty thousand taxis and four thousand business customers in Israel, England, the United States, and Russia and over a thousand employees worldwide, including three hundred in Israel. In May 2016, Volkswagen invested $300 million in Gett.

Another example of the Israeli entrepreneurial advantage is that of Ofer Feinstein, CEO of Co-op, a medium-sized retail chain, which was located mainly in residential neighborhoods throughout Israel and in the rural periphery of the country. When social protests focused on the cost of living were rampant in Israel, food producers and marketing chains were called to lower prices and have since been competing with each other. In the competitive environment, chains have risen and fallen, and those who have managed to convey to the public that their prices are the cheapest became a national hero. Co-op, as a network with high salary costs in comparison to the competing companies, was struggling to survive. "We are working differently," Feinstein says, and he tells the story of their unique development, aimed at retailing and managing midsize networks to significantly improve their efficiency. The chain developed a software that interfaces SAP's database management systems for efficient management of food chains. The software, which succeeded above the estimate, received the blessing of SAP worldwide to market it around the world, thus turning the co-op suddenly from a retail chain into a software house.

XI

THE SCIENTIFIC-
TECHNOLOGICAL ADVANTAGE

Israel serves as a fertile soil for scientific and technological achievements. According to the *Bloomberg Innovation Index*,[109] Israel ranks second in the world in R & D and fourth in the world in terms of educated labor force as well as in the quality of applied science researchers. According to IMD,[110] Israel ranks first in the world in terms of innovativeness and entrepreneurship, second in scientific research and public expenditure on education, and third for the rate of engineers in the workforce. It is in second place in the world in investor confidence in venture capital funds.[111]

The eight winners of the Nobel Prize have made Israel, from the beginning of the twenty-first century, the country with the largest number of winners per capita, with a large gap from the rest of the world, including the United State. Israel's Nobel Prize achievements are fifty times more than its weight in world population.

Israel is in the third-highest place in the world for winning Turing Computer Science prizes; 30 percent of the Gödel Prize winners for exceptional theoretical research in computer science are Israelis.

In the book *Start-Up Nation*,[112] the authors stress that Israel represents the greatest concentration of innovation and entrepreneurship in the world today. They are quoting some of the world's technological leaders. Google CEO Eric Schmidt said the United States is the best place for entrepreneurs in the world, followed by Israel. Bill Gates said, "The kind of innovation going on in Israel is critical to the future of the technology business." [113]

"In two days in Israel, I saw more opportunities than in a year in the rest of the world," said Paul Smith, executive vice president of Philips Medical. [114]

The authors of the book attempt to explain the origins of the techno-entrepreneurial ecosystem in Israel. They say that it is a result of distress and need that generates ingenuity, the Jewish-Israeli genius, the military and security needs, the rebellious-impertinent-unorthodox culture, and the nonhierarchical structure that characterize Israel. "It is not only a story of talent, but also of stubbornness, resolute questioning of the authorities and a determined determination, along with a unique approach to failure, teamwork, mission, risk taking and cross-domain creativity," they write.

"The embargo in the 1960s in which Israel needs for military supplies was refused pushed for the development of local weapons systems," says Menashe Sagiv, who, for many years, was IAI's [115] chief financial officer. "It was precisely the troubles that led to a breakthrough. The security needs, as well as the desire not to be dependent, to the extent possible, on external countries that may be politically biased against Israel, led to the existential need for developing technologies. The many military technologies developed during these periods were a critical catalysis for the development of civilian technologies that contributed greatly to the Israeli economy and to the main growth engine: export."

The Lavi Project was an attempt by the Israeli government, through the IAI, to develop Israel's first jet fighter. The project, although a technological success, was shut down due to economic and other reasons. "After the Lavi development project was closed, the IAI, like the other military companies involved, was in some sort of crisis. All of which continued with technological development based on the knowledge they accumulated in the development of the Lavi—for other technological products. Most military companies produced, at that time, only for the Israeli Ministry of Defense, who was unable to financially support them all. IAI has developed products that meet global standards, including missiles, satellites, communications systems, intelligence, and aircraft improvement. A few years after, IAI was already export oriented, with 85 percent of its revenues coming from exports and only 15 percent from sales to the Israeli Defense Ministry." The crisis was, again, a drive for a breakthrough.

THE TECHNOLOGICAL ENVIRONMENT

In the mid-1990s, I (A.R.) accompanied M-Systems as its financial risk management consultant. At that time, it was a fairly small high-tech company that employed fewer than one hundred employees. Dov Moran, the owner and CEO, caught me in the corridor one day and showed me something new they developed. He took me to a small room and took out a long, electronic stick made of glass. He explained at length what the new device was going to be. In retrospect, I found out that I was one of a handful of people who saw the world's first disk-on-key. Moran, one of the most prominent figures in Israeli high tech, submitted and invented more than forty patents.

The Israeli technological environment is formed around five focal points: the technological units of the military and the other security organizations, academics, Israeli startups, Israeli global technological companies, and R & D centers of foreign global companies.

Much of the success lies in the ties of these five focal points, together creating the technological ecosystem that feeds itself to increase its power. From academics flow knowledge, technology, and people. Startups must decide whether to be sold or grow. On the compost that the dead startups are creating, new companies grow. The R & D personnel of the big companies leave to build their own startups; they sometimes return after a failure, sometimes sell their startups to a larger company, and sometimes grow into a global Israeli company. The energy produced by this turbine increases its speed and energizes the Israeli economy as a whole.

The current technological environment in Israel reflects the character of Israelis: never satisfied, confident that they can solve any problem, have endless initiative, and love change and innovation.

There is no dispute that there is room for government involvement in high-tech industries since the public benefit is greater than the private. If a venture capital fund invests in the company and fails, it is a big pain for the company as well as its investors, but if a series of additional companies emerge from this failure, it is an important gain on a national level. An impressive and resonant example of this phenomenon was Better Place, which fell and lost billions, but from it emerged many knowledge groups that are now in the development centers of multinational companies and startups.

The deep governmental involvement in creating infrastructure and pushing for the establishment of technology companies in Israel began at the end of the 1980s, especially with the establishment of the government's Yozma program to encourage venture capital investments. This was designed to encourage the growth of the high-tech industry by investing in venture capital funds. The huge advantage for the entrepreneurs was that the government invested $1 per $1.50 of the entrepreneurs, which means that forty percent of the investment was covered by the government, and it also gave an exit door after five years to buy its shares at a convenient price, thus getting rid of the government partner. Each venture capital fund was comprised of Israeli venture capital investors (trainees), a foreign venture capital company, and an Israeli holding company or bank. Ten years later, it was estimated that the Yozma funds were invested in about 150 Israeli startups, and their survival rate was 65 percent, with the worldwide survival rate in this industry being only 40 percent. The program, dubbed the Israeli Model, inspired national projects in many other countries such as Ireland, Korea, Russia, Singapore, Australia, New Zealand, and Japan.

The captain who has for years been involved in encouraging Israeli high tech is the chief scientist of the Ministry of Economics, but he himself has concluded that there is a need for renewed thinking. The budget of the chief scientist was decreased over the years, while the needs for financing new, risky R & D projects increased. The time needed to develop governmental projects to deal with industry need was much too long; the fund never got to assist old industry and so forth.

The strategic work of the chief scientist, initiated by Avi Hasson, the former chief scientist, suggested that a new vision needed to be adopted, and the right governmental authority had to be established to develop it. There would be no more navigation of a small budget in the sea of companies' risk-financing requirements, but the economic impact of the high-tech industry would be expanded to more extensive audiences than the 9 percent employed in the industry, and economic prosperity would be brought across sectors and populations. In 2015, the government of Israel decided to establish the National Authority for Research, Development and Technological Innovation, which is designed to address all these challenges through six different unites, each focusing on different types of needs and customers.

The startup arena is designed to assist, encourage, and nurture startups and to develop unique work programs that operate within short, flexible time frames to meet these needs.

The growth arena, on the other hand, deals with mature companies and needs to address their unique challenges, such as reducing regulation that hinders their development, addressing the human capital issues required for them, and assisting in the acquisition of subsidiaries.

The traditional industry scene and its challenges are different. Here, there is a need for investments in the development of management infrastructure and in the implementation of innovative processes in production and supply lines.

The technological-infrastructure arena deals with the establishment of R & D infrastructures of nationwide advantages, such as a tissue banks, nanotechnology centers, magnet projects, and so on.

The public-social arena is designed to involve larger populations in the success of high tech, and it includes the integration of Arabs and Orthodox Jews.

The last arena operating in the new authority is the international arena. Cooperation in research and development demands continuous investment in order to integrate Israel in the global flow of information and capital by binational funds, such as the European R & D program, and strengthening Israel's cooperation in East Asia.

In the establishment of the National Authority for Innovation and the nomination of Aharon Aharon, former CEO of Apple Israel, and Ami Appelbaum, former president of KLA Tencor, to lead it, Israel sent a renewed and reinforced statement by the government and the Knesset that innovation is a national resource to which they are committed.

STARTUP NATION

Every eight hours, a startup is born in Israel; there are more than one thousand per year. These are huge numbers in every comparison. However, many of these startups operate at a high risk level, and most do not survive. The initial challenge is to turn small companies into small technology companies and grow them into medium and large companies. Startups are a breeding ground, but the challenge to survive and grow is huge.

Even though the large technological companies are the ones that bring the bulk of the exports, the advantages of small technology companies for economic growth are important for many reasons. Many new and growing companies are recruiting more workers than large, well-established companies. They create diversity and reduce risks to unemployment in case of crisis. They usually operate in niche areas where they are not exposed to fierce competition from international giants.

Nokia was the largest employer in Finland and provided, at its peak, direct and indirect employment for about 8 percent of the citizens of Finland, but its collapse brought the Finnish economy into a recession. As the economy consists of more companies in a variety of industries, the risk is lower. Yehuda Amichai, an Israeli poet and not an economist at all, described the situation well: "Not like a cypress, not all at once, not all of me, but as a grass."[116]

According to the IVC research, high-tech industry in Israel directly employs close to 10 percent of the Israeli labor market. From the beginning of the twenty-first century until the end of 2015, 10,604 startups were established in Israel, and 5,298 companies were closed. These numbers are not only very exceptional relative to the size of the population, but they are also dramatic in absolute terms relative to the world, with only large countries such as the United States and China able to present higher data. In the beginning of the century, over 60 percent of the capital raised came from Israeli venture capital funds; as of 2015, over 85 percent of the investments came from foreign funds, primarily those based in the United States.

The multiplicity of startups is a product of the environment in Israel, which is characterized by an extremely rapid pace, with an extreme array of initiatives and development directions with relatively low funding and a more high-tech environment than ever before. The time between the idea, the research, the approval, the funding, and the realization was greatly reduced. It took Waze less than four years to reach more than twenty million users.

In November 2015, the world's largest startup accelerator,[117] MassChallenge, announced that it was setting up its third center in Jerusalem alongside the accelerators in Boston and London. The program provides selected entrepreneurs, at no cost, with four months of consultation and guidance in order to help them break into international markets. John Harthorne, the founder and CEO of MassChallenge, was quoted in People & Computers saying that he sees Israel as an outstanding example of entrepreneurship and that the Jerusalem accelerator was launched in cooperation with the Israeli government, the Jerusalem Development Authority, and the Jerusalem Municipality, which will invest millions of dollars in the project. Choosing Jerusalem is not a trivial choice, but perhaps things are clearer when noted, for example, that it was the first city in Israel to have full Wi-Fi access.

The Junction is a unique accelerator, the product of a multidisciplinary collaboration among the venture capital fund Genesis, Bank Leumi, Deloitte, the law office Meitar Liquornik, and the global high-tech company SAP. It is located in a loft in south Tel Aviv and offers entrepreneurs a six-month program, during which companies are invited to sit in the common space, consult with members of Eco-Systems, and run the startup to the best of their abilities. To the testimony of the accelerator managers, 112 startups have used it so far. Fifty-three of them received financing, there were three exits, and $130 million was financed in total. Definitely an impressive achievement.

Along with the accelerators, the global phenomenon of joint workspaces is expanding quickly and includes a variety of programs for executives, workshops, investor clubs, and so on. The startups from the garage days, like Apple and others in Silicon Valley, have gone a long way to the stylized and trendy workspaces of the contemporary startup scene.

WeWork is an American company that provides shared workspaces, community, and services for entrepreneurs, freelancers, startups, and small businesses. Founded in 2010, it is headquartered in New York City. In Israel, the company operates six compounds in the cities of Tel Aviv, Herzliya, and Beer Sheva under the management of Benjy Singer.[118] One of WeWork's founders and its CEO is an Israeli-American entrepreneur, Adam Neumann.

Another shared workspace is the Library, with area allocated by the Tel Aviv municipality in Migdal Shalom; developers can use the area at a fair price for four months.

It is difficult to describe the interior design of the shared workspaces: from telephone booths for quiet, individual work to various spaces with weird sofas, chairs, bars, and buffets. The design is very eclectic and is supposed to influence the creativity of its residents, as if the space says, *I'm so crazy that everything is possible.*

There are workspaces in many places in Israel, and the philosophy is one—limited space density, multiple interactions, the ability to rub shoulders with experienced entrepreneurs, and the entrepreneurs' focus on a breakthrough.

Alongside the accelerators and workspaces, also technological incubators operate in Israel under the concession of the chief scientist of the Ministry of Economy. The expectation is that the entrepreneurial team will begin the startup with a joint workspace or accelerators, show the achievements at demo day at the end of the program, and then continue for another year and a half in the incubator.

Thus, in Israel, a framework was created to develop initiatives from their early stages until the completion of their growth, and then they move on to the next stage, which is usually a total failure of the idea, but sometimes it is a success. Although successes are the minority of cases, they are sufficient to excite and inspire entire generations of young people committed to developing their own ideas, as well as all the funding and financing industry supporting them.

Every innovative technology is a new country whose opportunities are unbelievable. In the old atlases, there were vast territories called "terra incognita," an unknown country. These territories attracted many explorers who settled and accumulated their wealth or died trying to do so. The Israelis, like those explorers, are targeted on every new horizon that opens. When the whole world is dazzled by the abundance of technological products and services, among the first to be found there are the Israeli startups.

It can be argued that in many cases, just like in the time of the Internet bubble, many funds are invested in applications where the technological depth is shallow. But one should pay attention to the words of Dov Moran:[119] "There are applications that changed the world, so it's a mistake to treat them all as one piece. Take WhatsApp for example; it changed the way we all communicate. In my view, it's a work of art."

If Israel is a habitat for startups, then the new crop must always be examined. The criteria for testing are the very growth of new crops. The pace, quantity, and technological depth are the correct tests and not, as is customary in more traditional markets, how one company or another jumps, grows, or wanes. This is a completely different philosophy.

The crop of the past few years includes, of course, the well-known Waze, Taboola, Outbrain, Gett, and also different startups. ZetaLabs, which develops a small, mobile printer that fits into any file holder. Kaltura has developed an open platform for online video, which is used today by all. Yevvo is an application that enables sharing in a live video stream. TapReason increases the usage of application in an non-invasive way by sending users a push message according to their personal features. Quando makes it easy to schedule service providers by coordinating customer logs with the merchant's calendar. BreezoMeter focuses on access to air-pollution information, Hi-Park deals with locating parking through information sharing, and on and on. The crop is huge.

Out of the shared work spaces and with the help of the accelerators and incubators, as well as venture capital funds and private angels, the Israeli startups operate in droves. New technological worlds yield new opportunities. In every new field that opens, you will find Israeli startups looking for their special value.

THE SPACE CLUB

It was a cold day on the White House lawn in Washington, DC, on March 26, 1979. The historic peace treaty between Israel and Egypt was signed by Egyptian president Anwar Sadat, Israeli prime minister Menachem Begin, and US president Jimmy Carter. The state of war, which began at the time of the Egyptian military's invasion of Israel, the day after David Ben-Gurion declared the establishment of the new state on May 15, 1948, ended on that cool day in Washington. The Egyptian anchor spilled in a lyrical moment when he quoted the poetry of the Israeli poet Naomi Shemer: "Tomorrow every man will build up with his own hands whatever he dreamed today."

This event of signing the peace treaty was, in the opinion of Maj. Gen. (Res.) Prof. Isaac Ben-Israel, the birth of the Israeli space project. "After the signing of the peace treaty with Egypt, it was not possible to send photo planes over Sinai, and therefore Prime Minister Menachem Begin decided to establish the space program," says Ben-Israel, who chairs the Israel Space Agency in the Ministry of Science and Technology and who initiated and established the National Cyber Headquarters in the prime minister's office.

Despite disasters along the way, the Israeli space industry is breaking through. Israel is the seventh country to enter the World Space Club. The Soviet Union was the first to launch a satellite into space with *Sputnik 1*, and it stunned the world. The second was the United States, which was shocked by the Soviet technological victory. Western European countries understood that each country on its own cannot compete with the two superpowers and established the European Space Agency (ESA). They were the third to send a satellite into space, followed by China, India, Japan, and Israel.

"It's not natural for a country the size of Israel to conduct activities in space," says Ben-Israel. Each of the other space agencies are from countries much larger than Israel, in their budgets and in their populations. But Israel had to do so because of the security needs. In 1988, the first Israeli satellite was launched. Since then, more than twenty have been launched.

However, it was not only the drawback of being small that acted against Israel. Because of its eastern neighbors, Israel's satellites could not be launched eastward, "as physics demands," notes Ben-Israel. An eastward launch, with the direction of the Earth's rotation, allows Israel to save energy and money, but east of Israel are vast countries like Jordan, Iraq, Saudi Arabia, and Iran—most of them hostile to Israel. Thus, it was necessary to launch west—in reverse of the Earth's rotation.

The budget challenge, together with the physical challenge, created the Israeli solution: lightweight satellites. "The Israeli satellites are more than ten times lighter than their counterparts, and the lightweight requirement of the satellite and all the hardware, required special solutions. There is a need to replace the glass of the camera lens with other materials that will be easy on one hand and enable high resolution on the other. Replacing the energy source used to operate the satellite engines from gas—whose balloons must be taken from Earth—to solar-powered electricity abundant in space," Ben-Israel says, and in retrospect, it turns out that Israel has created a very important economic asset. With the current launch costs of $50,000 per kilo of satellite, light satellites have an advantage, and Israeli technology on this issue has been beneficial.

A number of Israeli groups are currently developing microsatellites (ten to one hundred kilograms) and nanosatellites (one to ten kilograms). Israel's space industry focuses on high-resolution photo satellites placed in low Earth orbits (LEO) and geostationary (GEO) communications satellites.[120] In addition, Israel focuses on remote sensing, communications satellites, image decoding, and more. Israel's satellites are considered leaders in the global arena.

"Israel Aerospace Industries (IAI) serves as a national home for the Israeli space industry, both in the field of communications satellite and in observation satellite. Today, satellites are the 'eyes of the state,' hence, its strategic importance for the State of Israel in light of the changing threats," says Eyal Younian, CFO of IAI, and he adds that low governmental investment in aerospace is a huge challenge. "Which means that the entire burden of investment in the required infrastructure falls on IAI, which, with all due respect to being a government company, is required to work according to business standards, and the burden is heavy on its shoulders."

But the problems do not end there. To succeed, a critical mass production is needed to cover the enormous investments required in the satellite industry. IAI is limited in its export capabilities to certain countries, particularly in the security field, which, in turn, reduces the addressable market and the ability to return the basic investments.

"Adding to this the high labor costs in Israel, and you will get a clear picture. There is no economic possibility to continue to be a global player, without the state's own investment in the field of satellites," concludes Younian.

As far as space is concerned, Israel is a success—but it is not an island. Space is a place of global cooperation on one hand and civil, military, and local economic benefits on the other. There are huge egos in the field, ideas that inspire imagination, massive investments, and exciting people. The Israeli space agency focuses on creation and strengthening cooperation with other space agencies. Such collaborations help to divide the burden of development costs, allow for the use of advanced systems for research tasks, and enable researchers to be exposed to new research methods and international standards of R & D.

It goes without saying that promoting such cooperation creates many business opportunities and improves relations with countries around the world. Today, Israel cooperates with the American NASA, the European ESA, the Italian ASI, the French CNES, the Canadian CSA, the Indian ISRO, the Japanese JAXA, and the UN Space Office.

One of the most fascinating stories is the Venus project. It is a collaboration between Israel and France, focused on protecting the environment by sending to space a multispectral camera that has twelve different wavelengths, which will identify pollution factors on land and sea. Initially, the project defined Israel as building the lightweight satellite and the French supplying the camera. But due to the light weight of the satellite, an especially light camera was needed, which the French did not know how to build, and they published an international tender for the construction of the camera. This was won by an Israeli company, Elop. Thus, a cooperation project between Israeli and French technologies ended in a cooperation between one Israeli company and another Israeli company, financed half by Israel and half by France.

The Israeli space challenge is great. There is no end to Israeli innovation, but the R & D finance that Israel can invest is significantly lower than other countries. "Today there are Israeli space components on more than fifty satellites in the world," Ben-Israel says, adding examples such as the *Curiosity* probe on Mars, which digs rocks and analyzes their chemical composition and carries a cooling system manufactured by the Israeli company RICOR. AccuBeat's atomic clocks fly in dozens of satellites. ImageSat and Gilat are some of the world's largest providers of ground communications satellite stations.

"We are working on continuing to reduce the weight of the satellites, in order to reach one hundred kilograms, which would allow them to be launched from an aircraft. We have been working on unique satellite communications patents so that we can compete with US companies. Such as a digital satellite that will allow frequencies to be changed from Earth. Another example is the launch of a low-altitude satellite, which will be driven by solar energy to a high orbit. We have capabilities, we have technologies, we have knowledge," concludes Ben-Israel. "We lack only financial resources."

After the *Columbia* disaster, in which Col. Ilan Ramon, the first Israeli astronaut, was killed, Prof. Ran Ginosar founded the company Ramon Chips, with the aim of responding to Israel's strategic need for satellite chips and the many limitations on importing chips for space purposes, even from the United States. The chip developed by the company is considered one of the most advanced and fastest-performing chips in the world today.

We already see a future limitation in transferring too much data from satellites to Earth. Now, Ramon Chips is developing the next generation that will be able to support an "independent" satellite in its decisions, in which everything can be photographed, processed, improved, or discovered in predefined objects or features.

Academies also contribute to the definition of Israel as a space power. Dr. Maayan Soumagnac-Mor is a new immigrant from Paris who is currently doing her postdoctoral thesis at the Weizmann Institute's Faculty of Astrophysics. The specific area in which she deals is the separation of stars and galaxies—a vital step in understanding the sky images we receive. She is a young, impressive, and idealistic woman who shares her time with the Weizmann Institute's research programs and the establishment of an gender-equal synagogue in Jerusalem.

There seems to be no limit to the imaginations of the space scientists and developers, but as a result of budget limitations, Israel focuses on small satellites. As expected, some question the value of these satellites. In order to address this skepticism, the ULTRASAT initiative was launched in 2010 to produce light (about 100 kilograms) and cheap (about $100 million, including the launch) satellites. The main objectives of the mission are to understand the explosion process at the end of a supernova's life and to measure the mass and environmental conditions of massive black holes in galactic centers.

The future is in launching bands and swarms of nanosatellites. On this issue, Israel has a great advantage. Both swarms of satellites and separated satellites, when each part of the satellite flies separately, require the ability to fly a cluster or flight structure.

We would not be able to conclude this chapter on Israel as a space power without paying attention to the many public and educational activities that take place on this subject, such as the Ramon Foundation. The Ramon Foundation was established to encourage the future generation in Israel to realize its personal and social potential, combined with teaching about space and science in classes throughout the country. It even conducted the World Federation of Space Agency's International Conference in Jerusalem, in the midst of the October 2015 knife uprising, with the participation of the heads of the world's leading space agencies.

NEW TECHNOLOGIES, NEW OPPORTUNITIES

The cyber world is a new territory, open to all and is aware of terrorists threatening the assets of individuals and countries. The need for security and cyber protection has become critical throughout the world. In this field, the geniuses of each country compete against those of other countries. In search of geniuses, there is, of course, significance to the size of the population from which the geniuses grow—but also their quality.

To Israel's credit lies the special quality of its people for creativity in solving problems on one hand and for existential challenges on the other. Israel, which for years has been fighting Islamic terror, has developed special capabilities in this field. The knowledge flows rapidly in governmental security agencies and in the business sector.

IVC estimates that in 2017, about 430 cyber companies operate in Israel, which account for 20 percent of the global market. In comparison, for the size of the country, it is again a tremendous amount. Some of the best known are Check Point, the global Israeli company founded by Gil Shwed, and newer companies such as CyberArc, Imperva, Trusteer, and Radware.

———

Biotech startups are a whole and turbulent world in their own right. Check-Cap developed a capsule to photograph the inside of the intestine, Silenseed created a lozenge with a needle-assisted drug against cancerous tumors, and ReWalk has built a skeleton of metal limbs that supports wheelchair-bound people to stand erect and walk. Savicell engaged in the diagnosis of cancer through a blood test; Immunovative is focused on strengthening the immune system of patients. LipoCure improves the performance of drugs by inhibiting them in liposomes; MeMed provides pioneering diagnostic solutions, and its system differentiates between bacterial infections and viral infections for which antibiotics are not required. Optimata develops a simulation system and predicts the effect of drugs on a virtual patient. Brainsway develops and manufactures solutions for diseases and mental and neurological disorders. All of these are small examples of the biomedical R & D initiatives in various stages of development.

———

Another area in which Israel has a very strong global presence is in devices for aesthetic treatments. Technological development has revolutionized the global aesthetics market. Whereas once people needed to go to specialists for body hair removal, now they can do it themselves with a small, friendly device in the convenience of their homes.

Not only in body hair removal is the dominance of Israeli companies in major aesthetic treatments prominent. Some of the most recognized companies in the field of medical aesthetics are Israeli, such as Lumenis, Syneron, Home Skinovations, and Alma Lasers. "In international conferences, representatives from Israel make up 30 to 40 percent of those present in the auditorium," says a man involved in the field.

———

Avi Zeevi, a managing partner at Carmel Ventures, one of the largest venture capital funds, is considered to be the most well-known Israeli figure in the field of FinTech (creating technology-based financial services systems that will replace the human factor). Zeevi has been involved in high tech for over thirty-five years and believes that "Israel has a good opportunity to become a significant global player in the world of FinTech, since the success of Israel's industry has been widely recognized by leading financial institutions and investors, and the future is still full of possibilities."

How did Israel get to this point? Zeevi offers explanations: "It is important to remember that the financial-services industry is currently undergoing fundamental business and technological changes, creating many opportunities. Israel has knowledge and experience in technologies which rapidly become relevant for this field. Technologies such as real-time analytics, algorithmics, big data, risk management, fraud prevention, and security are all aimed to change the financial services to become more consumer friendly, mobile, and designed to reach even populations in remote areas who do not have access to all the services. Israeli FinTech companies became leaders in their fields, such as Actimize in the field of fraud prevention, Fundtech in the field of banking solutions, Retalix in point-of-sale solutions, Trusteer in the field of Internet crime prevention, and Sapiens in the field of insurance."

"There are thousands of Israelis who work in the global financial services industry, mainly on Wall Street and in London, and are at the forefront of the business and technologies demands in the field," says Zeevi. "Many of those Israelis return home with deep understanding and knowledge that helps the Israeli FinTech industry."

Barclays and Citi have large R & D centers in Israel. Visa has announced its willingness to develop cooperation with Israeli companies. J.P. Morgan opened a large innovation and R & D center, as have some of the leading players in the financial market such as SunGard, PayPal, and Intuit, who already have R & D centers in Israel that are growing steadily. Almost on a weekly basis, there are delegations from the world's leading financial institutions, eager to take advantage of Israeli technology and invest in Israeli FinTech. There is no doubt that outside the United States, Israel is one of the leading centers in the field.

––––––

The hottest technological field is autonomous vehicles. The future is already here, and the race for the development of autonomous vehicles is perhaps the most vivid race in the technological world. Ford, Peugeot-Citroen, Toyota, and General Motors, as well as technology companies such as Apple and Google, invest billions in developing technology capabilities. Google entered the race with an autonomous test vehicle already circulating on California roads, and there are also other companies, such as the Israeli Gett, in which Volkswagen invested $300 million; Lyft, in which GM invested half a billion dollars; Otto, which was acquired by Uber for $680 million; and European companies such as Thales and Valeo. Startup companies understand that the market is thirsty for relevant technologies.

Autonomous vehicle technologies are not only related to independent travel but also to vehicle information systems, navigation systems, fuel, and so on. The car companies are looking for any technology that can help them in development and provide them with an advantage over other companies in the industry.

Therefore, it is no wonder that many Israeli startups are rapidly jumping into this new field. The sale of the Israeli SAIPS to Ford, which acquired it in August 2016 for tens of millions of dollars to promote its autonomous vehicle project, is yet another milestone in the change that is taking place. There are many Israeli technology companies that develop exactly that: Innoviz, Nexar, Anagog, Valens, and Argus, which are still in their early stages, and of course the most famous, Mobileye, the NASDAQ Israeli company sold to Intel. All accelerate the entry of additional Israeli companies into the field.

XII

THE DEMOGRAPHIC ADVANTAGE

Israel has a significant advantage as a young country in an aging world. In recent years, there have been populations in the country that were excluded from the circle of employment, but now Israel is changing and experiencing a demographic revolution in relation to the world.

THE YOUNGEST COUNTRY IN THE OECD

According to a UN forecast, in 2050, twelve million people will live in Israel, compared to 8.8 million in 2018. This forecast is very different from the UN forecast for Europe (Western and Eastern), for example, that its population will decline from about 740 million today to only 700 million in 2050. In this sense, Israel is going against the tide.

Population age is of great importance to the economy. Economic growth is based on a young labor force that produces and has needs and establishes families that consume and help the economy, thereby helping the elderly population, which has ceased to work and produce.

Israel is the country with the youngest population in the OECD, and prominently so. The median age in Israel is thirty, while the median age in OECD countries is forty-two.

Not only that, but the fertility rate in Israel, which stands at 3.2 children per woman, is the only one in the OECD that passes, and significantly, the average of 2.2 children per woman—below which the population is reduced. In fact, apart from Mexico, all the other thirty-two OECD countries are in a process of erosion and population decline.

The average fertility rate for women in developed countries is only 1.7, which results an aging population and is followed by depletion of the population. According to demographic projections, in 2060, Germany will have sixty-eight million inhabitants, including immigrants, compared to eighty million today. According to the US Bureau of Statistics's annual census, in 2060, 55 percent of the US population will be over the age of sixty-five.

Analysis of the demographic projection for the most economically influential age group—the twenty-to-thirty-four age group—is very important. This age group is characterized by the fact that it works harder, builds families, and thus contributes more to consumer demand in the economy than any other age group, and it takes greater entrepreneurial risks. The combination of these factors leads to the economic contribution of this group being the highest.

According to a statistical study conducted by demographic researcher Yakov Faitelson, the weight of this important age group will be reduced in the OECD countries by an average of 14 percent between 2010 and 2030. The situation is especially severe in Japan, South Korea, and Europe. The only OECD countries that will experience an increase in this age group are New Zealand with 3 percent, Turkey with 4 percent, Mexico with 11 percent, and Israel with an exceptional increase of 28 percent in this group relative to its weight in 2010. According to the CBS forecast, the median age in Israel will rise from thirty to thirty-one in 2035, and in fact, Israel will remain the only young country in the OECD.

In Israel, there is also no problem of the "dependency ratio" that is so burdensome for aging countries. The dependency ratio is defined as the number of people who work and support the elderly population that depends on them. In 2035, Germany and Japan will have a dependency ratio of more than sixty-five elderly people per hundred workers, two and a half times higher than what will be in Israel. On average, in all OECD countries, this ratio will be higher than in Israel by more than double.

This extraordinary phenomenon has dramatic implications for economic trends. Israel is swimming against the current, and this will have a positive effect on its future economy, especially compared to developed countries.

JOINING THE LABOR FORCE

The ultra-Orthodox population numbers about 10 percent of the country's population, while the Arab population is about 20 percent. According to the poverty report of the National Insurance Institute for 2017, 48 percent of the ultra-Orthodox families and 51 percent of the Arab families live below the poverty line, which together constitute 83 percent of the Israeli families who live in poverty.

THE ULTRA-ORTHODOX WANT WORK

The separation of the ultra-Orthodox sector began with the establishment of the state and the desire of its leaders, with David Ben-Gurion at their head, to preserve some of this special way of life, which was mostly destroyed in the Holocaust. The original intention was for a minority of ten thousand people, but over the years, it grew to about 10 percent of the total population in Israel.

Between the ultra-Orthodox and the secular majority, which includes traditional and national religious Israelis who serve in the IDF and have a much higher participation in the workforce, there are tensions. The ultra-Orthodox were called upon to donate their share beyond being "the keepers of the ember." The arrangement that decrees that the state supports them so that they can focus on the study of the Holy Scriptures was relevant as long as their numbers were estimated at tens of thousands, not hundreds of thousands.

Paradoxically, for some time, the government has determined that anyone who does not enlist in the military cannot work without losing the government pension. This prevented young ultra-Orthodox men, who wanted to, from going to work legally. (Some of them worked in part-time positions and were paid in cash, thus contributing to the black economy.) This process also forced the ultra-Orthodox community to preserve among themselves a growing group of people who have dropped out of the holy studies who are not studying and prevented from working.

In addition, large-scale transfer payments to child allowances were a catalyst for the ultra-Orthodox sector, as well as the Arab sector, to have more and more children without parental financial responsibility. These transfer payments have become a major factor that encouraged entire populations, men and women, not to make a living and not to integrate into the circles of work and creativity. In many ways, this economic arrangement created a situation in which the State of Israel strengthened the ultra-Orthodox communities in the fields of society and economy and facilitated their isolation and separation for many years, turning them into parasites.

When an entire population prefers not to work, its poverty rates are also very high. Almost 50 percent of the families in the ultra-Orthodox sector live below the poverty line, compared to only 5 percent of the secular and national religious population. Additional funding methods that enabled many of the sector not to work over the years were funds received through countless nonprofit organizations that deal with "charitable donations," which are based on large-scale donations of rich Orthodox Jews from abroad.

Hence, political and religious reasons, as well as serious governmental errors, contributed to this.

In early 2003, child allowances were cut to yeshiva students. Then finance minister Benjamin Netanyahu led the move. Later on, income tax was also reduced in order to encourage the exit to work, and a financial instrument that promotes employment was created—a negative income tax that subsidizes working people. The social and political ability to do so stemmed from a severe recession that the Israeli economy was in at the time, that was effected by the bursting of the dot-com bubble in 2000 and the second intifada that began in 2001 as well as changes in the internal political structure. The goal was threefold: to save the state budget, to increase the percentage of participation in the labor force, and to reduce the poverty rates that characterized the late 1990s.

———

The *Poverty and Social Gaps* report for 2013 formulated this as a change in historical trend: "The multi-year approach proposes to see the development from 2008 in light of the breakdown of stagnation in the state of poverty," the National Insurance Institute wrote. This is the case in view of the extraordinary findings of the poverty report, which attest to an improvement in almost all the poverty data in Israel. National Insurance Institute researchers pointed to the reason for the decline in poverty data. Low-paid workers began earning more, thanks to the increase in employment. The increase in wages neutralized the cuts in child allowances. The increase in employment (and the decrease in unemployment) was sharp, especially among the populations that are usually excluded from the labor market.

———

"My mother did not work, my wife does not work, but I have three working daughters, four sons, the older one doing national service, the second in the Golani Brigade, the third wanting to be a combat paramedic, and the youngest wanting to join the 8200 unit. The young people are stronger than the adults, because with them it comes from recognition and not from the commandments of learned people...I signed an Eddie card [a card signed in agreement to donate your internal organs to people in need in case of your own demise, to save their lives]...A while ago, my daughter-in-law asked me if it was Halacha [Jewish law] permissible to sign," says Yehuda Meshi Zahav, who was a Neturei Karta (the most extreme ultra-Orthodox sect) officer and led large demonstrations of the ultra-Orthodox street against the state of Israel. Today, he is chairman and president of the ZAKA organization that he founded.

"There were ideological arguments, but the young people who were born into the country do not want to raise another generation of poor people; their worldview has changed...Today, there are ultra-Orthodox studying in universities, colleges, and even at the Technion. It's still not sweeping, but the trend is clear. Today, over 50 percent of ultra-Orthodox men participate in the labor force," adds Meshi Zahav.

As Meshi Zahav says, processes of change, slow but significant, are taking place among the ultra-Orthodox population. These include exposure to the Internet, general studies, and vocational training. The improvement in the economic situation and the change in the consumption habits of large groups in the ultra-Orthodox population led to social and political changes that have an impact on the lifestyle. The Internet and smartphones give them a glimpse of the possibilities that exist beyond the walls. Wikipedia opens up an entire world to which they were unaware of its existence. The departure of the "great leaders of the generation" and the disintegration of the "society of learners" also contribute to what is commonly referred to as the ultra-Orthodox spring.

———

Rabbi Yaakov Litzman is considered one of the leaders of the ultra-Orthodox in Israel. He was born at the end of World War II in a rescue camp in Europe. His father, a Holocaust survivor who lost a wife, a daughter, and a large family who were murdered by the Nazis, married his mother in the rescue camp. At the age of seventeen, Litzman moved to Brooklyn, where he grew up. He later became a rabbi, Knesset member, chairman of the Finance Committee of the Knesset, and minister of health of the Israeli government. He has five children—three sons and two daughters—innumerable grandchildren, and even one great-grandson. Rabbi Litzman calls on the ultra-Orthodox to go to work. "Those who do not study will go to work," says the rabbi, adding that "we do not need people who will just walk around in yeshivas."

The engine for the process is, of course, life itself: the economic distress of many ultra-Orthodox families, the possibilities that today are open to ultra-Orthodox men and women, and legal, political, and other reasons. In Brooklyn, 90 percent of ultra-Orthodox men work; there is no reason why, in Israel, only 50 percent should work.

Ultra-Orthodox society is undergoing a major change, first of all, in its perception of the state, about which its people did not know. "This is not the Zionist state that is against religion; it is the state of all of us and we must take part in its leadership," says Litzman.

As of 2017, the participation rate of ultra-Orthodox women in the labor force jumped from 40 percent a decade ago to 72 percent. This rate has already reached the target set by the government for 2020 and is significantly above the participation rate of all Israeli women in the labor market, which stood at 60 percent in 2017. Ultra-Orthodox men's participation rate also had a jump, from 32 percent to 50 percent. More ultra-Orthodox join the academies and study subjects relevant to the labor market.

ISRAELI ARABS AS AN OPPORTUNITY

Al-Qasemi College for Science and Engineering was established in 2004 next to the Great Mosque of Baka al-Gharbiyye and the College of Teachers. Unlike the College of Teachers, which was successful throughout its history, the College of Engineering and Science failed, and in 2012, it was time to decide whether to close it or to implement a change that would jump it forward. Dr. Dalia Fadila, who was the first woman to be accepted to the college faculty and later became the president of the Teachers College, was appointed head of the Engineering and Science College. She decided to separate it from the teachers' campus and moved to a new building, far from the mosque.

Under the management of Dr. Fadila, the college has been successful in its program of promoting practical engineers, complementary medicine school, vocational training, medical training school, finance school, and, more recently, a BSc program in engineering together with Ruppin Technological College.

"The problem of Arab society is that we do not have a liberal-progressive leadership that will lead the way to the vision of a developed society that has a clear institutional, educational, and ethical infrastructure, and not just a conflict," said Dr. Fadila. "We must take responsibility for ourselves."

"The academy is a meeting place for all of us," adds Marwan Anabosi, director of the Bank Leumi branch in Baka al-Gharbiyye.

Dr. Fadila was born in Tira to a family of six children, and her father, who was head of the education department, instilled in his children the concept she is trying to instill in the entire Arab sector, which says that the Arabs are a minority in the country, and "the minority must excel."

"As soon as you decide that you live in Israel, part of the Israeli entity enters your identity." She defines herself as a Muslim and an Israeli and an Arab and a Palestinian, and all these identities sometimes collide and sometimes live in peace. Certainly, but above all, Dr. Fadila understands the damage of submission to the thinking of the clan, as opposed to the independent thinking of modern man. She has written many books for the English education network she founded, and every one of them starts with *I am.* "Only giving legitimacy to the individual can bring about change," she says, adding, "Until when will we cry that others are to blame in our situation? Even if so, now is the time to take responsibility for ourselves and develop ourselves."

"There are seventeen point five percent Arabs in the population; where are they?" Yoram Yaacovi, Microsoft's R & D CEO, asks, adding, "Why, until recently, did we get zero resumes of Arabs as candidates for Microsoft? It was explained that they do not send a resume to Microsoft 'because there is no chance they will be accepted.' We devote a lot to learning the subject, and there are various evaluations. One of the arguments is that the concentration of the Arab population is not synchronized with the concentration of jobs in high tech. But the distance between the Arab villages and Herzliya is not only geographic, but in Arab culture, the first refusal to accept work is a hard blow to the ego. When we understood this, we changed our approach, and today, the result of all our actions is that we receive Arab resumes. In addition, we did a house check and found that our recruiters, as well as the managers, would very much like to see Arab employees at Microsoft, but they have an 'unconscious bias' that makes it difficult for Arabs to pass the sieve. The Arabs did not have military service and lack the maturity and experience that ensued. They are younger, and their backgrounds are different. In order to deal with this issue, we have recruited an Arab woman, and we are also sending the managers here to a course on 'unconscious bias.' We do not have any solutions on the subject, but there is work and hope."

Dr. Subhi Basheer, who initiated and developed Enzymotec, which was issued on NASDAQ in 2013, was born in Sakhnin, the city where he still lives with his wife, a social psychologist, and his three daughters. "The Israeli system does not take advantage of 20 percent of its population, and there are very successful people here in the Arab sector, and the fact that they miss them is a loss for the entire industry," says Dr. Basheer, emphasizing to us all the demographic advantage inherent in the Arab population.

DIVERSIFICATION OF THE EMPLOYMENT MARKET

The largest story of employment is women (only some ultra-Orthodox). In 1969, about 70 percent of men participated in the labor force compared with 30 percent of the women. In 2014, about 70 percent of the men still participate in the labor force, but the share of women is almost equal to that of men. This dramatic increase is one of the leading reasons for the rise in the labor force participation rate in Israel. On this issue, Israel is now the leader of many of the OECD's high-income countries.

Another statistic attests to the trend of equality between men and women in the labor force: since 2009, there have been no significant differences in the rate of unemployment between men and women. In the past, women's unemployment was higher than that of men. In 1991 to 1992, the unemployment rate for men reached 9.2 percent, and that of women was 13.9 percent. The thought of not firing a man "because he is the provider" has passed, and since 2009, there are almost no gaps in this area.

Another unique group that has made a dramatic change is the older population. In 2014, it was found that 65 percent of those aged fifty-five to sixty-four work compared to 50 percent of this group a decade earlier. Part of the explanation is, of course, raising the retirement age. However, in a long-term perspective, it is clear that this is the trend that will lead in the coming years.

"One of our biggest challenges is to integrate the ultra-Orthodox and the Arabs into the job market, including high tech," says Prof. Amnon Shashua, chairman of Mobileye, in an interview with Eti Aflalo, deputy editor of Capital Markets at *Calcalist*. "They too understand that they have to integrate into the economy, and the allowances are not enough for the growth rate there. The high tech entices them to be a high-tech entrepreneur. This means designing a business with your organizational culture and preserving the values of ultra-Orthodox society, along with meaningful work and livelihood. This is a revolution from below. The Torah establishment does not interfere. I'm not saying something they do not know, and there's a change that is not talked about. I participated in the competition for business proposals for ultra-Orthodox startups. We offered NIS 20,000 to six winners in the first places. Two hundred forty startups have come to the competition; that's a lot, and they're all startups of ultra-Orthodox, not secular. Five thousand people attended the ceremony. It would seem like a Nobel Prize. The ceremony started at 8:00 p.m., and I thought to myself that this was what had to open the news broadcasts."

The employment challenge does not apply only to the ultra-Orthodox and Arab sectors. Thus, for example, Kobi Altman, CFO of ICL - Israel Chemicals Ltd., says, "We must not give up the periphery. These populations have not yet enjoyed relative success from Israel's success. As someone who works in a company that constitutes almost a quarter of the economic activity in the south of the country and is also the largest employer of the Arab and Bedouin minority, I think this is a national mission. It is inconceivable that a thirty-five- to forty-year-old who lives in Dimona and works for ICL knows that if he loses his job, he will probably be unemployed for the rest of his life."

PART IV
AN ISLAND OF THE FUTURE

XIII

THREE REVOLUTIONS
IN THE MAKING

THE FIRST REVOLUTION: ABUNDANT WATER

Ze'ev Lishnitzman, later Ze'ev Yaar, was a child in the Yavne'el village in the Galilee. His father, Haim Lishnitzman, immigrated to Palestine in 1882, bringing with him his parents, brothers, and sisters. They bought two estates and worked the land, "black soil like in the distant Russia homeland." Like the Arab fellahin who lived beside them, the children walked barefoot every day after school to the fields for stone removal and to create the land for sowing. They piled the heavy stones, plowing them with a hand plow. The children returned home only in the evening, hungry and very tired.

In the corner of the room, their mother made them pitas she had baked in the *taboon* in the courtyard. They dipped the hot pitas in olive oil. Fatigue took over the hunger and overwhelmed them until the next day.

Their father, Haim, was not with them. He worked in Tel Aviv, trying to earn sufficient money to buy seeds for the next sowing season. "When Father returned," Ze'ev testified, "we would look at the seeds that were planted in the open furrows and wait for the rain to fall, but the sky was like steel; not even a drop of rain fell, and the seeds from which we could make bread were wasted for nothing in the dry ground." The father returned to Tel Aviv to earn money to buy more seeds for the next season, and the children returned to the stones and the hand plow.

Israel is a state on the edge of the desert, bordering the global belt of deserts that surrounds the Earth and spreads with global warming. The desert belt, including the Sahara and the Arabian Peninsula, lies between the twentieth and thirtieth latitudes. The State of Israel is located between the latitudes thirty and thirty-three. Two-thirds of the rainfall descends on one-third of the country's surface. Especially in the north and part of the center, almost nothing falls in the Negev and on the mountain. Thus, the State of Israel is at the forefront of the global desertification process.

Israel's water balance is negative. Throughout its existence, and even before, the state needed more water than the average rainfall could supply. In particular, the lack of water has increased in the face of the challenges of the rapidly growing population. Approximately seven billion cubic meters (BCM) of rain a year are lost in Israel, and most of the water (70 percent) evaporates into the atmosphere. Only 30 percent of rainwater can be collected and used. The natural norm in Israel is 1.4 to 1.8 BCM per year, and the norm in the semidesert climate is that there is a series of years of blessed rain and a series of drought years.

About one-third of the world's population, according to the World Bank, the International Monetary Fund, the National Intelligence Council, and other research bodies, will be facing severe water shortages by 2025. We hear of more drought and more dehydration of aquifers. There is such a shortage that there are assessments that in the future, wars will be held around the water sources, which is not the exclusive domain of desert countries but also of countries with suitable water sources.

The main reasons why water will become a more precious and rare commodity are indeed related to the growth of the human population on the planet, the increase of the middle class in third-world countries (mainly China, India, and Central Africa). The main effect of improving the standard of living is the transition from rice and wheat consumption in India and China to meat consumption. The production of a kilo of vegetables requires about two thousand liters of water, while producing a kilo of meat requires about ten thousand liters of water.[121]

Climate change and groundwater pollution as well as large-scale leakage of municipal water-transport systems in an urbanized world will make water an expensive commodity. In this last section, it is surprising to know that a modern city such as New York is losing about 30 percent of the water passing through the municipal pipeline, and Chicago is losing about 25 percent. In major cities in the Middle East and Southeast Asia, these rates can reach 50 or even 60 percent.[122]

One in eight people worldwide has no access to clean water. Other facts published by the World Health Organization are that 3.5 million people will die from contaminated water every year, of whom 1.5 million will be children under the age of five; 98 percent of all these deaths will occur in the developing third world. At any given time, half of the beds in hospitals around the world are occupied by patients suffering from diseases related to lack of access to safe drinking water, poor sanitation, and hygiene. A major factor is the fact that about 80 percent of the sewage, especially in developing countries, flows to rivers, lakes, and coastal areas without any initial treatment. The problem usually perpetuates itself.

According to international studies, the global population is expected to grow from 7.4 billion people in 2015 to 8.3 billion in 2030. This figure is expected to increase demand for drinking water, hygiene, and especially for the food industry. For example, according to the Water Footprint Network, the amount of water needed to produce one piece of bread is forty liters. The amount of water required for one kilogram of wheat is thirteen hundred liters, and the production of a sheet of paper requires ten liters of water. Producing one megawatt per hour requires thirty thousand liters of water.

The water crisis has a far greater impact than the absence of clean water, which is destructive in and of itself. Women and children have to spend hours every day chasing this basic need, with very little time available for something else. Children are neglected, and things like learning and personal development are thrown on the sidelines as well as basic concepts of forgotten human brotherhood. In fact, the health of the whole community is in danger when a basic commodity such as clean water is in short supply.

Israel's population has grown thirteenfold since its inception. The severe shortage of water over the years, and especially with the growth of the population in the early years of the state, placed the water problem at the top. Coping with it took place on two parallel lines: coping with demand on one hand and the supply side on the other. On the demand side, a long campaign of "water discipline" was conducted. Myriam Ben Arush, who immigrated to Israel from another arid country, Morocco, remembers vividly how, for many years since she was a child in Jerusalem, everyone was educated to save water: "Many would refrain from taking baths and making do with the shower, and they would close the water when soaping themselves. We would immediately inform the municipality of every explosion in the irrigation water pipe lines that watered gardens in the public spaces. We also made sure to water the gardens fairly." However, even exemplary civilian savings in water and sophisticated irrigation methods are insufficient, and the water problem also has to be dealt with on the supply side.

Two major periods are notable in Israel's attempts to deal with the water issue. The National Water Carrier and the previous Yarkon-Negev line responded by pumping water from the north, which is relatively abundant in water, to the dry south. It used the waters of the Sea of Galilee in rainy years to bring water to the mountain aquifer and even to the coastal aquifer. Parallel to that, a saltwater carrier was established around the Sea of Galilee, which directed the salty springs to other paths.

The level of the Sea of Galilee has become an obsessive national concern. The Sea of Galilee has been the main source of water for Israel since the country's inception, and for many years, therefore, it influenced the national mood. In drought-stricken times, the fear of dehydration of the main water source would have taken on the dimensions of a national epidemic, with the press and television following the level day by day. Although it is the largest water source, in international terms, the

Sea of Galilee is only a very large lake. In addition to being a source of water, it is also used for vacations and camping, as a pilgrimage spot for Christians, and even for commercial fishing. At that time, according to the same way of thinking, significant portions of the streams were also "caught" and transferred to the expanding population. At the same time, expertise has been developed in locating water sources in desolate areas. Current technologies allow us not only to locate the water reservoir but also to determine its size, water quality, and the best way to drill and reach it. Researchers in the Department of Atmospheric Sciences at the Hebrew University of Jerusalem developed a unique technology to extract all the potential rain in the clouds mainly by spraying planes with silver iodide.

However, none of these was sufficient to address the water needs of the growing population. A critical crisis was at hand. The level of the Sea of Galilee, over the years, rises in the winter and descends in the summer. The general trend of the water level is characterized by a multiyear decline as a result of years of drought in which more was absorbed than what has remained. The change was the transition from the "upper red line" to the "lower red line" until the water level dropped to a "black line." Every year, the State of Israel drew more water. The same picture was seen in the groundwater, the mountain aquifer, and the coastal aquifer, where the level reached a state lower than sea level, and these penetrated and salted the groundwater. Water quality has also decreased both in the Sea of Galilee and in the groundwater. The saline processes caused damage to agriculture. At the same time, groundwater was polluted from domestic effluents, treated wastewater, pesticides, agricultural fertilizers, landfills, toxic industrial metals, micro-organic pollutants, and so on.

The repercussions of the water crisis on the environment were severe. At the beginning of the twentieth century, Israel had seventy thousand acres of wet habitats (lakes, streams, swamps, and winter pools). Since then, most of the areas have become dry, and in the early 2000s, they were almost completely lost. It was a severe environmental crisis, affecting the variety of animals and plants.

VICTORY OVER THE DESERT

Against this backdrop, it is difficult to find the intensity of the words that will describe the revolution that Israel succeeded in creating with regard to water—from a country in real danger of dwindling water supply to one where there is no shortage of water. Today, water is being returned to nature and aquifers as well as rivers. The humid habitats are being rehabilitated, the agricultural areas and green lungs are expanding, and swimming pools and parks are being built. Saline land and the process of desertification change direction.[123]

Avshalom Felber, CEO of the desalination engineering company IDE, divides the water revolution over fifty years into three subrevolutions: First was the revolution of the effluents of the 1960s. Second was the economic rationalization of water prices, as defined in the mid-1980s, which created a proper economic price for water for the urban consumer and the reduction of water subsidies for agriculture. Third came the desalination revolution of the early twenty-first century.

Felber claims that only because of making water an economic cost came the push to save it. "In countries such as India or China, the price of water is very cheap, and therefore it is a resource that is not being tried to save." Many third-world countries are watering the fields by flooding methods because countries are not trying to raise the price of water. But it happens even in the developed countries; the City Hall of London says that 50 percent of the water is lost in its old pipeline, but there is still no serious treatment in England because the water there is "too cheap." Felber estimates that the increase in water prices in Israel has accelerated the establishment of entire industries that built technologies designed to save water. Examples for this phenomenon are the manufacturers of drippers such as Netafim and NaanDan, and water meter manufacturers such as Arad Technologies, a world leader in the field, Amiad water-filtration solutions, and high-tech companies such as TaKaDu, who are building innovative technologies to detect explosions in pipelines.

Water crises are increasing in the world, and even countries such as the United States, Russia, Australia, and Bulgaria and certainly the Middle East and North Africa are all suffering from a growing water problem, which Israel has dealt with. In Kazakhstan, the area of Aral has dried up, and hundreds of thousands of residents have become refugees. There are those who claim that part of the problem of the refugees in Syria could be solved with several desalination plants and that many of the current refugees in Europe from Africa are actually refugees of water scarcity. Is it Europe's fate?

In Israel, in contrast to other water laws in many parts of the world (for example, contrary to American law), three basic principles were established. According to Israeli law, all water sources are public property; there is no ownership of private water sources, and they are all managed by the state. In comparison, we note that US law states water belongs to the owners of the land, who historically hold the rights to it. As a result of the severe drought of recent years in vast areas in California, the water pumped from the Colorado River to the city of Los Angeles was reduced, since the farmers historically own it, they receive all the water they want. They water their fields by flooding them, which is an extremely wasteful irrigation system due to the evaporation of water. This kind of inefficiency produces absurdity, and Los Angeles city residents pay the price.

Quite impressively, success is reserved for the Ministry of Finance, the government, and the Knesset in Israel for their wise and determined actions to change. The Water Law was amended in 2006 so that the Water Authority was established as a closed economy of NIS 9 billion, which is not subject to the government and the Knesset. The purpose of establishing the Water Authority was to concentrate the administrative and regulatory powers that were represented by many bodies with different interests and goals. The government ministries and public representatives hold decisions that are made at one table and in a majority of opinions, and the government ministries cannot oppose them. A series of decisions and administrative arrangements has changed the course of history, and it has been decided to stop subsidizing the price of water and raising it to its real economic price. In the required investments and the establishment of desalination plants, it was decided to pump water for the rehabilitation of the aquifers and nature reserves and streams. The Water Corporations Law was passed, which took responsibility for municipal water issues from all the local authorities.

Within eleven years, five of the largest seawater desalination plants in the world were built with a total output of about 600 MCM (million cubic meters) of freshwater annually. The first desalination plant was built in 2005 in Ashkelon and supplies 120 MCM a year. In 2007, the Palmachim facility opened with 45 MCM, and two years later the Hadera facility with 145 MCM. In 2013, another 45 MCM were built in Palmachim, and the largest facility of all, of some 150 MCM, opened in Soreq. In 2017, the last facility was inaugurated with a capacity of 100 MCM per year, in Ashdod.[124] These facilities supply some 90 percent of urban water consumption in Israel.

Due to relatively high energy consumption, the costs of seawater desalination are usually higher than the alternatives (pumping freshwater from tunnels or groundwater), but alternatives are not always available, and the rapid depletion of water reservoirs is a critical problem in the world. According to Global Water Intelligence, around 1 percent of the world's population receives desalinated water for its daily needs, but in 2025, the UN expects 14 percent of the world's population to be dependent on desalinated water.

There are close to twenty thousand desalination plants in the world.[125] Soreq is the largest reverse osmosis desalination plant in the world and the second largest in the world in terms of output (the largest is in Saudi Arabia). There is worldwide criticism of desalination plants that result from their high energy consumption, but the Soreq Desalination Plant has the lowest energy consumption in the world for its size.

The desalinated water is of much higher quality than the natural water, both in salinity and in cleanliness. If aquifers have two hundred to three hundred milligrams of chlorine per liter, desalinated water has twenty to forty milligrams of chlorine per liter. Mixing the desalinated water with water from natural sources raises the quality of water in Israel. For example, in Beer Sheva, there were 225 milligrams of chlorine per liter in 2005, and in 2010, the figure dropped to sixty milligrams per liter.[126]

Following the desalination plants, the transportation system in Israel has also been upgraded. The pipeline was expanded so that it could absorb and transfer the new quantities of water, and a water line was constructed from the seawater desalination plants west of Jerusalem in the east.

The return of treated wastewater is another important dramatic achievement in the struggle for water. In addition to the fact that effluents are an important alternative source of water for the water sector, recycling itself has important values, both in sustainable development and in the preservation of nature and the environment of land and sea. Of the approximately 500 MCM of wastewater produced each year in Israel, about 460 MCM are treated each year, and about 425 MCM of effluents are taken annually to agriculture; more than 90 percent of waste water are recycled. This is an extraordinary achievement and is even more striking in view of the fact that Israel is a world leader in this field, while in second place, far behind, Australia has a recycling rate of about 22 percent, followed by Spain with 18 percent and the OECD average of 5 to 15 percent.

"Even California, whose southern part is completely drying up, is returning only 12 percent of the treated wastewater," says Felber. "However, Israel has an advantage because of its small size, there is economic logic in establishing a separate water network for agriculture." It is no wonder that delegations from all over the world come to examine how Israel did this. It should be noted that although the quality of treated wastewater is excellent and can be consumed, it is used only by farmers in Israel. "If in the 1980s, out of 1.7 billion cubic meters, over 1 billion cubic meters of fresh water went to agriculture, today it is only 300 million cubic meters, out of 2.2 billion cubic meters that Israel produces in all," adds Felber.

Mekorot, the government company that handles the issue, has set itself an ambitious goal of reaching full utilization of all the effluents in

Israel and completely stopping the discharge of untapped wastewater. At the same time, in this activity, the sources established professional standards at the international level, which are now used as role models in many countries.

The annual report of Deloitte, in which the countries ranked Israel's water-quality indices, ranked Israel in the water sector in first place with the perfect score of one hundred. The score weighs excellence in the areas of water reclamation, water loss, the national water system, advanced technology, and transportation in the field of desalination.

"We belong to a small group of countries where citizens can open the tap and drink water directly from it, without further purification. We are world leaders in returning water to agriculture; 90 percent of the water for domestic consumption [is] treated and returning back for agriculture of high quality. Our water depreciation is one of the lowest in the world—about 3 percent over twelve thousand kilometers, and we have two national carriers," Shimon Ben-Hamo, former CEO of Mekorot, boasts.[127]

Of course, the greatest advantage of agriculture from the use of effluents is to increase farmers' forecasting ability, since they are no longer dependent on the mercy of the skies. The boy Zeev Lishnitzman will no longer have to pray for rain in order not to be hungry.

PEACE WATER

The year 1998 is remembered by Jordanians as particularly challenging. The severe water pollution crisis that hit Amman, their capital, that year led to a real political crisis. Water supplied from the main treatment facility to domestic consumers fell below the minimum quality standard, and due to the pollution in question, a parliamentary committee of inquiry was established in Jordan, leading to the dismissal of the water minister and the Jordanian prime minister. The government was also replaced by the crisis, and the fear of government instability was heavy.

As part of the 1994 Israel-Jordan peace accords, it was decided to allocate 50 MCM of water to Israel each year (even in years when Israel itself had no surplus of its own). The necessity of ensuring optimal water quality for the Jordanians is clear to the Mekorot Water Company, which transfers water to the neighboring state, following Israel's commitment to the peace agreements. Mekorot decided to take all the necessary measures so that the water transferred to Jordan would be of the highest quality. Since 2016, in order to prevent contact with the ground and the air, Mekorot is building a new pipeline after Israel has committed to transfer another 50 MCM per year to the Hashemite kingdom in addition to a similar quantity currently transferred from the Sea of Galilee. In return, water will be transferred to Israel from the Jordanian desalination plant that will be built in the southern city of Aqaba on the Gulf of Eilat.

The Jordanians will receive drinking water for the northern part of the country, and Israel will receive water for agricultural irrigation in the southern Arava region, which will come from southern Jordan. This is critical for Jordan because following the ongoing civil war in Syria, millions of refugees settled in the north of the country, and water became essential.

As for the PA, until 1967, during the Jordanian period, the ancient aqueducts built during Herod's reign (37 to 4 BCE) and the period of the kingdom of Israel (928 to 722 BCE) were used. The Jordanians also drilled 350 small drills of narrow diameters. In total, the supply stood at 66 MCM per year. Most of this water was used for agriculture, and only four Palestinian cities had running water in their houses.

During the period of the Israeli Civil Administration, prior to the Oslo Accords, the National Water Carrier's arms were built to supply water to the new Israeli settlements, connecting all Palestinian villages and cities on the way to the national water system. Deep-drilled wells were also drilled in order to assist the Palestinian cities. Thus, during this period from 1967 to 1995, Israel increased its water supply to the West Bank from 66 MCM a year, mainly to agriculture, to 118 MCM per year, which were transferred mainly to the cities.

Since the Oslo Accords, there has been a long period of development. Lines and pools were built, and counters were placed on every point of convergence between the Israeli system and the Palestinian system. Many villages and towns were connected to the water system, water distribution networks were built for houses, and the momentum of investment in water development led to an increase in the water supply from 118 MCM per year in 1995 to 180 MCM per year in 2006 and 210 MCM in 2015. Thus, while the Oslo Agreement states that upon the signing of a permanent agreement between the sides, Israel will supply 200 MCM a year to the PA, Israel has already fulfilled its part, although no permanent agreement has been signed.

In addition, in accordance with the Oslo Agreement, a joint committee was established with four subcommittees: a hydrological committee that determines and approves drilling, an engineering committee that determines what to do above the surface (piping, counters, and so on), a sewage committee, and a pricing committee. This committee, as others, is not functioning on the Palestinian side, and the price of water remains as determined by the Oslo Accords and is significantly subsidized by Israel.

The management on the ground by the Palestinians is still very poor. Some of the approved drillings do not work, engineering and hydrological errors occur frequently, and there is technical negligence. At the same time, there are hundreds of pirate drills that have not been approved by the joint committee, which—although the PA claims that it has no responsibility for them—connected them to the electricity grid and thus enabled their activities.

The Joint Committee on Wastewater did not function until 2015 because the Palestinians refused to build any treatment facilities, despite the increase in their population, the substantial international donations they received, and the growing needs of their people. The sewage of the West Bank has become sewage channels; the Nablus River, Hebron, Kelt, Kishon, Alexander, Kidron, and more have become contaminated and are significant health hazards. In the years 1996 to 2002, the donor countries gave the PA more than $500 million for water and sewage projects, of which only $25 million was invested in a sewage treatment facility in Al Bireh and some $32 million at a Jericho purification plant,[128] and plans have been approved in Nablus, Tulkarem, Jenin, Salfit, Ramallah, Kidron, Hebron, and elsewhere. In the past two years, the Israeli government has succeeded in influencing the construction of several sewage facilities in Ramallah, Nablus, and Hebron, but other local authorities still pollute rivers and the surrounding areas.

One of the main problems that prevent any solution is that Palestinian consumers do not pay for the water they receive. The main water meters, located on the same line between Israel and the Palestinians, are paid to Mekorot by the Israeli government, which offsets part of the debt from tariffs collected from the PA. Of course, there is no value for water, and the Palestinians have no incentive to save, neither the people nor their municipalities. The water is wasted, and Palestinian reports speak of more than 33.6 percent of water leaks and waste in cities. Many Palestinian farmers water their fields by flooding, which is the most wasteful irrigation method.

Today, there is no international law on water, especially since in many countries, there are arguments about rivers flowing from country to country or shared water bodies. A proposed international law has not been approved. However, even if there were international law, agreements between states prevail over it, and between Israel and the PA exists the Oslo Agreement, which, as we have noted, was fully filled by Israel.

The draft international law speaks of three criteria: natural indices, that is, the length of the river or coast relative to the countries, historical uses, and alternative sources. The mountain aquifer is the subject of dispute between Israel and the Palestinians. The Palestinians say that the area of Judea and Samaria, where the extraction origin is, determines their right to the mountain aquifer. Israel says that the storage areas and the natural springs are the ones that determine the area, which is mainly in the area west of the Green Line border, just as it exists in many other countries in the world.

The second criterion indicates preference for Israel, both from possession and from historical uses. Israel's possession of the mountain aquifer is from the 1950s. The historical uses also stood at 80 percent Israeli use versus 20 percent Palestinian use. Today, Israel gives 35 percent to the Palestinians and 65 percent to itself.[129]

The third criterion, the most interesting one, speaks of alternative sources faced by the parties. The Palestinians have the eastern mountain aquifer; from it they can produce 70 MCM per year, and it is determined that they are invited to do so. Prevention of leaks in the pipeline can bring them at least another 10 MCM per year, all in areas of demand for water in existing cities and villages. In addition, a more sophisticated irrigation system will provide additional 30–50 MCM per year. An additional 15 MCM per year can come from desalination (to Gaza and northern Samaria). All are waiting for the Palestinians to say the long-awaited "yes" they refuse to say. The PA can double the water supply, without any dependence on Israel, from 200 MCM to almost 400 MCM per year. If only they would want their welfare more than their desire to harm Israel.

―――

Israel's coping with the demand for water has also gone through various technological developments, including the invention of the drip irrigation method by Simcha Blass, which dramatically reduces the amount of water consumed in agriculture. One story is that after examining a row of trees planted at the same time and living under the same conditions, despite the alleged equality of the surroundings, one of them was unusually large. A closer examination showed the reason: tiny holes in the pipe near the tree caused a slow but constant drizzle. Another story relates to a farmer who showed Blass the plants he grows almost without irrigation while digging the pipes near their roots. Whatever the story, the drip method dramatically changed the water consumption of crops while improving their yield.

On the basis of the invention of the dripper, Netafim was founded. In a world where the population is growing, Netafim's vision of growing more crops with fewer inputs such as water, fertilizer, and pesticides seems increasingly critical. Seventy percent of the world's water goes to agriculture, and in developing countries, it's over 80 percent. Only 20 percent of the world's agricultural areas are irrigated; the rest are still dependent on the mercy of the rains. Of the irrigated areas, 80 percent are irrigated with flooding, which, in addition to water waste and crop reduction, also has an adverse effect on greenhouse gas emissions. In an interview with Netafim's CEO, Ran Maidan, he said that the world can be improved by changing the watering methods, such as increasing the amount of water supply by desalinating or recycling wastewater.

"A good dripping system should not be affected by the length of the pipe [the field] or the amount of drips in it or the slope of the field. The flow rate of each drip should be the same, and it doesn't matter if there are different qualities and lower water pressure," he says. "Netafim invests significant R-and-D resources in drip irrigation in order to meet these challenges and to stand at the forefront of drip-irrigation technology, while investing in the pipes themselves so that they are light, thin, and will withstand extreme temperature differentials at times, and they can survive and be useful for ten years and more. We invest significant amounts in remote command and control systems, so that from Israel, for example, we can control the irrigation and fertilization of the orchards in real time in China."

India's prime minister, Narendra Modi, who, in his election victory speech, defined the vision of "more crop per drop" as a national goal, declared that within a few years, all of India's agricultural lands would be irrigated with advanced systems. The goal is food security in India and economic improvement as a result of increasing the number of agricultural cycles from one to three per year.

The same rule applies to China, which invests billions in infrastructure and irrigation systems. The quality of life of farmers in developing countries, especially rural women, who are usually responsible for irrigation, is dramatic. The difference between a woman walking with a hoe to open the flood, pumping water from the stream or well, or even opening the irrigation tap, and the woman who controls the irrigation from her cell phone is significant.

In recent years, there have also been developed detectors that are "sitting" on the roots of plants and are giving orders to the irrigation systems to transfer water only in accordance with the thirst of the plants—a real science fiction.

Netafim Israel, which was born out of the water shortage, has become a world leader in the field. In conclusion, we will quote Seth M. Siegel, a member of the American National Security Council, who wrote in his book,[130] "The Struggle for Every Drop—How the Israeli Experience Rescues the World from Thirst", that Israel holds the key to preventing a crisis that could change the lives of four billion people. Siegel argues that the innovative developments are not only a solution to the global water crisis and have no other alternatives, but they are also a response to attempts to isolate Israel diplomatically. More than 150 countries use technologies born in Israel to save their citizens from thirst. "Water diplomacy," writes Siegel, "opens a new gateway for cooperation, in the face of the campaign of hatred and de-legitimization that Israel faces."

THE SECOND REVOLUTION: ENERGETIC INDEPENDENCE

Israel has been an energy importer since its establishment. Its dependence on external sources of energy was almost complete, mainly for refined products of oil and coal. Although it lies in the heart of one of the world's richest oil and gas regions, its political isolation and many confrontations with the Arab states have prevented it from importing oil or gas from the Gulf states or Saudi Arabia. Israel, therefore, had to import the necessary oil from distant sources for its needs, and the oil was brought by ships sailing in the Mediterranean Sea. This was a serious security and geopolitical problem that the state had to deal with throughout its existence. There was always the fear that when a war broke out in the region, Israel would be isolated. Ships would not be able to reach its ports, and the country would suffer from a shortage of energy that would cause serious economic and social damage to the economy and to the nation's residents.

Both the existing potential in the region and the geopolitical isolation pushed for hectic oil and gas exploration, but until the beginning of the twenty-first century, finding such energy sources in its territory was no more than a dream. Many experts have provided estimates of the feasibility of significant oil and gas reservoirs in one area or another. The Israeli stock exchange has been a conduit for raising funds for drilling, but the result has always been that the well is dry. All this changed in 2000 with the success of the project called Yam Tethys, where the rights holders in the partnership were Noble Energy and a number of Israeli companies. The name of the project was derived from the ancient ocean, which played an important role in the geology and marine environment of the region. As a result of the project, a number of marine gas reservoirs were discovered; the most important of which was the Mary Gas Reservoir, which was discovered thirty kilometers west of Israel's southern coast and estimated at thirty BCM.

Since early 2004, gas became the new energy source for the operation of some of Israel's power stations instead of the oil used in the past. That reduced the number of power plants polluting the air and lowered the cost of electricity generation. The Mary B Gas Reservoir became dry after supplying some twenty-three BCM of gas, equivalent to about 87 percent of the volume of the entire reservoir and similar to the purchase of 142 million barrels of oil. In 2012, it was decided that the gas balance in the reservoir would serve Israel only in emergency situations. It should be noted that due to the strategic significance of the supply of electricity in Israel, most of the Israel Electric Company (IEC) units operating on natural gas are able to use coal, too, for reasons of redundancy and even to operate by fuel oil and diesel oil when necessary.

Another source that was developed was the Arab Gas Pipeline, a land pipeline owned by Egyptian companies that used to export natural gas from Egypt to Jordan, Syria, and Lebanon on a long route that bypasses Israel for political reasons. A small branch of it was built quietly through an underwater pipeline from El-Arish on the northern Sinai coast to the city of Ashkelon in Israel. At the beginning of 2008, the pipeline began to supply the IEC, and after the signing of agreements for the transfer of 7.5 BCM, Israel became one of Egypt's largest export markets, and it became Israel's largest natural gas supplier (about 40 percent of the gas consumed).

In 2010, Egyptian activists claimed that the price of gas sold to Israel was too low, but the Mubarak administration rejected these ideas. After the coup in Egypt in 2011, there was a demand by the Egyptian public to stop the flow of gas to Israel for political reasons. In the following months, dozens of acts of sabotage on the land line crossing the northern Sinai were carried out by terrorist organizations that wanted to harm Israel economically (and in a way that also harmed Egypt) and succeeded in intermittently stopping the flow of gas, which was subsequently halted also to Jordan, Syria, and Lebanon. IEC had to import more fuel oil and coal, which cost billions of dollars more than the company's budget. The IEC was forced to approve a sharp increase in electricity prices, and it cost the Israeli economy billions of dollars in damage. In 2012, the Egyptian company officially announced the unilateral cancellation of the agreement to sell gas to Israel.

ECONOMIC MIRACLE

At the beginning of 2009, the Tamar Gas Reservoir was discovered off the coast of Israel, and at the end of 2010, the Leviathan Reservoir was as well. The Tamar Reservoir contains about 306 BCM and the Leviathan reservoir about 622 BCM, which made it the world's largest natural gas reservoir discovered in deep water in the first decade of the twenty-first century. Additional discoveries of several small reservoirs, such as Karish and Tanin, found accumulated total gas reserves of about 980 BCM, and within a few years, Israel had become owner to 0.5 percent of the world's gas reserves. This may not sound like much, but experts agree that in any calculation of future electricity consumption, these amounts will be enough for Israel for decades to come.

Gas discoveries have dramatically changed the rules of the game: from a country based on energy imports, Israel has quickly become one that is increasingly based on energy from its own resources and can export gas in the future. Finding gas brought another blessing—unlike oil or coal, gas is a relatively clean source of energy.

At the Herzliya Conference in June 2016, Energy Minister Yuval Steinitz said, "According to our estimates and estimates made by the Americans and the European Energy Commission, we have another 2,200 BCM of gas that has yet to be discovered. It's like four other Leviathan reservoirs or eight Tamar reservoirs."

According to various estimates, the state's revenues from the gas reservoirs will amount to approximately $80 billion over the next thirty years as a result of royalties and direct and indirect taxes.[131]

It should be noted that due to the great distance between Israel and large consumers of natural gas, mainly in Europe, it is an "energy island," and it is difficult to import or export natural gas easily. As the distance grows, longer pipes are needed. In discussions held at a ministerial level in September 2016, regarding the export of gas to countries in central and western Europe, Israel, Greece, and Cyprus have developed guidelines on how to promote this common gas pipeline. Large deposits have also been discovered in Cyprus, and Greece is supposed to be the base of the pipeline's entry into Europe. The discussions were important in light of the completion of an economic and engineering feasibility study for the pipeline, financed by the European Union, which is interested in diversifying its gas sources by importing gas from Cyprus and Israel.

But there are also consumers in the region. In September 2016, the Leviathan partnership signed a gas contract with the National Electric Company of Jordan for a period of fifteen years at an estimated value of $10 billion. According to estimates, the basic gas contract will amount to forty-five BCM (about 7 percent of the gas reserves in the Leviathan Reservoir). For this purpose, a pipeline will be built through the Jezreel Valley and the Beit She'an area and will be connected to a pipe belonging to the Jordan Electric Company. The Jordanians estimate that the gas will save them about $600 million a year. The supply of gas is expected to begin with the start of supply from the Leviathan Reservoir and the completion of the systems required for the transmission of natural gas. Additional plans also exist for export to Turkey.

In 2017, 65 percent of Israel's energy consumption comes from its own sources. Over 90 percent of the autonomous sources are based on natural gas from the Tamar Reservoir. IEC provides about 60 percent of Israel's energy consumption and uses gas for about 50 percent of the total power it produces. Private electricity suppliers and large plants use gas to produce electricity for their needs at a rate exceeding 90 percent.[132]

Israel's leaders can start thinking in a different way: from the perspective of a country that is looking to save electricity to one where electricity will be relatively cheap so that its price could encourage the establishment of energy-intensive plants such as petrochemicals and aluminum in the deep, desolate Negev (where there are no urban localities, so pollution is bearable). Israel could thereby turn from a country that imports petrochemical and aluminum products into one that exports them. The Israeli transportation sector will also be able to enjoy this in the future and establish some of the public transit running on gas. In 2020, gas-generation facilities are expected to operate at a total capacity of 13,500 megawatts. Some forty-eight hundred megawatts of coal facilities will still be left.

In this context, it is interesting to note that there has been a halt in the constant increase in demand for electricity in Israel since 2013, and on the other hand, there has been a steady rise in production capacity by private electricity producers.

THE PRICE OF THE BARREL

Israel is in a small group of countries where high oil prices are not only an economic problem but also a geopolitical problem because oil enriches their enemies. (This group includes, for instance, the Eastern European countries threatened by Russia, the gas and oil giant.) Some Arab countries and oil exporters, as well as Iran, have been and still are Israel's adversaries. When we add this to the fact that some of these countries are the largest arms importers in the world who spend a considerable portion of their revenues on the strengthening of their armies, it is clear that Israel would prefer the price of oil to be as low as possible.

Perhaps the reason that oil-producing countries are more paranoid and therefore possess large armies is that they have to protect their rich oil reserves. Libya, where a high percentage of GDP is derived from oil (80 percent), dedicates 8 percent of GDP to defense expenditure; Saudi Arabia, where 45 percent of the product is oil based, devotes 12 percent of its GDP to defense; Iraq, with 42 percent of oil revenues, dedicates to security 5 percent; and Iran devotes the same percentage to security when its revenues from oil are some 26 percent of GDP. For the sake of comparison, the global average is 3 percent of oil revenues in relation to GDP, and global defense expenditure stands at an average of 1.7 percent of GDP.[133]

It is therefore not surprising that the freefall of oil prices from the average $100 level in mid-2014 to which prices have moderated to an average of approximately $50 per barrel since then serves Israel on both economic and geopolitical levels. Israel is not in a direct arms race with Saudi Arabia, but it will not regret if the IMF estimates of the end of October 2015 show that the foreign currency reserves of the world's third-largest oil producer (after the United States and Russia) will fall from $660 billion to zero by 2020 if oil prices remain at these levels. It should be noted that oil producers around the world lost about $360 billion per annum between 2015 to 2017. Even Iran, which has been removed from the sanctions regime and has returned to export oil to Western markets, cannot celebrate due to these historically moderate prices.

Libya and Iraq have other concerns: Libya can no longer be called a state after it has broken apart, and various tribes control its parts and fight among themselves over the oilfields. In Iraq, the situation is unstable. In the north, the Kurds also control the autonomy they have created for themselves and use their revenues to export oil from the region and do not transfer them to the central government in Baghdad. Thus, this dismantled state, which is at the center of a world war between the Sunnis and the Shiites, lost and continues to lose significant oil revenues.

The main reason for the decline in the price of a barrel of oil is the transformation of the United States into being the world's largest energy producer following the oil and gas shale revolution. It is difficult to underestimate the importance of the enormous influence oil producers still have on the foreign policy of their trade partners, including the impact on their voting in UN institutions, when the issue of a resolution concerning Israel arises. The victory of Donald J. Trump in the presidency reinforces US oil and gas producers.

The second part of the equation is related to the improvement in Israel's economic situation as a result of the decline in oil prices. Today, Israel is an importer of oil distillates, mainly for transportation purposes. The Israeli economy is enjoying the new situation immediately when the gas prices at the stations go down, public transportation prices are reduced, and the transport companies save money.

THE ELECTRICITY FLOWS

Israel is an energetic island. Unlike many other countries, there are no power lines between Israel and its neighbors. The purpose of these lines is mainly to support peak hours or malfunctions that can occur in the system. This is a huge challenge for the IEC, which is committed to providing continuous electricity without backing from another country when necessary. Peak electricity consumption in Israel occurred on August 3, 2015, with 12.8 thousand megawatts. However, despite the slight panic the press broadcast, the consumption was far from the production capacity of the IEC and the private production companies, which is estimated at fifteen thousand megawatts.

One must say that the Israeli public is not accustomed to psychological long-term power cuts; randomized power cuts are fixed relatively quickly, usually within hours or, in exceptional cases, within a few days by IEC employees, and the damage caused to the economy is negligible. In any event, there is a steady increase in electricity reserves above the peak demand of some 25 percent.[134] Even when Hamas from the Gaza Strip or Hezbollah in 2006 fired rockets and missiles aiming at power plants, there were no power outages because the power plants and emergency teams were skilled. In any case, since 2011, Iron Dome missile systems have entered the picture and prevented it.

RENEWABLE ENERGIES

David Ben-Gurion, the first prime minister, envisioned renewable energies in 1955: "Our scientists and research should concentrate on new research fields to sweeten the sea with cheap processes, to exploit solar energy in our country, and especially in the Negev, to exploit the force of the winds to create electric power."

"The concept of sustainability, first and foremost the concept of renewable energies, is engraved on the flag of a number of Israeli companies," says Tal Raz, chief financial officer of the Shikun & Binui group, a major player in the field. "We chose to promote an advanced electricity and renewable energy strategy for environmental reasons and the strengthening of the Israeli economy." Various renewable energy projects are scattered throughout the Israeli Negev. "The Ashalim project for the construction of a large solar thermal power station in the Negev, which is currently under construction, is a real fulfillment of Ben-Gurion's vision of the Negev, which will provide 110 megawatts and cost about $1 billion," continues Raz. "The facility is kept at a high international standard in the fields of the environment, protecting employee rights, sharing stakeholders, and creating jobs and economic development for residents of the region."

Upon its accession to the OECD in 2010, Israel undertook that by 2015, at least 5 percent of its total energy sector will be based on renewable energy. In practice, the goal has been achieved later than that. The commitment to the OECD to reach 10 percent by 2020 does not seem realistic. According to Israel Rosen, a senior engineer at GE Israel who manages renewable energy projects, "this is an unattainable goal." It can be explained that the goal will not be achieved by the discovery of gas, which is a relatively clean and cheap source of energy and has cooled the enthusiasm of government officials to invest in renewable energies that are expensive for the Israeli consumer.

SOLAR ENERGY

Most of the electricity in Israel that comes from renewable sources is produced by solar energy.[135] These are photovoltaic power producers, and as of 2017, production reaches some six hundred megawatts in the peak of summer demand. About twenty-five fields provide solar energy, from a few megawatts in the small fields to tens of megawatts in the large fields. Energy production varies according to the intensity of the sun's radiation during the day and the seasons and is affected by clouds, haze, and other disturbances. The location of the fields in the Negev, "the land of the eternal sun," enables them to supply high yields, even in the winter. The tariff for solar fields is subsidized when there is an obligation to purchase electricity produced from these fields at a certain rate. The subsidy rate is gradually declining over the years as the prices of solar panels worldwide and the cost of installation decrease.

There is no Israeli who does not know the "solar boiler" on the roof of almost every house. These thermosiphon systems are Israeli patents, which heat water to high temperatures with the help of the sun's rays in a way that saves large amounts of electricity and energy. As early as the 1970s, Israel was the country that, more than any other country, took advantage of solar energy, thanks to binding legislation to install solar water heaters on the roof of every new apartment. The legislation took place in 1976 as a result of the energy crisis following the Arab oil embargo. This is an interesting Israeli example of the consequences of necessity. According to data from the Knesset Research and Information Center, in 2012, solar water heaters were placed in 85 percent of all households in Israel, and these resulted in about 80 percent savings in electricity consumption in homes and about 4 percent of electricity consumption in general.

———

Even before the world thought of solar energy, it was Dr. Harry Zvi Tabor who developed the field in the 1950s and was the pioneer of solar energy utilization in Israel. Internationally recognized for his research and applications, he developed a black coating for solar absorption and emission prevention in 1955, which was responsible for the first breakthrough in solar technology in Israel: the development of the selective surface that significantly improved the efficiency of solar energy absorption (compared to the less-efficient mirror technology). This made Israel a global leader in solar technologies and has allowed widespread use of solar water heaters in the Mediterranean, Australia, and many other countries, which has led to a reduction in air pollution and reduced political and economic dependence on oil. It is estimated that from the beginning of the century, China has spread nearly one hundred million solar heaters and India about thirty million, especially in sunny areas in these countries.

THE THIRD REVOLUTION: INFRASTRUCTURE AND TRANSPORTATION

Many economic studies provide clear evidence that investment in infrastructure brings about long-term growth. Infrastructure projects in general—electricity, roads, ports and airports, water systems, and telecommunications—are the foundations of modern economics. They have a multiplier effect because every dollar spent on infrastructure leads to more than one dollar in future revenue. When building a power plant, for example, the idea is not only to create employment through construction activity at the power station but also to create an industrial base around the station for anyone who wants to take advantage of energy and that future revenues will be higher than the total expenditure at source. One must emphasize at this point that the multiplier effect of investment in infrastructure is higher in developing economies than in developed economies.

Israel promotes infrastructure projects of all types, from the installation and improvement of water and sewage systems through the diversification of electricity sources, the addition of telecommunications infrastructure, and the addition of railways and roads to an additional airport and two additional seaports. The sums invested are tens of billions of shekels a year every year. Since it happens all the time and for a long time, the endless construction around it is seen as a normal phenomenon to every Israeli. But this is a revolution that will move Israel forward economically and build infrastructures that will serve a country of 11.5 million residents in 2035 (compared with 8.75 million in 2017).[136]

In the subsection "Victory over the Desert," we showed the return on investment in water infrastructure: desalination and recycling. In the energy chapter, we have shown the return on investment in these areas, but there are other areas of investment, the main one being that in transportation infrastructure.

Transportation infrastructures in the State of Israel are in the midst of a revolution, but as of the date of writing this book, they are still lagging behind international needs and comparisons. This disadvantage exists in land, sea, and air transport. Its treatment, which began in recent years, will bring great value to the economy.

LAND TRANSPORT

Israel is a long, narrow country with a large (too large) part of the economic activity in one city—Tel Aviv. Entry and exit to and from there are problematic. The huge volume of new car purchases in Israel, many of them by cheap credit, cause endless bottlenecks, despite the tremendous contribution of the Waze application. The development of road and rail infrastructure is a harbinger of growth and increase in the standard of living, and it enables transportation of people and, to a large extent, happiness resulting from the sense of freedom.

Adding an additional route to the road is supposed to bring workers to their jobs faster, saving them time. Already, many researchers disagree: there are studies that have not necessarily found a link to growth in modern economies, especially in terms of road and rail infrastructure.[137] In most modern countries, much of this infrastructure already exists, and the huge financial investments in multiplying and tripling transport routes do not provide the expected growth.

In recent years, investments in roads have reached a high volume compared with the rest of the world, focusing on the addition of interchanges and improvement of the existing infrastructure. This contributes both to the comfort and speed of travel and to the decrease in the number of road accidents.[138] An analysis of trends in investment in road infrastructure shows that in recent years, with a decline in investment in the central region, emphasis has been placed on the periphery, with an increase in investments to the south and to greater Jerusalem as well as to Haifa and the northern regions. Still, this expansion is not enough in light of the steady increase in the purchase of private cars.

The solution to this problem is to increase public transportation, but from 2000 to 2014, the rate traveled by private vehicles increased by about 4 percent per year, while the volume of public transport—the number of seats on fixed bus lines and the number of buses and their kilometers traveled—rose by only 2 percent. The rate is similar to the increase in the rate of increase in the number of persons aged fifteen and over—the main consumers of public transportation. However, these characteristics began to improve in the last three years.

As for trains, the length of the tracks relative to the territory of the state is slightly below the distribution centers in OECD countries. The level of investment increased since the 1990s, and with it, the use of the train also increased. However, the railway network is still relatively small, and Israel is below the median of the developed countries in terms of the ratio between using the train and traveling on the roads. In the field of railways, as in all areas of mass transport, there are significant advantages to the network, and therefore, additional investments may be of greater marginal benefit.

For many years, there was criticism of meeting the railroad schedule, a justified argument for the time. Today, it is less prevalent. It turns out that Israel Railways has significantly improved its performance in meeting timetables and has subordinated itself to the accepted standards in developed countries. Between 2005 and 2015, despite doubling the number of trips by passengers on trains from twenty-seven to fifty-three million, the accuracy of the arrival of trains, as measured by international parameters, increased from 83.8 percent to 95.4 percent, one of the highest in the world and comparable to the level of precision measured in Switzerland and Germany.[139]

The railway also contributes to the transport revolution, says Husam Bishara, the chairman of the railway, adding that the train has shortened travel times and increased the frequency and accuracy of trains in recent years and that the number of passengers is expected to double by 2020, reaching about eighty million a year. Improving railway service, Bishara says, is based on streamlining work methods, important developments in the functioning of the workers' committee, concentration of trains and locomotives, and especially the assimilation of new technologies in general and control in particular.

METROPOLITAN TRANSPORTATION

In spite of the grandiose plans, mass transportation is still lacking, especially in some of the metropolitan areas. In a study that assessed the level of public transport, the use of public transport was examined in forty-one metropolitan areas in twenty-three OECD countries.[140] It was found that the use of public transport in two of the metropolitan areas in Israel—Tel Aviv and Beer Sheva—is far from the level customary in the OECD countries.

Among the amendments that Israel has made in recent years to deal with the issue of transportation in metropolitan areas are the Metronit in Haifa, the light railway in Jerusalem, and the light railway under construction in Tel Aviv.

One of two revolutions in transportation is cycling. Slowly, the urban roads are filled with bicycles, and unique paths are built; they are a safe and friendly way to reach the centers of employment, recreation, and residence in the metropolis.

The joint shuttles are in early development, with regulatory barriers going on, while more and more technologies are being implemented.

MARINE TRANSPORTATION

Modern shipping and ports are an important part of a country's trading life and a necessary existential condition. The efficiency of the ports depends directly on the level of the land infrastructure: roads, railways, and storage warehouses for goods reaching the ports and the quality of the communications and logistics involved in their operation. Only a country with advanced land transport and infrastructure enables the existence of efficient and modern ports.

The movement of passengers from and to Israel by water transport is considered thin in international terms. The port's importance is related to the fact that approximately 99 percent of the goods are imported and exported through Israel's seaports:[141] about seventy million tons a year, of which twenty-seven million tons are fuel and coal (most of them through the two Hadera and Ashkelon energy ports) and Eilat. The volume of foreign trade in Israeli goods is estimated at $130 billion in 2015, of which about $70 billion imported and about $60 billion exported.

"The vision is that Israel will be a hub, a regional center that will serve as a port to other destinations. This will bring a lot of value to Israel's globalization, to its status in the region, to places of employment, and to Israel's soil," says Isaac Blumenthal, CEO of Ashdod Port, adding that he is committed to the long-term vision of the State of Israel. "My commitment as CEO of the port fits in with my civic commitment."

In order to increase competition in the two ports, the government decided to establish a southern port, which would compete with the port of Ashdod, and the Bay Port, competing with Haifa Port. This reform is progressing in full swing, and the work is underway in Ashdod by the Chinese company China Harbor, and the tender was won by the Dutch company TIL. In Haifa, there is a joint group of Shafir Engineering and

Ashtrom, and the operating tender was won by the Chinese company SIPG. Expected operating date for the ports is 2021.

AIR TRANSPORTATION

The Ben-Gurion Airport 2000 project has changed the ability to handle the entry and exit of passengers from Israel's main and almost exclusive airport in order to further improve these capabilities. The Ilan and Assaf Ramon Airport will serve as a secondary port for Ben-Gurion International Airport in 2018. The field will be used for domestic and international flights and will enable large jet aircraft to take off, mainly for flights to and from Europe, but also for flights to more distant destinations such as the United States and the Far East. The field was built with green perceptions. For example, it was decided that a compound will be built for decorative purposes in the heart of the terminal in a kind of patio, and it will have cooling systems that will enable the accumulation of water that will condense from the cooling air. The development of the environmental landscape will be based on local desert vegetation that does not require multiple irrigation.

The three revolutions on the way, demography, energy, and transportation, have not yet exhausted their full effectiveness, and there is a point in continuing to empower them. The same is true for projects that have already been launched and are being conducted with full vigor and for those that are still shuffling. There is no doubt that as soon as the encounter between the relative advantages and the emerging revolutions is created, the situation of the Israeli society and economy will be much better than the already existing good situation.

XIV
Challenges—There Is Plenty More to Do

Grumbling but Advancing

"Satisfaction with the current situation does not allow for change," quotes Eli Assraf, former CFO of Makhteshim Agan and currently entrepreneur and director, from the words of Prof. Michael E. Porter, who is renowned for his research on the competitive edge of companies and countries. "Dissatisfaction is a driving force, smugness—paralyzing."

This perception is one of the national traits of the Israelis, who express their dissatisfaction with the current situation and are moving forward with impressive strength the Israeli economy and society.

Businesses are not satisfied with the world; they want growth and improvement of the bottom line. The media is not satisfied; it wants more discoveries and more exposures and influence. The workers are not satisfied; they want to raise wages and improve their working conditions. Unhappy parents want their children to be the best. The Israelis want better treatment in hospitals and they want the food to taste better and be healthier and they want the Internet to be faster. We want the leaders to be honest and smart and strong and more attentive.

The aspiration for excellence has a reward, but it also has a price. A society that is not satisfied is a society that progresses and achieves; on the other hand, it is also a persecuted society that blackens the gray and defines itself as a corrupt state whenever a politician is thrown to prison, and it is one that people must emigrate from and live elsewhere and better. This is a mood prevalent among the Israeli public, and everyone is aware of it and feels it.

Eli Assraf's father used to say, "Look back proudly, and look forward intently." The alertness is what will improve things. Pride is the one thing that will give you the knowledge that you are capable of achieving the best.

An elder from one of the kibbutzim, on a trip to England, was thrilled by the green, soft, and well-kept lawn of one of the queen's palaces. When he asked the royal gardener what the secret was, the gardener replied, "I water, fertilize, and mow."

"I do that too, but your lawn looks better, much better," said the kibbutznik.

"How many years have you been doing this?" the British man asked.

"Forty," replied the Israeli.

"We've been doing this for four hundred years," he told him.

This story illustrates the Israeli approach, which demands results of excellence in a very short time without distinguishing between the areas in which it is possible and those in which time has meaning.

Israel's demand for immediate excellent statehood can be demonstrated in the context of its membership in the OECD. In 2010, Israel was accepted into a club of the world's top thirty countries. Its comparative results relative to other countries place it in the middle for the most part, in some areas slightly higher and others slightly below the middle. Its results are certainly reasonable—but not in the eyes of the Israelis. They are insulted to the depths of their souls every time comparative data are published according to which Israel is not among the top three. Israel is ranked high in the various fields that express growth, but these figures do not compensate for the terrible insult Israelis feel against the less favorable figures. Israelis do not want to be average. They strive to be the best—in every field and immediately.

There is no doubt that this is a praiseworthy feature of achievement. It is also burdensome, oppressive, and can discourage. Balance, perspective, coolness, and patience are what Israelis should practice. They may not be as good as they wanted to be, but they are much better than they think.

ETHICAL CHALLENGES

The fact that in Israel everyone is justiciable, there are no sacred cows, and no one is immune to the law is a tremendous strength, even if it sometimes seems to be a problem for the Israeli public. The Israelis are not more corrupt than everyone else, nor are they more righteous than others. They have the wisdom and maturity as well as the public power to deal with it.

Many economists believe that trust is the factor that explains the gap between poor and rich countries, writes *Forbes*.[142] This approach is also held by Steve Knack, chief economist of the World Bank, who has been researching the issue for over a decade. The economic value of trust includes many elements, from direct security to physical and digital and to improving the functioning of government systems, but trust is what makes it possible to do business, and businesses create wealth. Trust is what allows us all to give credit card numbers to strangers as well as to invest in businesses we have never seen and sign contracts with people and partners in distant lands. The personal trust in one another and the trust of everyone in the system, both local and international, are intertwined to bring economic value to all.

Prof. Dan Ariely, a behavioral economics researcher, says in his book[143] that he became interested in the subject of cheating in 2002, a few months after Enron collapsed. We all cheat but not to the extent that it weighs too much on our consciences and on our image, in our own eyes as moral and decent people, Ariely says. This is especially true of creative people who have the ability not only to find innovative solutions to difficult problems but also to bypass laws and interpret information in a way that will serve our interests. According to him, the combination of the positive and desirable aspect of creativity on one hand and the dark side of creativity on the other is pushing us into a problematic corner. Ariely also claims that people tend to believe that their country is far more deceitful than other countries. "Because I grew up in Israel, I was particularly intrigued to see how many Israelis are cheating, compared to other places in the world. (I admit that before I did the experiment, I thought the Israelis would cheat more than the Americans.) But it turns out that I was wrong—our Israeli participants cheated just like the Americans, Turks, Canadians, and Englishmen."

As far as corruption is concerned, from the publication of the International Transparency Organization from January 2017, Israel is ranked twenty-eighth, with the OECD average twenty-second out of the thirty-four developed countries.[144] From the Israelis' point of view, it is not good enough, and there is definitely more to improve.

CULTURE AND DISCUSSION

In-depth public discussion, as well as intersectional meetings, are critical to the success and prosperity of Israeli society and economy. Maintaining respect for the debate and reducing aggression, populism, and McCarthyism[145]—are a significant challenge.

Yossi Shain, a political scientist at Tel Aviv University and Georgetown University in Washington, argues[146] that in Israel, "the language of corruption" has become a tool in cultural struggles on religious and ethnic grounds. "The culture of political admonishment in Israel has gone out of control," writes Shain. In Israel, the obsession with corruption breached the limits of criticism necessary to preserve the foundations of democracy, and it impairs the brakes and balances needed to manage the affairs of the state and the economy. Among the "moral agents" who profit from the widespread discourse of corruption, Shain described the "arrogant bureaucratics" and the anticorruption organizations in Israel. Shain says the rhetoric of the fight against corruption is disseminated and nurtured not only by investigative journalists and by headline hunters who rely on scandals but also by senior journalists, legal commentators, and columnists from the mainstream. It must be remembered that in every organization against something, there is a built-in need for something to exist and even to be strengthened. This is an engrained absurdity. What is the need for a union that fights against something if that something is marginal or disappearing?

As a result, Israelis live in a populist and violent society in which there is quick judgment of public figures in the media, even before the court decides whether they are indeed to blame.

POVERTY AND SOCIAL GAPS

Inequality in Israel is much higher than its residents can bear. It is very high compared to the OECD average. Add to this the dimensions of poverty and the intensity of social gaps, and an unacceptable social picture materializes in front the eyes of the Israeli society, which requires a high level of social fairness. After all, this is the country that invented the kibbutzim—the most interesting experiment that was created in the areas of equality, classes, and individual solidarity.

The reasons for inequality are mainly gaps in participation and accessibility to work as well as gaps in the level of education in general and relevant vocational education. In a different section of this book, we referred to the nature, characteristics, and components of poverty in the population and the cycle of poverty to which generation after generation has been enslaved without being able to extricate itself.

———

In 2010, the government of Israel set employment targets for 2020 for the entire population, detailing the goals for special populations (ultra-Orthodox and Arab). The motivation for this is based both on the goals of increasing the GDP and the overall standard of living and on reducing poverty and narrowing the gaps. The employment of these populations is still far from fulfilling its potential. There is no doubt that the more ultra-Orthodox Jews and Israeli Arabs will join the labor market, the more we will witness a reduction in income gaps, which is an important economic, social, and moral challenge. The increase in participation in the labor force of weakened and disconnected populations, which increase within a developed and educated environment, will bear fruit beyond the existing conditions in the other OECD countries. For this to be fruitful, Israel began a government policy that has a broad public consensus. This plan is helped by the business sector, targeting education and increasing employment of these sectors.

The challenges of education are the key to social mobility on one hand and the preservation of Israel's relative advantage in the world on the other. The state must continue to invest in nurturing educational excellence in the center as well as in the geographic and social periphery. The indicator must be the ability of each child to utilize his or her skills, regardless of age, religion, sex, or geographical location.

The challenge of equality also requires attention to equal pay for women and appropriate representation of them in positions of power. Beyond being a value-based violation, the gap between men and women is a burden on society and the economy in Israel.

———

According to the *Gini Index*, an important measure of inequality in income distribution, the situation is improving. When measuring inequality in economic income, which measures monetary income and nonmonetary income (income deriving from self-use in an apartment), inequality in Israel is constantly improving, from 51.5 percent in 2000 to 47.2 percent in 2015.[147] Again we have to remember: the trend is important.

STRUCTURAL CHALLENGES

Employment costs in the business sector in Israel are high in international comparisons with competing countries. The cost of programmers, engineers, production workers, economists, accountants, and other middle-class workers is similar to that in France and Japan and about 85 percent of the standard wage in the United States and Germany in parallel professions.

On the other hand, the gross wage is relatively low. The difference between the employers' costs and the employees' salaries stems from high pension payments, which are paid by the state, health insurance and national insurance, holiday gifts, corporate events, summer camps for children of workers, car expenses resulting from continuing difficulties in effective public transportation, and other expenses that are the result of encouragement of the Histadrut labor federation, which benefits the strong workers instead of protecting the weak.

Thus, despite the high costs of employment to the business sector, the net wage for workers is relatively low. This difficult equation is compounded by the high cost of living, which is also the result of heavy legislation on businesses. Retail prices are high despite the fact that the marketing networks are barely making a profit, and producers are slowly becoming importers because of the high production costs. Training, municipal taxes, labor and rest law, restitution, guarding— all these factors cause a very expensive consumer basket and expensive prices for food and housing.

The State of Israel has indulged in taxes on apartments, cars, and fuel. Thirty percent of the cost of a new apartment is taxation, and 50 percent of buying a car or fueling it is taxation. Some 65 percent of Israeli workers do not pay income tax imposed mainly on middle- and high-income earners.

The high cost of living in Israel, according to the OECD report for 2016, stems from the control of monopolies or oligopolies in many sectors, the most important of which are the food, banking, electricity, gas, railway, and ports industries. Many are handled by the government or are under its close supervision. Of the aforementioned branches, the vast majority are dominated by strong workers' committees, managed by the Histadrut labor federation, which maintains a strict protectionist policy against the consumers.

The report also refers to the high costs of kosher food and argues that there are more efficient ways to enforce kashrut (kosher) laws so that food prices can fall.

Another problem is the decline in the number of workers in the traditional industry who find it difficult to cope with cheap imports from abroad. "The food industry is an excellent example of a traditional, profitable industry with technology and efficiency," says Harel Beit-On, a managing partner of the Viola Group. "If the plant has a sufficient domestic market and can be profitable, why should not it benefit from capital investment? For some reason, all the programs for government encouragement for investments are in the direction of technology and exports, as if the country does not have foreign currency."

Eli Assraf adds some critical challenges such as the huge gap between the center and the geographic-social periphery in Israel, the government monopolies, the unbalanced power of the security establishment, and the norms that fall in the public and business sectors. "I am optimistic that these issues can be dealt with; it is imperative to deal with these issues," says Assraf.

———

Regulation and bureaucracy have hurt, on a daily basis, the efficiency of doing business in Israel. A study by the OECD found that the legal barriers to business entry compare with the most daunting barriers among the organization's members. Other comparative studies show that an anti-competitive regime tends to impair the adoption of international improvements that increase labor productivity.

For example, the Ministry of Economy has initiated a move that will enable companies to employ foreign experts—whose salaries are at least two and a half times the average salary—when they need their special expertise. The cumbersome regulation of the Immigration Authority prevents its implementation without the Ministry of Economy being aware of the obstacles that have been blocked on its good intentions.

A well-known example that the state comptroller has drawn public attention to is the enormous difficulty in connecting the gas infrastructure to small and medium enterprises,[148] the result of regulation and bureaucracy created by officials.

The barriers to entry and exit of businesses in Israel are among the highest in the OECD. They prevent proper allocation of resources in the economy and make it difficult for successful companies to grow, and make it hard for failing businesses to clear space for new and fruitful companies. In seven out of the eleven indices examined, Israel is in the top three.[149]

REAL ESTATE PRICES

Israel is a relatively small country, similar to OECD countries like Belgium and the Netherlands. The trends of demographic growth will make it, within a few decades, the most crowded. Most of the construction takes place in the central region, as the majority of the population wants to live near the main employment areas. One of the main components of the cost of living in Israel is the price of housing. The fact that an Israeli has to pay an average of 140 salaries to buy housing for his family in comparison to less than ninety average salaries in the OECD is intolerable. Endless studies have been conducted on the subject, countless programs have been formulated, and the problem is far from being resolved. Among the important factors contributing to this situation are the low interest rate that reduces the return received from investments in other channels, the high taxation on apartments, which the state does not want to lose, the constant increase in population size, and the high land costs demanded by the Israel Land Administration.

REGULATION, BUREAUCRACY, AND ENFORCEMENT

Inefficient regulation and cumbersome bureaucracy are two of the main factors in the cost of living and housing in Israel. The government ministries and the Knesset have well-intentioned people who lack contact with the market, sometimes shoot in the dark at unidentified targets, and achieve the opposite of their goals. For example, when the price-marking law, whose meaning was undoubtedly good, was passed on products, it raised the cost of living in Israel.[150] Another example is the law that re-quires a lifeguard in every hotel pool, regardless of the size of the hotel and contrary to what is customary in European countries. An important law for saving lives or another component of the cost of living in Israel? This explains, among other things, the high cost of hotels in Israel compared to their competitors in the world. "The main point is that the State of Israel has very heavy regulation over hotels that does not exist in Germany," said Noaz Bar-Nir[151] during his tenure as director general of the Tourism Ministry. "We have about 20 percent more costs only because of govern-ment regulations, security guards, and lifeguards. Go to hotels in Berlin; there is a pool and no lifeguard. I do not say that you do not need to have a lifeguard, but when there is no pressure on the pool and there is not a lot of tourism, you do not always need a lifeguard, and the hotels have to make the decision."

This is the result of a crisis of confidence in the possibility of con-structive discussions that are free of all corrupt intentions between the business sector and the government. The ineffective regulation resulting from this, as well as the growing paternalism of the regulators over the seemingly small consumers and employees themselves, is a major problem.

———

The OECD report for 2016[152] states that among all OECD countries, Israel is in first place in the severity of regulation in the product market.

Members of Knesset throughout the generations like to legislate laws. In order to comply with these rules, the officials like to make a lot of regulations. No wonder countless laws and regulations are superfluous. Israel suffers from too many laws and regulations, and as a result, there is a need for battalions of inspectors and policemen to enforce them all. On the other hand is the public's disdain for regulations, enforcement ability, and its necessity in general.

THE SECURITY BURDEN

The security burden, despite its many years of contraction and the tremendous socioeconomic value of the military, still weighs heavily on the state budget. In recent years, the discussion on the size of the defense budget, which stands at approximately 4.5 percent of GDP, has been overshadowed by the broad public exposure to the issue. About a quarter of the defense budget goes to retirees and pensioners, rehabilitation of the disabled, and payments to the families of the fallen. The Ministry of Finance claims that "the defense budget is too large for the economy," while the heads of the defense establishment claim that the budget is too small to be able to cope successfully with Israel's security needs.

The defense expenditure,[153] in the overall calculation of the IDF, the Shabak (*Shin Bet*, General Security Services), the Mossad, and others, stood at some NIS 55 billion in 2017, which is some 4.4 percent per GDP. Defense consumption has increased in real terms in some of the last few years, despite the increase in the public's awareness of social needs. The main reason for this was Operation Protective Edge and the uncertainty regarding the direction of the unstable Middle East. In addition, there is potential for friction with the PA. In such an unstable system, it is necessary to maintain high security margins.

The level of defense expenditure maintained its real value in the last five years, about NIS 7,000 per capita. The percentage of Israel's defense expenditure, relative to the GDP,[154] was the lowest in its history, "from the lowest to the lowest—the broad spectrum that the IDF has to contend with," said the head of the planning department, Colonel Eyal Harel, the IDF's streamlining program at the CFO Forum in Eilat in the summer of 2016. The IDF's diverse defenses at this time include protecting Israel's economic waters and its gas wells, cyber warfare, and a line of defense against the spillover of the wars of the Middle East.

The IDF's multiyear plan, called Gideon, which was declared by the Chief of General Staff, Lt. Gen. Gadi Eisenkot in July 2015, presents a revolution, first and foremost, with its very existence, as well as its priorities. From an initial focus on equipping, it turned to a focus on training, and nurturing the human resource. The name chosen for the program, Gideon, is thought-provoking. Gideon is the name of the Israeli general from the Bible who fought against the Midianites, a period of struggle between the permanent inhabitants of Canaan (the Israelites) and the nomads, (the Midianites), who carried out raids of terror and looting. Gideon sought to recruit some thirty-two thousand fighters initially; then the number went down to ten thousand and finally to only three hundred. Finally, the success in combat was a result of the proper classification of those three hundred. Similarly, the current Gideon multiyear plan handles budget cuts while streamlining orders, flattening the organization, merging units, and increasing the use of outsourcing. "The IDF has defined itself as a vision of a quality military, young and dynamic, as well as proud, ethical, and effective," concluded Col. Harel.

Israel was born out of a historical rift between the weakened Ottoman Empire and the British Empire that wanted to replace it. The two empires that replaced the British, the Russians and the Americans, saw Israel as a way to broaden their influence: the Russians hoped to do so because of the sociocommunist orientation of the founders of the state and the Americans because of the large Jewish minority in the United States that they hoped would influence Israel.

In the emerging confrontation between the weakening United States and the growing Russia, Prof. David Passig argues that Israel will once again be a plaything between the superpowers and that after the growth of regional powers, Iran and Turkey, they are expected to have another clash over spheres of influence.

"The past has already proved[155] that Israel has a strong enough force to deal with threats from the peoples of the region, but because of its smallness, it cannot cope with world powers," says Passig. "The second threat, it needs clever diplomacy—which is a major challenge to Israel's existence."

BOYCOTTS AND BOYCOTTERS

In recent years, Israeli diplomacy has faced a new challenge: the proliferation of anti-Israeli or anti-Zionist anti-Semitism. The idea of the beginning of Zionism, according to which the Jewish state would be like all other nations and, with its establishment, would cease to be under anti-Semitic attacks, turned out to be an overly optimistic thought. The Jewish state undertook being the flagship of the Jewish people. Israel's central vision of a refuge for all persecuted Jews in the world has become the object of accusations, envy, and demonization from some of the world's nations. Anti-Semitism did not disappear from the world. The memory of the Holocaust did not destroy it, and it flourishes with the enthusiastic encouragement and funding of the Arab countries[156] and is supported by some European countries. "Anti-Semitism is the projection of the fears of people and religions about the Jew, stemming from the Jew's ability to change, to wear local national belonging without harming his Jewish identity," says A. B. Yehoshua.[157]

Against this backdrop, the strength and success of the State of Israel, despite all the difficulties it faces, is perceived as mysterious and is believed to rely on a hidden and threatening Jewish force. This fear links anti-Semitism to anti-Israelism and anti-Zionism, which nurture one another.

For example, a 2012 Anti-Defamation League survey found that large sectors of Europe believe that Jews have too much power in the business world and that they are more loyal to Israel than to the countries in which they live.

The strength of the Jews, at its core, stems from their national-territorial weakness. This weakness provided adaptability, and it helped them to spread the risks. It was not Sabbath that kept Israel but the fact that they kept the Sabbath in hundreds of communities around the world.

Anti-Semitism is the fear of this weakness-power, which is perceived as a Hydra with a thousand heads.

If so, what is the need for the Jews in the existence of the State of Israel? Does it weaken this power that has been proven throughout history? The history of the Jewish people throughout the generations proves that whenever Jews felt safe and protected, whether by a kingdom, special territories, or a state, there was growth and prosperity in Jewish demography, and Israel was a key factor in the growth of the Jewish people.

As of 2017, 165 countries recognize Israel and maintain diplomatic relations with it. Thirty-five countries do not have diplomatic relations or, even worse, do not recognize Israel, most of them Muslim nations. Despite the relatively large list of countries that do not recognize it, this is a very good political situation compared to what Israel was accustomed to in the past.

Boycotts of Israel are nothing new. They are not the result of the "occupation" of the territories. It is a fact that even in 1945, an official Arab boycott was imposed by the Arab League for what was not even the State of Israel, which was only established in 1948. It was declared that "the production of Jews and Jewish products from Palestine is unwelcomed in the Arab countries" and called on Arab associations to refuse to buy, in any form, any kind of Zionist production. With the establishment of the state, the boycott was expanded and, in fact, on a number of levels, when even third parties who had business relations with Israel were boycotted. There is no doubt that the boycott has harmed Israel, but it is also clear that the it did not succeed in harming the country at the level planned by the Arab League.

From the beginning of the 1970s, with the strengthening of socialism and anticolonial, anti-imperialist, and anti-Western movements in Latin America and the Middle East, the leftist movements joined the Islamic movements, in cooperation with the Soviet Union, against the West and adopted Israel as a symbol of all this. During this period, Israel became more and more isolated from the Latin world and the Soviet Axis countries and their satellites (including China and India) and became the punching bag of the leftist movements in most countries of the world.

The boycott and the great harm it caused to Israel as well as to many other countries in the world was during the oil embargo that took place during the global energy crisis in October 1973. The official aim of the boycott was to pressure Western countries not to support the Israeli side in the Yom Kippur War. This was an opportunity for the OPEC countries, most of them Muslim, to raise the price of oil aggressively because they believed it was too low for them. The boycott was effective for two main reasons: the industrialized countries became almost completely dependent on oil, and even the oil reserves in the United States were dwindling, and Israel became an importer of oil.

From the political point of view, the oil embargo has partially achieved its goals: countries that were considered neutral on the Arab-Israeli conflict began to adopt a clearly pro-Arab view, such as Japan, Canada, and Western European countries, while the United States continued to back Israel and supplied it with arms during and after the 1973 war.

The results of the boycott were also felt many years later, when many multinationals were afraid to operate in Israel. But just as nature does not tolerate a vacuum, so did the Israeli economy: Pepsi-Cola refused to enter, but Coca-Cola entered and eventually pulled Pepsi in after it. Japan's Mitsubishi and Toyota did not agree to export cars to Israel, but the Japanese Subaru agreed, as did all the European automakers, and finally brought Mitsubishi and Toyota into their wake. More and more, it has been proven that the multinational companies do not want to and cannot boycott Israel.[158]

In the 1980s and until the early 1990s, there was a trend of loosening of the Arab boycott, mainly in light of the signing of peace agreements with Egypt in 1979 and later with Jordan in 1994. As of 2017, there are even commercial companies in Muslim countries that do not have diplomatic relations with Israel, but they indirectly buy Israeli goods and services while turning a blind eye to the authorities.

The state has learned to live with economic boycotts over the years out of lack of choice. Often, boycotts have spurred the Israeli economy to operate in areas and places where the boycott effect does not touch. As the Israeli defense industry, for understandable reasons, is unfamiliar to the Arab countries, many Israeli companies have found and developed new and additional markets and ignored Arab markets that may be close to them. But countries that do not recognize the State of Israel are a fait accompli, and the Israelis have nothing to do in this matter.

What about organizations that were established specifically with the aim of exerting pressure on Israel through boycotts? The BDS movement,[159] for example? If you ask the average Israeli, who feeds on the newspapers, he will surely tell you that the boycott of the BDS does hurt the Israeli economy. But it turns out that reality is very far from that. Contrary to what is reported in the press, the real economic impact of the BDS organization and its like is entirely marginal. Perhaps the most interesting example of this lack of success is Israel's extensive trade with Turkey. In 2010, following the military conflict between Israel and the Gaza Strip, Turkish president Erdoğan, who, in many ways, led the wave of countries screaming against Israeli policy, demanded that his people and other countries stop economic ties with Israel. In practice, despite these boycotts, trade between the two countries increased almost 50 percent in five years from $3.1 billion in 2010 to $4.5 billion in 2015. In an article published in Bloomberg in June 2016, the authors have shown that between the time the BDS boycott was established in 2005 and the end of 2015, foreign investment in Israel has tripled, and foreign holdings in shares of major Israeli companies marked by the BDS have increased significantly.

The struggle against the boycott takes interesting forms and, for example, mobilizes the support of Israel's supporters in the American Congress. A member of the House of Representatives, Republican Peter Roskam, first promoted the initiative to wage a war against boycotters of Israel, and he raised a bill on the matter.[160] Congress further passed the law that boycotts, denunciations, and sanctions on Israel by governments, government bodies, and international organizations are contrary to the principles of nondiscrimination of the GATT, which regulates trade agreements and reduces tariffs between countries.

At the same time, as part of the drafting of a free-trade agreement between the United States and Europe, called the Transatlantic Trade and Investment Partnership (TTIP), there is a clause that obliges the EU countries to refrain from boycotting Israeli goods as well as governments and organizations acting to boycott Israel. Local legislators are adding regulations and laws that foreign countries will not be able to operate within the United States if it turns out that they have boycotted Israel.

Financial Immunities conducted a multiyear study to examine the effects of the economic boycott on companies in the Israeli economy. The fact is that most of the companies are completely under the radar of boycotts. Financial Immunities estimates that about 98 percent of Israeli companies are not vulnerable to consumer boycotts.

There are many reasons for the strength of Israeli companies, but the most important of these is Israel's high technological level, with products embedded in the devices and systems that constitute the core of the global technology. The contribution of Israeli technology companies is critical to the worlds of computing, communications, the Internet, security, space, research, and medicine. Among the additional reasons for the Israeli companies' immunity to boycotts is the fact that most of them sell their products to businesses (B2B) rather than to the end consumer; their product or service is a small component in a "product in process" or "finished product" of non-Israeli companies. In other cases, it is not possible to "mark" the product because it passes through wholesalers and retailers until it reaches the sales stalls. The products are not written as "Made in Israel," and if they are, not prominently.

Other solutions come from white-label sales. The fact that many Israeli companies sell a large part of their products under the brand names of their subsidiaries in the target countries, which are difficult to link with Israel, also helps. Israeli companies are also subsidiaries of large, well-known international companies. What will the boycotters do? Will they not buy General Electric's products because the company's grandchild subsidiary is in Israel and produces a component that is a quarter of a percent of the product that General Electric sells? In addition, the fact that Israeli companies operate in many niche industries in a wide variety of products and services makes it very difficult for boycotts to mark a specific industry. The days in which Israel's main exported goods were oranges that could be boycotted and instead oranges exported from Spain were bought, are over.

In any case, Israeli companies operate on a practical level by managing this risk while implementing solutions such as not emphasizing their "Israeliness," focusing their future development on niche and OEM products, partnerships, or sponsoring strong multinational companies. In the countries that are indifferent to the phenomenon of "anti-Israelism," such as most of Southeast Asia, this focus is also consistent with the fact that this region is the engine of future growth of the global economy.

In saying all this, we do not make light of this phenomenon of boycotts of Israel, which are nothing more than anti-Semitic stupidity in all its ugliness.

Another type of boycott that Israelis are concerned about is a cultural boycott. Like the economic boycott, here, too, the Israeli newspaper headlines scream and inflate every artist, junior and senior, who has decided not to perform in Israel. However, for every foreign artist who announces with great noise that he will not come, there are fifty, if not more, who are happy to come—and they come from all over the world. The data show that there is no less than an inflation of performances by foreign artists, and all the stories about the cultural boycott of Israel are nothing more than a bluff. Thus, in 2010, there were twenty-two performances by foreign artists in Israel; in 2012, the number rose to forty-two, and in 2014, the number jumped to seventy. The numbers are 122 foreign artists who appeared in Israel in 2016 and 140 in 2017.[161]

Within seven years, the number of performances by foreign artists in Israel jumped sixfold. Not only are all the stories about a cultural boycott of Israel inflated disproportionately, but they simply mislead the Israeli public, and that's a shame.

———

Still, after we have said all this, we can only agree somewhat with some of the "standard" risks that many Israeli economic forecasters look at with concern. These include Israel's high dependence on foreign trade and the implications of a global recession on the economy, especially considering that a significant portion of its growth in recent decades was based on exports. The "drying up" of the Israeli stock exchange and the decline in trading volumes in hundreds of shares increases the liquidity risks to institutional investors' portfolios. One can also add new geopolitical risks, which have recently surfaced around the world, with an emphasis on the tension between the United States and China and the United States and Russia.

XV

SO WHY ARE THE ISRAELIS HAPPY?

The happiness indices of citizens worldwide repeatedly point to the following: Israelis are happy relative to other nations, despite their repeated complaints and existential challenges throughout all the years.

The *Gallup World Poll* places Israel in eleventh place in terms of its happiness level, a survey by the OECD places Israel in seventeenth place, and the *World Happiness Report 2017* published by the UN ranked Israel again in eleventh place out of 156 countries.

This ranking puts Israel in a better place than the United States (thirteenth place), Germany (sixteenth place), Britain (twenty-third), France (thirty-second), and Japan (fifty-third). The index was conducted by researchers from the University of British Columbia, the School of Economics and Political Science in London, and the UN Development Group. The Happiness Report was first published in 2012, when Israel reached fourteenth place.

It should be noted that Israel is ranked as one of the countries with the lowest standard deviation in the index—that is, the gap between respondents' answers was not very high, which demonstrates that most Israelis are almost equal in their happiness compared with other nations.

The report was composed of responses from three thousand participants in each country listed in the report. Respondents were asked to rate their lives between zero (totally unbearable life) and ten (the best possible life). The average level of happiness in the world reached 5.3 points. The score Israel received in the report is 7.3, and it rises in the happiness index from year to year.

But not surprisingly, most Israelis are not aware of their good position in regard to other nations. We call it "the Israeli paradox." How can it be that people are happy but are unaware of it?

According to the *Social Survey* of the Israeli Central Bureau of Statistics (2013), 88 percent of the Jewish population and 73 percent of the Arab population are satisfied with their lives. The rate of those satisfied with their lives is steadily increasing.

But it is not only the polls that point to this trend. Many Israelis, who have the choice whether to live in Israel or in other countries—Europe or the United States—prefer to live in Israel. For example, why did Eyal Waldman, the successful Israeli entrepreneur, not stay in the United States? Why he did not build Mellanox there? "First of all, because I'm an Israeli, and no less than that the biggest chance of succeeding in setting up a high-tech company is in Israel," he replies. "When I recruit people, I know what unit they were in the military, I understand what their experience is, and I can trust their CV. Israel is my home, and this is the only place I was sure I wanted to build a company that would succeed."

Waldman describes the Israeli employee as one "who has more commitment to the team, has an almost obsessive striving to touch goals and make success. Israeli employee is much more loyal, have courage, and not afraid of failures."

"Living in Israel is a choice, not a necessity," says Prof. Amnon Shashua, who founded Mobileye, one of Israel's most exciting high-tech companies. "I lived in Boston for five years, in my doctoral and postdoctoral studies, and a year in Palo Alto. I saw the best that the American empire can offer, and I really enjoyed it, but Israel is the best thing there is. You are connected to the place where you were born. Here you have your real friends, not virtual but real. Here you have common history. This is something that a person has only in his country of origin."

The economic situation steadily improving is one of the possible causes of happiness. Since the mid-1950s, the standard of living in Israel has steadily increased. In addition, most of the immigrants to Israel improved their personal economic situations relative to their countries of origin, mainly new immigrants from Arab countries and the former Soviet Union. Israelis feel that today is better than before, and there is room for optimism that improvement will continue. The sense of continuous economic improvement has a strong impact on satisfaction.

Another explanation comes from ties with families and friends. Ninety-five percent of Israelis are satisfied or very satisfied with family relationships, according to the Social Survey of the Central Bureau of Statistics. Families and friends are a very significant support network. Raising children has a positive effect on the self-satisfaction of parents and grandparents. Most families in Israel have up to three children, and 19.9 percent families have four or more children.

Dr. Anat Shoshani is a researcher at the School of Psychology at the Interdisciplinary Center Herzliya and an academic director of the Center for the Study and Application of Positive Psychology. She explains[162] that the reason for high solidarity within Israeli society is rooted in cultural elements in Judaism as well as in the military. "Israeli society is organized from an early age in groups. Young people join the military, are educated to protect each other, and get the feeling that they are not alone in this world," she says.

Personal influence and meaning in life are well known as predicting satisfaction. The high level of creativity that exists in Israeli society among many employees and certainly in technological companies results in high satisfaction with work and a sense of meaning. When you feel your contribution is well recognized, you have a high sense of satisfaction and pride in yourself. It also has to do with the general feeling of Israelis who build a state together, when people feel the high importance of their contribution for something greater than themselves.

Prof. Aaron Ben-Ze'ev, former president of Haifa University, who is president of the European Philosophical Association for the Study of Emotions, explains that the feeling of happiness in Israel is largely the result of the challenging nature of the state. "Happiness is measured, among other things, by our ability to realize ourselves, to feel belonging, and to instill meaning in our actions, as well as to overcome obstacles." According to him, the young age of Israel and the ability of the individual to be significant in shaping his or her way increase the sense of happiness. Overcoming obstacles creates a sense of ability based on proven experience. There is no doubt that the past and present of this young country are fraught with opportunities for the individual to strengthen his or her abilities and personal power.

An important variable in Israelis' explanation of happiness is dystopian feeling. Dystopia is the opposite of utopia. It is the land of the underworld, the place of disasters and sorrow. As sons of a nation that has undergone countless persecutions, murders, and physical abuse, Israelis know that their position in the Jewish history perception is the best ever.

The last explanation for Israeli happiness, and not the least important one, is genetic design, which explains, researchers say, about 50 percent of a person's ability to be happy. Can Israelis and Jews have a genetic structure for happiness?

WHERE WOULD YOU LIKE TO BE BORN?

In 1988, a team of multidisciplinary experts created an index, done for the first time, ranking fifty countries in the world by asking where is the best country to be born in order to live there at the age of eighteen. In other words, it was an attempt to anticipate the future of these countries. Not surprisingly, the United States came first.

But the situation was very different twenty-five years later. In 2013, the Economist's Intelligence Unit (EIU) has decided to reevaluate this and see which countries will provide the best opportunities for a healthy, safe, and prosperous life and where a baby should be born.

The EIU quality-of-life index connects the results of surveys to subjective satisfaction with life—that is, how well people say they are happy, along with objective quality-of-life factors in different countries. It turns out, not surprisingly, that being wealthy helps more than anything else, but that's not all that matters. Things like the level of crime and security to walk the streets, trust in public institutions, and health security are also relevant and very important. Overall, the index of the EIU took into account eleven statistically significant indicators, some of them fixed factors, such as geography; others change slowly over time (demographics, social and cultural characteristics), and a number of factors depend on policy and the global economic situation. Forward-looking elements also entered the game.

The results of the index showed that although it was only five years after the crisis of 2008, in some ways humanity had never been better. Although GDP growth rates have entered a lower stage worldwide, average income levels have reached record highs. Life expectancy continued to rise steadily, and political freedoms spread throughout the world. On the other hand, the 2008 crisis left a deep impression in the Eurozone and in other places, especially in terms of unemployment and personal security, and in many places, family and community life were eroded.

The quality-of-life index's results for 2013 showed that the luckiest baby would be born in Switzerland, followed by Australia, Norway, and Sweden. In general, small economies dominate the top ten. When it came to Israel, it was a surprise: it reached twentieth place, ahead of countries such as Italy, Japan, France, and Britain, which appeared in the index after that. Israel was also one of the countries that jumped the highest number of places. Since the 1988 survey, Israel jumped ten places.

It is very good for a baby to be born in Israel. Israel is a success story.

ENDNOTES

1. Matt Ridley, *The Rational Optimist* (New York: HarperCollins Publishers, 2010).

2. Eilat Cohen-Castro, *Immigration to Israel 2015* (Jerusalem, Israel: Central Bureau of Statistics, 2016).

3. Eilat Cohen-Castro, *Immigration to Israel 2007–2010* (Jerusalem, Israel: Central Bureau of Statistics, 2012).

4. Eric Weiner, *The Geography of Genius: A Search for the World's Most Creative Places from Ancient Athens to Silicon Valley* (New York: Simon and Schuster, 2016).

5. OECD/European Union, *Indicators of Immigrant Integration* (Paris: OECD, 2015).

6. A facility for intensive Hebrew language studies for new immigrants.

7. Prof. David Passig, *Israel 2048* (Israel: "MISKAL" Yedioth Books, 2010).

8. The collective body of Jewish religious laws from the written and oral holy scriptures.

9. *Here and There*, directed by Darko Lungulov (2009; Serbia: Modifier Group, 2010), DVD.

10. A native Israeli; also known as a term used for the strong "new Israeli" who worked the land of Israel at the time that new Jewish immigrants arrived to the land.

11. Col. (Res.) Yesha'ayahu (Shaya) Harsit, *A New Sky and a New Land* (Tel Aviv 2012).

12. *One Flight for Us*, directed by Haim Hecht (2005; Israel: Radio Kol Rega, 2005), DVD.

13. A Polish military force loyal to the Polish government in exile in London, established in the Soviet Union in World War II to fight the Nazis.

14. Azrieli's journey to the land of Israel, as well as his first experiences in Israel, were documented in his book *One Step Forward*, written by his daughter, Dana Azrieli (Jerusalem: Yad Vashem, 1999), 77–83.

15. From an interview to Amir Kurtz, "Dana Azrieli, the business successor of the mall empire: "I have what it takes","" *Calcalist*, 2008.

16. Felix Zandman, *From Vishay to Vishay—From Youth in the Holocaust to the Matriculation Exams of Science and Industry* (Beit Shemesh, Israel: Keter Press, 1995).

17. A round piece of textile worn on the head to fulfill the requirements of the customary Jewish law (Halacha).

18. Resolution 185, 2008.

19. Resolution 1544, 2002 and 1250, 2003.

20. King James Bible.

21. The Jewish sages from the times between the final three hundred years of the Second Temple in Jerusalem to the sixth century CE (250 BCE to 625 CE), who composed the oral holy scripture (Mishna, Tosefta, and Talmud).

22. A set of precepts and commandments given by God.

23. Yehuda Amichai, *Also Fist Was Once an Open Hand and Fingers* (Tel Aviv: Schocken, 1989).

24. A Jewish institution that focuses on the study of traditional religious texts, primarily the Talmud and the Torah.

25. Dr. Inbal Abu, *Social Responsibility in Business Organizations* (Beer Sheva: The Israeli Center for Third Sector Research, Ben-Gurion University, 2013).

26. 2011 Israeli social justice protests: a series of demonstrations in Israel involving hundreds of thousands of protesters from a variety of socio-economic and religious backgrounds opposing rise in the cost of living (particularly housing) and deterioration of public services such as health and education.

27. Navit Zomer, "I Got Up in the Morning and Suddenly I Was the Bad Guy," *Yedioth Ahronoth*, June 10, 2016.

28. Discount Bank, *Social Report 2014* (Tel Aviv: Discount Bank, 2014).

29. The first major written redaction of the Jewish oral traditions (536 BCE to 70 CE).

30. Bloomberg L.P. 2013.

31. OECD, *CIA World Factbook*, published by the CIA, 2012.

32. *The Face of Israeli Society*, No. 6, CBS.
33. International Agency for Research on Cancer (IARC), 2015.
34. http://data.oecd.org/healthcare/caesarean-sections.htm#indicator-chart
35. C. Meydan, Z. Haklai, B. Gordon, J. Mendlovic, and A. Afek, "Managing the Increasing Shortage of Acute Care Hospital Beds in Israel," *Journal of Evaluation in Clinical Practice* 21, 1 (2015): 79–84.
36. https://en.wikipedia.org/wiki/In_vitro_fertilisation#Success_rates
37. http://www.informationisbeautiful.net/visualizations/because-every-country-is-the-best-at-something
38. Eric Weiner, *The Geography of Bliss* (London: Transworld Publisher, 2008).
39. The documents that comment and expand upon the Mishnah (the first major written redaction of the Jewish oral traditions), the first work of rabbinic law, published around the year 200 CE. A specification in scripture and a learning material from the Oral Torah.
40. M. Botticini and Z. Eckstein, *The Chosen Few* (Princeton, Princeton University Press, 2012).
41. https://www.reddit.com/r/dataisbeautiful/comments/20k5dk/top_40_countries_by_the_number_of_scientific
42. The Jewish text that sets the order of the Passover Seder, a Jewish holiday that commemorates the liberation of Jews from slavery in Egypt by God.
43. A spectrum of strictly Orthodox Jews.
44. https://freedomhouse.org/report-types/freedom-world
45. Noah Efron, Nazir Majli, and Amitai Shaharit, *Israel in 2048—A Place for Hope* (Tel Aviv, Israel: Shacharit, 2011).
46. *Charlie Hebdo* is a satirical weekly that publishes cartoons, reports, and jokes of an anti-racist nature that focus on the radical right, Christianity, Islam, Judaism, and so on. In January 2015, masked Islamic terrorists broke out and murdered ten journalists and six police officers and wounded ten because of cartoons of the Prophet Muhammad published in it.

47.   Thomas Friedman, *The Lexus and the Olive Tree, Globalization—A View into a Changing World* (Israel: Hed Artzi, 2000).

48.   Uri Ram, *The Globalization of Israel, McWorld in Tel Aviv, Jihad in Jerusalem* (Beer-Sheva: Resling, 2005).

49.   Asa Kasher, "The Jewish Democratic State," in: Yossi David (ed.), *The State of Israel Between Judaism and Democracy* (Jerusalem: The Israel Democracy Institute, 2000), 116.

50.   Palestinian Authority.

51.   *Ynet* and *the Association for Religious Freedom and Equality*, October 2016.

52.   Talmud, Eruvin 13,2.

53.   Prof. Gad Yair, *The Code of Israeliness: The Ten Commandments for the 21st Century* (Jerusalem: Keter Books, 2011).

54.   Prof. Gideon Dror, *Elective Methods and Values of Democracy* (Matach).

55.   Sebastian Junger, *Tribe: On Homecoming and Belonging* (New York: Twelve, 2016).

56.   Book of Numbers, chapter 23.

57.   Noga Kainan speech to CFO Forum, 2007.

58.   The Israel Democracy Institute, *The Israeli Democracy Report* (Jerusalem: The Democracy Institute, 2015).

59.   Prof. Ronnie Ellenblum and Prof. Yuval Noah Harari, "Discussion on the Topic: Man—Environment—World," moderated by Prof. Moshe Sluhovsky. January 25, 2017, Hebrew University.

60.   From "A Voyage to the Holy Land: Pleasure Excursion to the Holy Land," a chapter of a journey by the American author Mark Twain, in 1869, from the book by Mark Twain, *The Innocents Abroad or the New Pilgrim's Progress* (Cleveland: American Publishing Company, 1869).

61.   1857: British consul James Finn reported, "The country is in a considerable degree empty of inhabitants and therefore its greatest need is that of a body of population."

62.   1867: Charles William Elliott, president of Harvard University, wrote: "A beautiful sea lies unbosomed, among the Galilean hills in the mist of that land once possessed by Zebulon and Naphtali, Asher

and Dan. Life here was one idyllic…now it is a scene of desolation and misery."

63. Samuel Manning, *Those Holy Fields* (London: The Religious Tract Society, 1890), 14.

64. Shlomo Ilan, "Traditional Arab Agriculture in the Land of Israel in the Ottoman Period," *Kardom—Monthly Bulletin of the Land of Israel* (Ariel: Ariel Press, September 1984).

65. An accident in which a bridge over the Yarkon River collapsed during the opening ceremony of the fifteenth Maccabiah sport games on July 14, 1997, in which four athletes were killed and sixty-nine were injured. Due to the impact of the bridge on the water, poisonous substances from the bottom of the Yarkon rose up, and the damage to the health of those in the water was more severe than it would have been had it not been for the pollution in the Yarkon. The rescuers who entered the water to rescue the athletes were also injured.

66. Navy soldiers who served in the naval commando have been practicing in the Kishon River for years, unknowing of the dangerous effect of diving in the polluted river. Large numbers of cases of cancer occurred among former Israeli navy divers.

67. Baruch Kimmerling, *Immigrants, Settlers, Natives* (Israel: Am Oved, 2004).

68. According to the Israeli National Library's data for the book week of 2014, 82 percent of the books published are original Hebrew books, and only 18 percent are translated. In international comparisons, the sources of the data are as follows:
https://en.wikipedia.org/wiki/Books_published_per_country_per_year
https://jakubmarian.com/number-of-books-published-per-year-per-capita-by-country-in-europe/
http://www.bbc.com/culture/story/20140909-why-so-few-books-in-translation
https://www.theguardian.com/books/2014/oct/22/uk-publishes-more-books-per-capita-million-report

69. Maya Nachum Shahal, "An Excelent Joke," Calcalist, 2010.

70. Avraham Carmeli and Hila Maimon, *Musical Bodies in Israel 2014* (Tel Aviv: Ministry of Culture and Sport, 2014).

71. Avraham Carmeli and Menachem Lazar, *Public Theaters in Israel— Summary of Annual Activity Ministry of Culture and Sport* (Tel Aviv, December 2014).

72. The Irgun (The National Military Organization) was a Zionist paramilitary unit whose goal was to end the British Mandate in Palestine.

73. Haganah (The Defense) was a Jewish paramilitary organization in the British Mandate of Palestine, which became, later on, the core of the IDF.

74. Ahuzat Bayit was founded in 1906 by a group of Jews at the initiative of Akiva Aryeh Weiss in order to build a new Hebrew city in the land of Israel (later the city of Tel Aviv).

75. Ecosystem is term borrowed from biology, which relates to the business environment associated with a product or technology. This environment includes suppliers, marketers, customers, service providers, and so on. Without an appropriate ecosystem, it will be difficult for technological startups to develop.

76. Rafi Eldor, Shmuel Hauser, and Rafi Melnick, *The Impact of Terrorism and Anti-Terrorism on Capital Markets* (Jerusalem: Israel Securities Authority, 2005).

77. K. Peleg, J.L. Regens, J.T. Gunter, and D.H. Jaffe, "The Normalization of Terror: The Response of Israel's Stock Market to Long Periods of Terrorism." *Disasters*, 35, 1 (January 2011): 268–283.

78. David Goldman, *How Civilizations Die (And Why Islam Is Dying Too)* (Washington, DC: Regnery, 2011).

79. From G-Planet site, 2016.

80. Institute for Economic & Peace, *Global Terrorism Index 2015* (Sydney, Australia: Institute for Economics & Peace, 2015).

81. Israel Security Agency, "Shin Bet" report of 2015.

82. https://www.youtube.com/watch?v=lbgt2FhggOQ

83. shoebat.com/television.php?PHPSESSID=f361733d98074ae8e77f7d b6048fe01f

84. A British Commission managed by Sir John Hope Simpson, to address Immigration, Land Settlement and Development issues in the British Mandate of Palestine.

85. http://www.jewishvirtuallibrary.org/jsource/History/hope.html

86. Ilan Kfir and Dani Dor, *Iron Dome* (Modi'in, Israel: Kinneret Zmora Bitan, 2014).

87. "During the fighting in the north, Rafael knew quite a few alarms and falls nearby. But they did not stop. One of the shelters had a nursery school and kindergarten, and everyone continued to work. I was there on a management visit at the same time, to strengthen them. I was and saw."—N.K.

88. Daniel Rosenman, *Changes in Indicators of the Israeli Economy Compared with OECD Countries* (Jerusalem: Bank of Israel, 2014).

89. Owned by coauthor of this book (A.R.).

90. Stephen D. King, *When the Money Runs Out: The End of Western Affluence* (New Haven: Yale University Press, 2013).

91. Researches by: Bloom and Williamson (1998); Bloom, Canning, and Malaney (2000). D. E. Bloom, D. Canning, and J. Sevilla, *Economic Growth and the Demographic Transition* (Cambridge, MA: National Bureau of Economic Research (NBER), 2000). D. E. Bloom, D. Canning, G. Fink, and J. E. Finlay, *Does Age Structure Forecast Economic Growth?* (Cambridge, MA : National Bureau of Economic Research (NBER), 2007). D. E. Bloom, D. Canning, and G. Fink, *Population Aging and Economic Growth* (Cambridge, MA: Harvard Initiative for Global Health: working paper, 2008).

92. Yuval Noah Harari, *Homo Deus: A Brief History of Tomorrow* (Modi'in, Israel: Dvir, Kinneret Zmora Bitan, 2015).

93. https://forward.com/articles/161803/microsofts-steve-ballmer-to-visit-israel/

94. Gallup Poll. "Americans' Views Toward Israel Remain Firmly Positive." February 29, 2016.

95. Michael B. Oren, *Ally: My Journey Across the American-Israeli Divide* (New York: Random House Trade Paperbacks, 2016).

96. Stephen Mansfield, *Lincoln's Battle with God: A President's Struggle with Faith and What it Meant for America* (Grand Haven, Michigan: Brilliance Audio, 2012).

97. During Obama's visit to Israel, 2013.

98. http://www.u-s-history.com/pages/h1971.html

99. New York Times, "better than 5 C.I.A.'s", March 6, 1986.

100. Israel Hayom, The Ettinger Report, "Senator Daniel Inouye – Did They Break the Mold?", December 20, 2012.

101. ZAKA is an ultra-Orthodox Jewish voluntary organization that assists the Israel police and the rescue forces in dealing with disaster scenes; their main function is to identify victims of disasters and bring their bodies for burial.

102. Jewish penitential poems and prayers said in the period leading up to the High Holidays and on days of fast.

103. Teva announced in 2017 that it plans to lay off nearly 25% of its global workforce, including 1,700 Israelis. It also intends to close its two plants in Jerusalem.
read more: https://www.haaretz.com/israel-news/business/1.830063

104. GEM: Global Entrepreneurship Monitor, 2013.

105. Based on the GEM study, conducted at the Ira Center for Business, Technology, and Society at Ben-Gurion University, Beer Sheva, 2007.

106. GEM: Global Entrepreneurship Monitor, 2013.

107. PitchBook's index, IVC 2016.

108. Thomas Malthus, *An Essay on the Principle of Population* (London: Joseph Johnson, 1798).

109. The Bloomberg Innovation Index, 2015.

110. IMD World Competitiveness Center, *IMD Competitiveness Yearbook* (Lausanne, Switzerland: IMD World Competitiveness Center, 2014).

111. Deloitte, 2014.

112. Dan Senor and Saul Singer, *Start-Up Nation* (New York: Hachette Book Group, 2009).

113. Israel21C, "Bill Gates – Israel is a high tech superpower", October 30, 2005.

114. Dan Senor and Saul Singer, *Start-Up Nation* (New York: Hachette Book Group, 2009).

115. IAI, Israel's Aerospace Industry.

116. Yehuda Amichai, "Not as a Cypress Tree."

117. Accelerator is an acceleration program for projects designed to bring them from the initial product stage to any advanced stage. The program includes a combination of group work with the nurturing of a personal mentor from technology and investment, product development assistance, exposure to work methodologies, development of a strategic plan, dating with angels and factors legal, marketing, accounting, and financing.

118. https://en.wikipedia.org/wiki/WeWork

119. Testified in an interview with Adi Rubinstein in September 2014.

120. Satellites that are positioned at a point where their orbital duration is equal to the circumference of Earth on its axis so they are perceived as standing still.

121. According to the UK's Institution of Mechanical Engineers; IME

122. Some of the information in this section is taken from the book by S. M. Siegel, *Let There Be Water* (New York: Thomas Dunne Books, 2015).

123. The global desertification process is a phenomenon in which populated areas become desert areas. Thus, for example, the Sahal, located on the border of the Sahara Desert, was made, by the process of desertification, to be impossible to live for people who experienced hunger and thirst. The phenomenon of desertification occurs in many places in the world. In Israel, we found an antidesertification process when a southern city such as Beer Sheva moved from an average annual rainfall of about two hundred milliliters a year between 1930 and 1960 to almost three hundred milliliters of rain in the years

1960 through 1990. Kiryat Gat went from less than four hundred to almost five hundred milliliters, Ashdod from four hundred fifty to more than five hundred milliliters. Arad went from one hundred to two hundred, and so on. The meteorologists who worked on the study concluded that the National Water Carrier project in the northern Negev, which has become a cultivated place, has changed the color of the area, from yellow to green and brown; changing the color of the soil changes the radiation (Alpert and Mendel, 1985). Some claim that this is not a statistical error but that the phenomenon is noteworthy and that it is a follow-up; in any case, it is a unique documentation of antidesertification in the world.

124. Source: Israel Water Authority.
125. http://idadesal.org/desalination-101/desalination-by-the-numbers/
126. Prof. Haim Gvirtzman, Department of Environmental Sciences, The Hebrew University of Jerusalem. https://www.youtube.com/watch?v=JoP7DCtGd1Y
127. From an interview on Israeli "Globes" website, October 13, 2016.
128. The data is based in part on independent research conducted by a researcher who previously worked for B'Tselem and asked to remain anonymous on the basis of data received from the PA and international organizations.
129. Prof. Haim Gvirtzman, "Cornerstones." (Lecture 11, Department of Environmental Sciences, The Hebrew University of Jerusalem, Jerusalem, 2015).
130. Seth M. Siegel, *Let There Be Water* (New York: Thomas Dunne Books, 2015).
131. These estimates are based, inter alia, on analysis of analysts in the Israeli capital market and assessments of the Bank of Israel and the Ministry of Finance. Indirect taxes mainly refer to tax revenues that the state will collect on capital gains on the stock exchange, which will come against the background of an increase in the value of holdings of private investors in shares of gas companies.

132. According to a source in the management of Israel Natural Gas Lines, who asked to remain anonymous.

133. Estimates of financial immunities, average for the years 2012 through 2015.

134. Electricity Authority, *State of the Electricity Sector Report for 2015* (Haifa: Electricity Authority, 2015).

135. Electricity from sources such as hydroelectric, biogas, and wind are negligible and together produce less than twenty-five megawatts annually.

136. According to the CBS forecast.

137. There are also projects that lead to "antigrowth," such as Valley Railroad, in which the financial investment will probably never be covered, even according to the most optimistic scenario. www.ynet.co.il/articles/0,7340, L-4360580,00.html

138. L. Brown, N. Sussman, and R. Shaharabani, "Causes of Road Accidents on Interurban Roads in Israel" (Discussion Paper Series, Bank of Israel, Jerusalem, 2014).

139. *Accuracy of Passenger Trains and Travel Volume 2005–2015* (Lod, Israel: slide from internal presentation, Israel Railways, 2016).

140. Bank of Israel, the level of infrastructure in Israel and investment in them: international comparison and long-term analysis, March 18, 2015.

141. Statistical Abstract of the Shipping and Ports Authority.

142. Tim Harford, "The Economics of Trust," *Forbes*, July 21, 2010.

143. Prof. Dan Ariely, *The Honest Truth About Dishonesty: How We Lie to Everyone-Especially Ourselves* (New York: HarperCollins Publishers, 2013).

144. https://www.transparency.org/news/feature/corruption_perceptions_index_2016

145. McCarthyism is a term used to accuse people for no reason or on the basis of questionable evidence to label and distance that person and infringe on his civil rights.

146. Prof. Yossi Shain, *The Language of Corruption* (Modi'in, Israel: Dvir, Kinneret Zmora Bitan, 2010).
147. Kohelet Forum publications, January 2017.
148. *The State Comptroller's Annual Report* (Jerusalem: The State Comptroller, November 2016).
149. "OECD Barriers to Entrepreneurship," 2013.
150. Daniel Levy, "The Price Marking Law: A Review of the State of the World, Trends and Assessing the Impact of the Law on Consumer Prices, Research and Economics Administration." Ministry of Industry, Trade and Labor, May 2008.
151. http://www.ynet.co.il/articles/0,7340, L-4682939,00.html
152. OECD Economic survey of Israel 2016.
153. Shmuel Even and Eran Yashiv, "The Defense Budget for 2017–2018," INSS, The Institute for National Security Studies, December 2016.
154. https://www.siri.org/yearbook/2015
155. Prof. David Passig, *Israel 2048* (Israel: "MISKAL" Yedioth Books, 2010).
156. Saudi Arabia and the Gulf states used petrodollars to finance, among other things, "research institutes" in various countries, including the United States, to influence public opinion and policy makers there.
157. A. B. Yehoshua, "An Attempt to Understand the Infrastructure of Anti-Semitism" (lecture, Haifa University, Haifa, 2009).
158. The only industry in which this phenomenon continues to hold is the global oil and gas exploration industry due to the weighty interests of many international players in Saudi Arabia and the Persian Gulf.
159. The BDS (Boycott, Divestment and Sanctions) movement is a global campaign attempting to increase economic and political pressure on Israel to end what it describes as violations of international law.
160. Roskam: A bill to promote trade and commercial enhancement between the United States and Israel and for other purposes. 114th Congress, First Session.

161. Sources: Cards Online website, Mako website, City Mouse website.
162. Yael Gaton, "So Why the Israeli Are So Happy," *WALLA*, May 21, 2015.

Made in the USA
Lexington, KY
27 April 2018